STAR WARS®

KNIGHTS OF THE OLD REPUBLIC

VOLUME TWO
FLASHPOINT

THE OLD REPUBLIC
(25,000—1,000 YEARS BEFORE THE BATTLE OF YAVIN)

The Old Republic was the legendary government that united a galaxy under the rule of the Senate. In this era, the Jedi are numerous, and serve as guardians of peace and justice. The **Tales of the Jedi** *comics series takes place in this era, chronicling the immense wars fought by the Jedi of old, and the ancient Sith.*

The events in this story take place approximately 3,963 years before the Battle of Yavin.

STAR WARS®

KNIGHTS OF THE OLD REPUBLIC

VOLUME TWO
FLASHPOINT

SCRIPT JOHN JACKSON MILLER

ART DUSTIN WEAVER, BRIAN CHING & HARVEY TOLIBAO
WITH SPECIAL THANKS TO CRYSTAL FAITH CELESTIAL

COLORS MICHAEL ATIYEH & JAY DAVID RAMOS

LETTERING MICHAEL HEISLER

COVER ART BRIAN CHING & MICHAEL ATIYEH

Dark Horse Books™

PUBLISHER   MIKE RICHARDSON

COLLECTION DESIGNER   KRYSTAL HENNES

ART DIRECTOR   LIA RIBACCHI

ASSISTANT EDITOR   DAVE MARSHALL

EDITOR   JEREMY BARLOW

Special thanks to Elaine Mederer, Jann Moorhead, David Anderman, Leland Chee, Sue Rostoni, and Amy Gary at Lucas Licensing.

STAR WARS KNIGHTS OF THE OLD REPUBLIC VOLUME TWO: FLASHPOINT

This volume collects issues seven through twelve
of the Dark Horse comic-book series *Star Wars: Knights of the Old Republic.*

Published by
Dark Horse Books
A division of Dark Horse Comics, Inc.
10956 SE Main Street
Milwaukie, OR 97222

darkhorse.com
starwars.com

To find a comics shop in your area,
call the Comic Shop Locator Service toll-free at 1-888-266-4226

First edition: May 2007
ISBN: 978-1-59307-761-7

3 5 7 9 10 8 6 4
Printed at Midas Printing International, Ltd., Huizhou, China

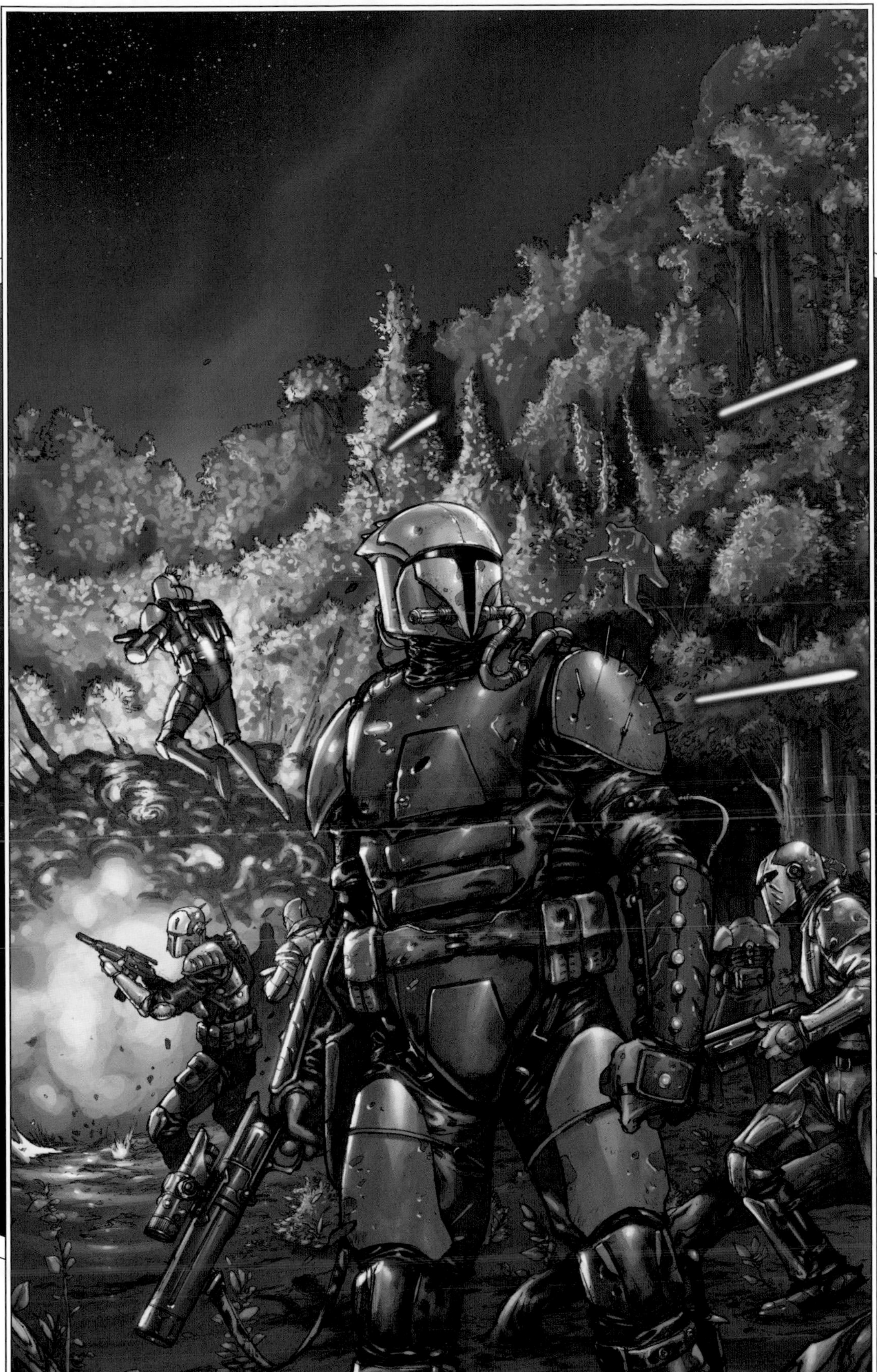

ILLUSTRATION BY BRIAN CHING AND MICHAEL ATIYEH

FLASHPOINT

art by Dustin Weaver

In the OLD REPUBLIC, the JEDI KNIGHTS form the backbone of law and order, just as they would nearly 4,000 years later in Anakin Skywalker's time. But there are factions within the Jedi—including a cabal that fears young ZAYNE CARRICK may unleash THE SITH upon the galaxy.

Framed by his former Masters for murder, Zayne becomes a fugitive, joined by GRYPH, a literal partner in crime. They take flight aboard the ramshackle *LAST RESORT* with the addled inventor CAMPER, his fierce protector JARAEL, and the confused droid ELBEE.

To escape the reach of the law, they make for the battlefront where Mandalorian and Republican forces have been bogged down. But the chaos they left behind on Taris may have repercussions for the war itself . . .

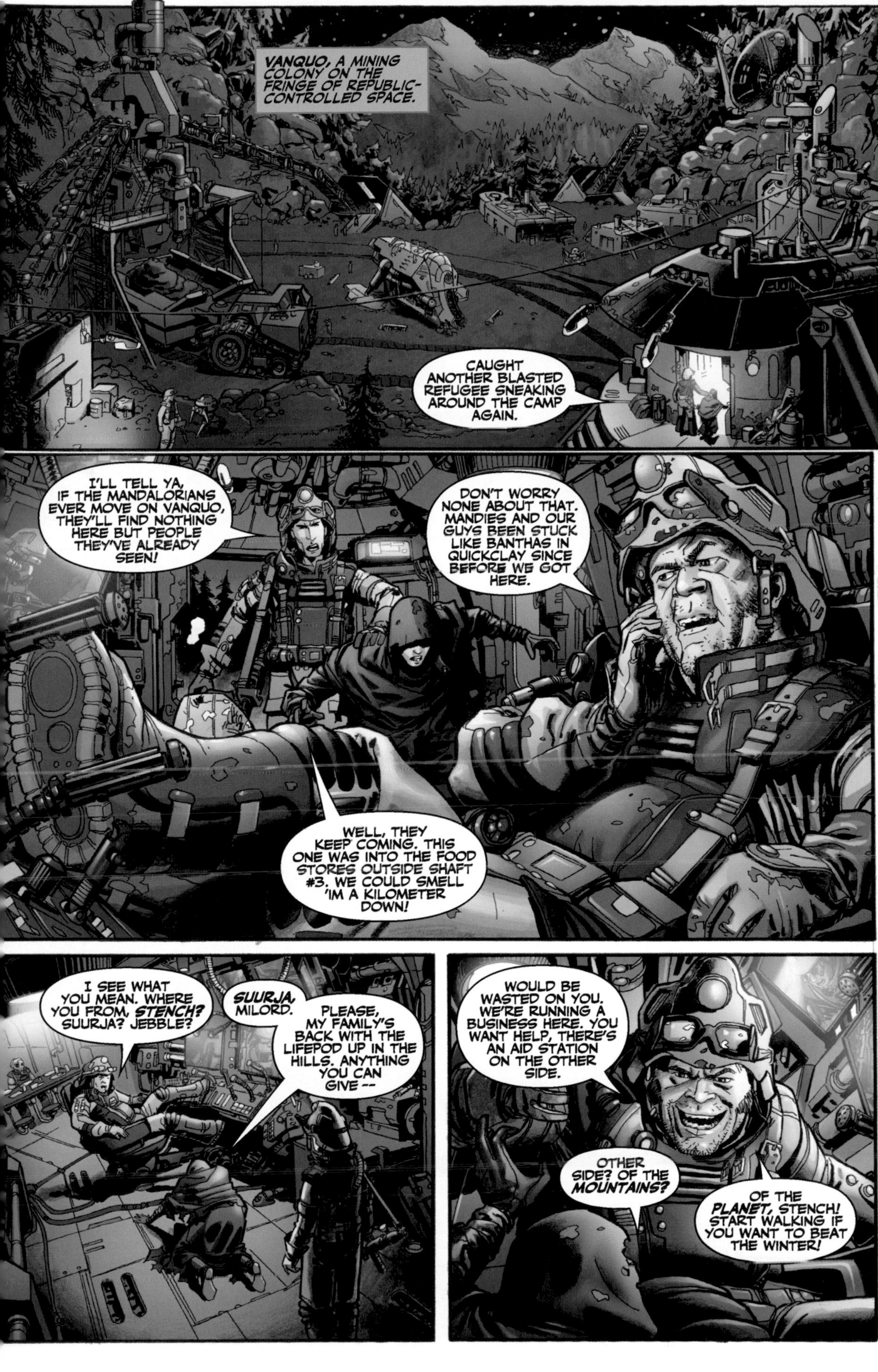
VANQUO, A MINING COLONY ON THE FRINGE OF REPUBLIC-CONTROLLED SPACE.
CAUGHT ANOTHER BLASTED REFUGEE SNEAKING AROUND THE CAMP AGAIN.
I'LL TELL YA, IF THE MANDALORIANS EVER MOVE ON VANQUO, THEY'LL FIND NOTHING HERE BUT PEOPLE THEY'VE ALREADY SEEN!
DON'T WORRY NONE ABOUT THAT. MANDIES AND OUR GUYS BEEN STUCK LIKE BANTHAS IN QUICKCLAY SINCE BEFORE WE GOT HERE.
WELL, THEY KEEP COMING. THIS ONE WAS INTO THE FOOD STORES OUTSIDE SHAFT #3. WE COULD SMELL 'IM A KILOMETER DOWN!
I SEE WHAT YOU MEAN. WHERE YOU FROM, STENCH? SUURJA? JEBBLE?
SUURJA, MILORD.
PLEASE, MY FAMILY'S BACK WITH THE LIFEPOD UP IN THE HILLS. ANYTHING YOU CAN GIVE --
WOULD BE WASTED ON YOU. WE'RE RUNNING A BUSINESS HERE. YOU WANT HELP, THERE'S AN AID STATION ON THE OTHER SIDE.
OTHER SIDE? OF THE MOUNTAINS?
OF THE PLANET, STENCH! START WALKING IF YOU WANT TO BEAT THE WINTER!

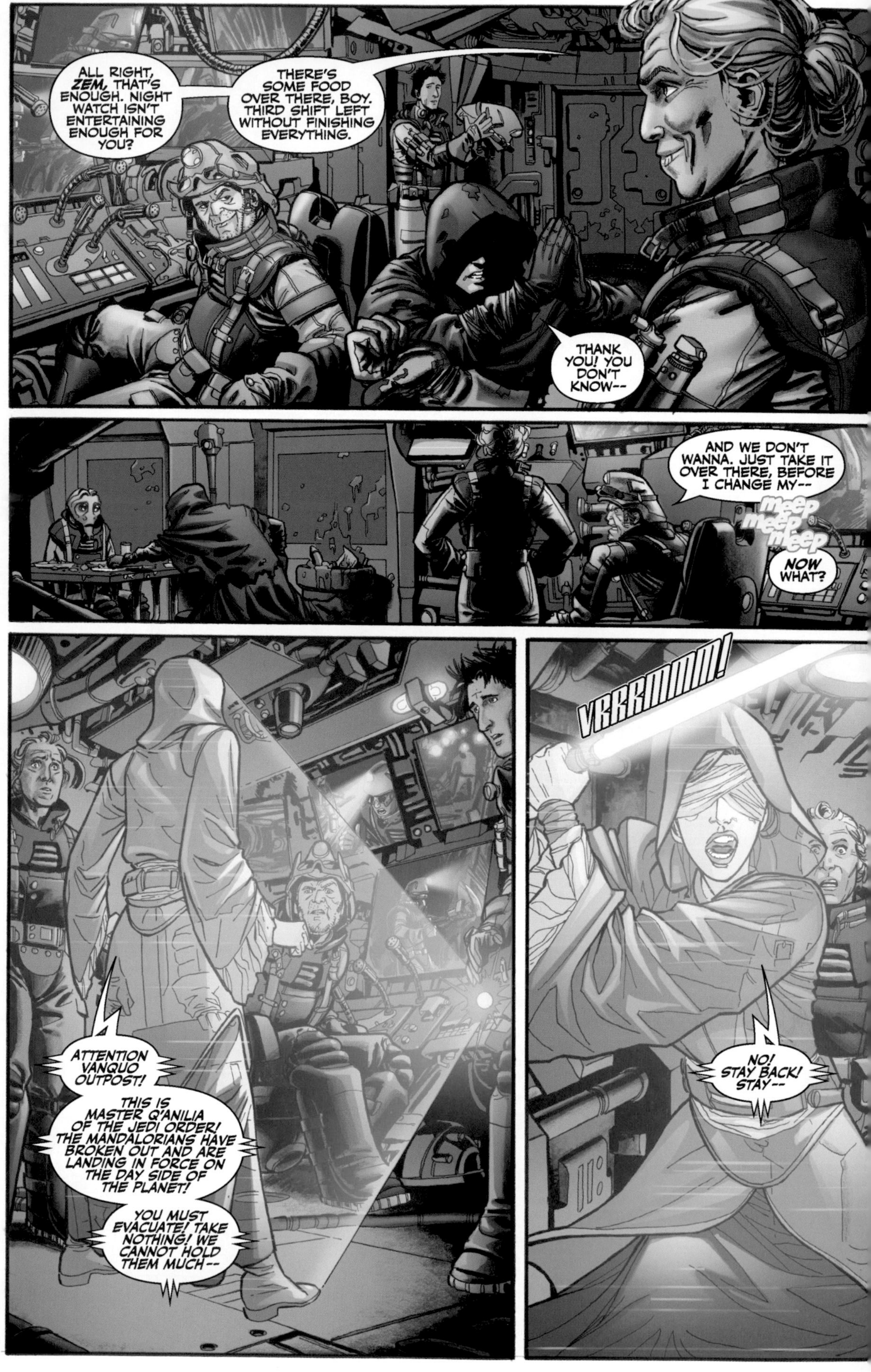
ALL RIGHT, ZEM, THAT'S ENOUGH. NIGHT WATCH ISN'T ENTERTAINING ENOUGH FOR YOU?
THERE'S SOME FOOD OVER THERE, BOY. THIRD SHIFT LEFT WITHOUT FINISHING EVERYTHING.
THANK YOU! YOU DON'T KNOW--
AND WE DON'T WANNA. JUST TAKE IT OVER THERE, BEFORE I CHANGE MY--
meep meep meep
NOW WHAT?
ATTENTION VANQUO OUTPOST!
THIS IS MASTER Q'ANILIA OF THE JEDI ORDER! THE MANDALORIANS HAVE BROKEN OUT AND ARE LANDING IN FORCE ON THE DAY SIDE OF THE PLANET!
YOU MUST EVACUATE! TAKE NOTHING! WE CANNOT HOLD THEM MUCH--
VRRRMMMM!
NO! STAY BACK! STAY--

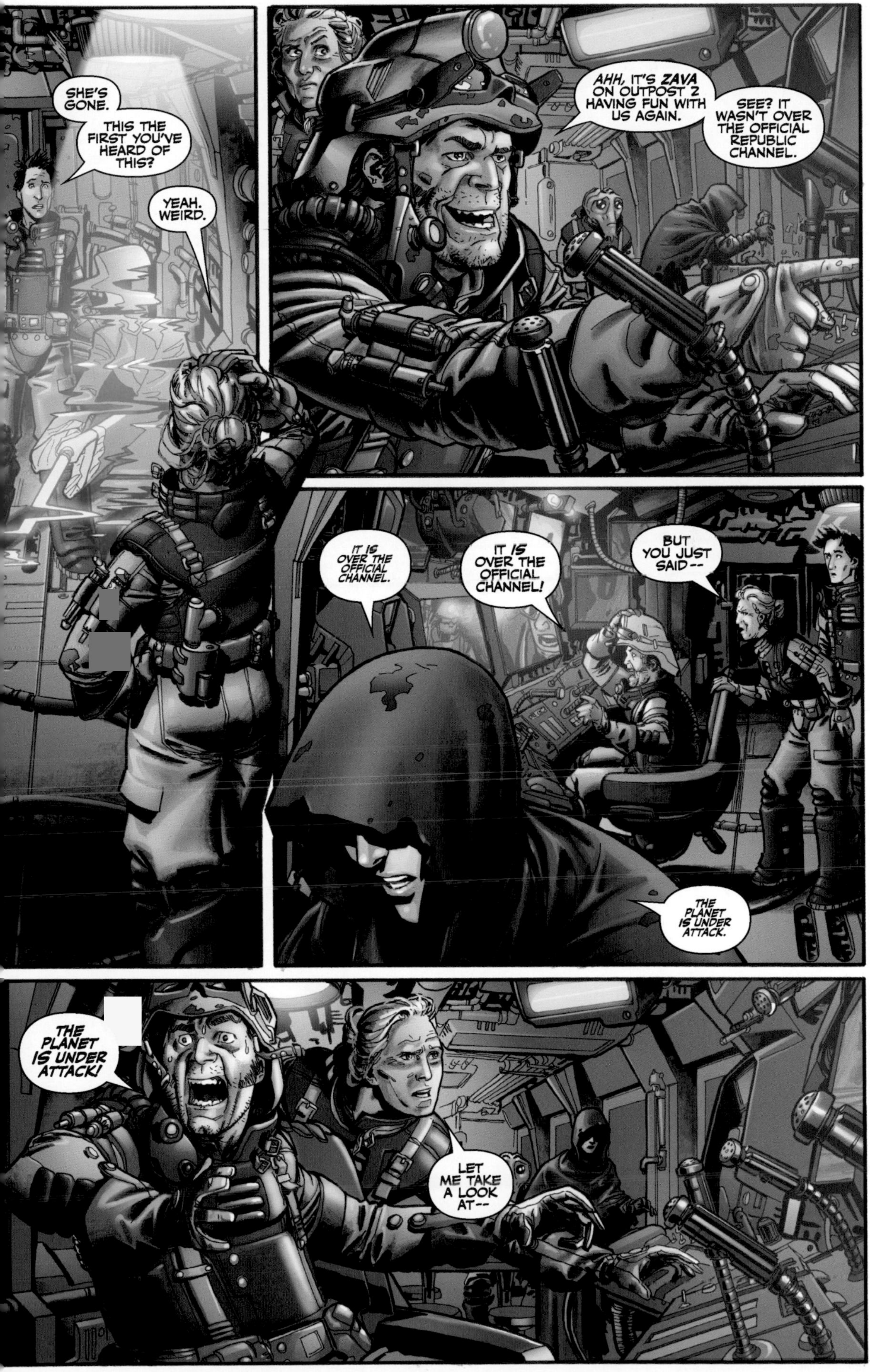

SHE'S GONE.
THIS THE FIRST YOU'VE HEARD OF THIS?
YEAH. WEIRD.
AHH, IT'S ZAVA ON OUTPOST 2 HAVING FUN WITH US AGAIN.
SEE? IT WASN'T OVER THE OFFICIAL REPUBLIC CHANNEL.
IT IS OVER THE OFFICIAL CHANNEL.
IT IS OVER THE OFFICIAL CHANNEL!
BUT YOU JUST SAID--
THE PLANET IS UNDER ATTACK.
THE PLANET IS UNDER ATTACK!
LET ME TAKE A LOOK AT--

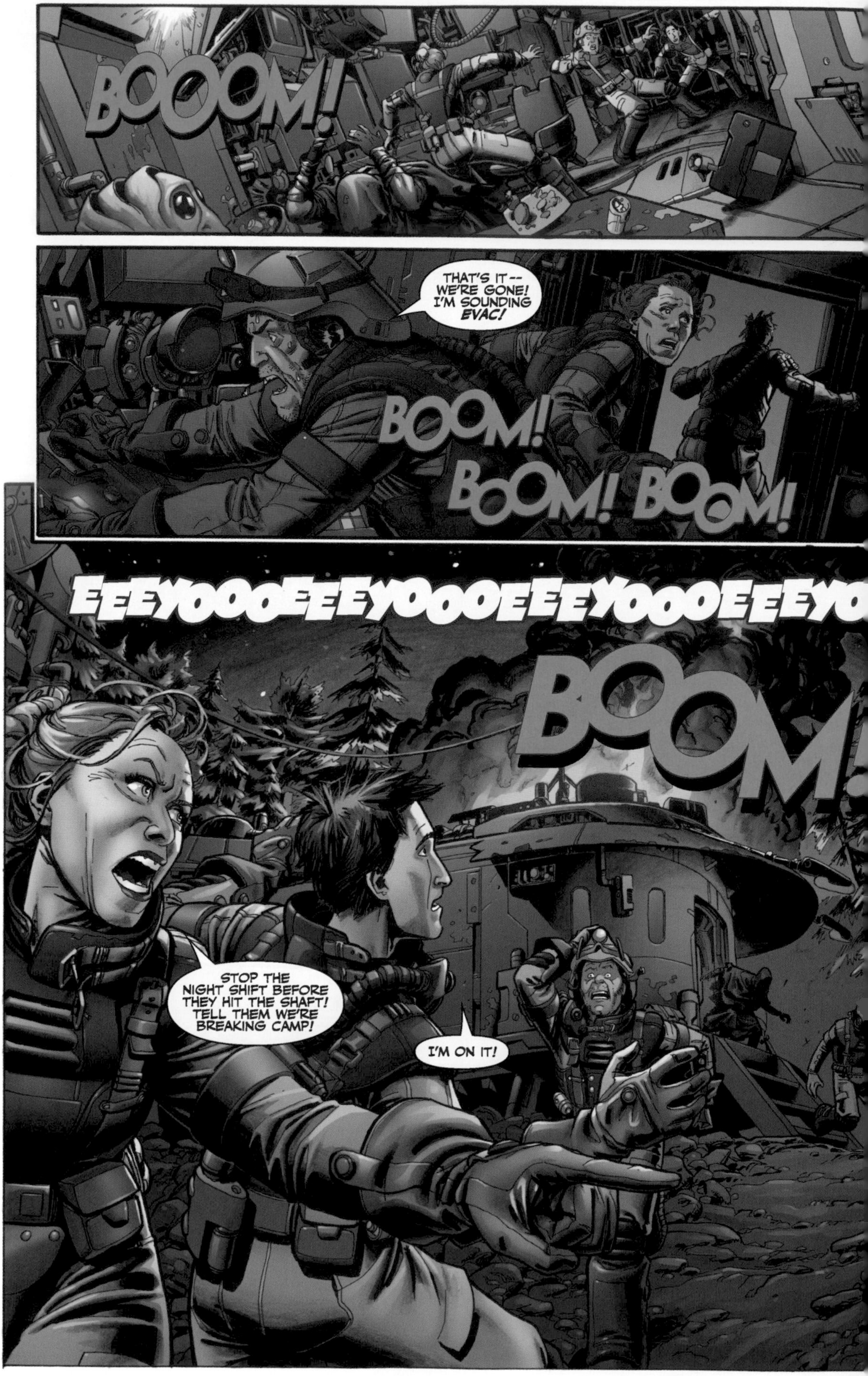
BOOOM!
THAT'S IT -- WE'RE GONE! I'M SOUNDING EVAC!
BOOM! BOOM! BOOM!
EEEYOOOEEEYOOOEEEYOOOEEEYO
BOOM!
STOP THE NIGHT SHIFT BEFORE THEY HIT THE SHAFT! TELL THEM WE'RE BREAKING CAMP!
I'M ON IT!

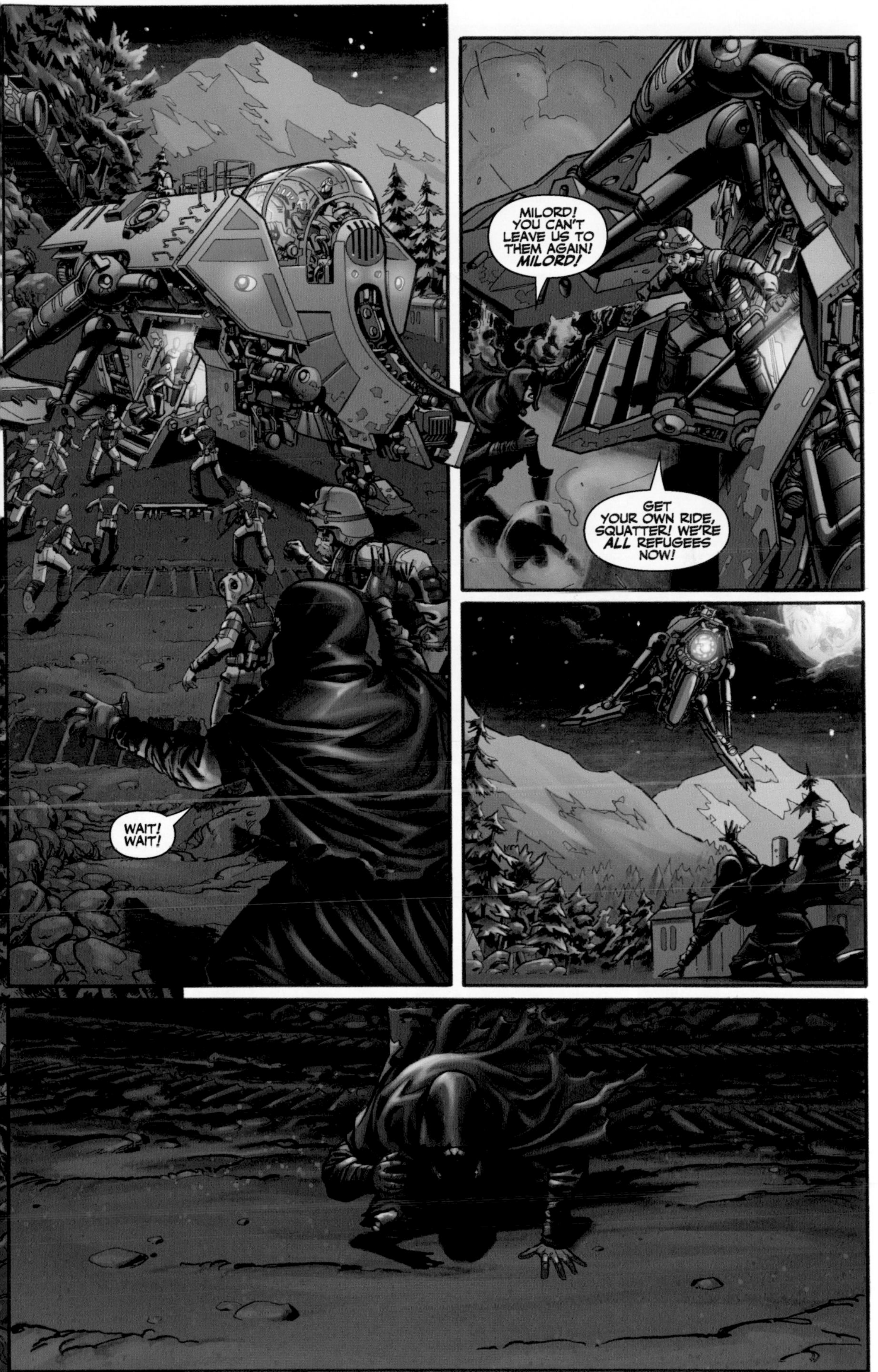
WAIT! WAIT!
MILORD! YOU CAN'T LEAVE US TO THEM AGAIN! *MILORD!*
GET YOUR OWN RIDE, SQUATTER! WE'RE *ALL* REFUGEES NOW!

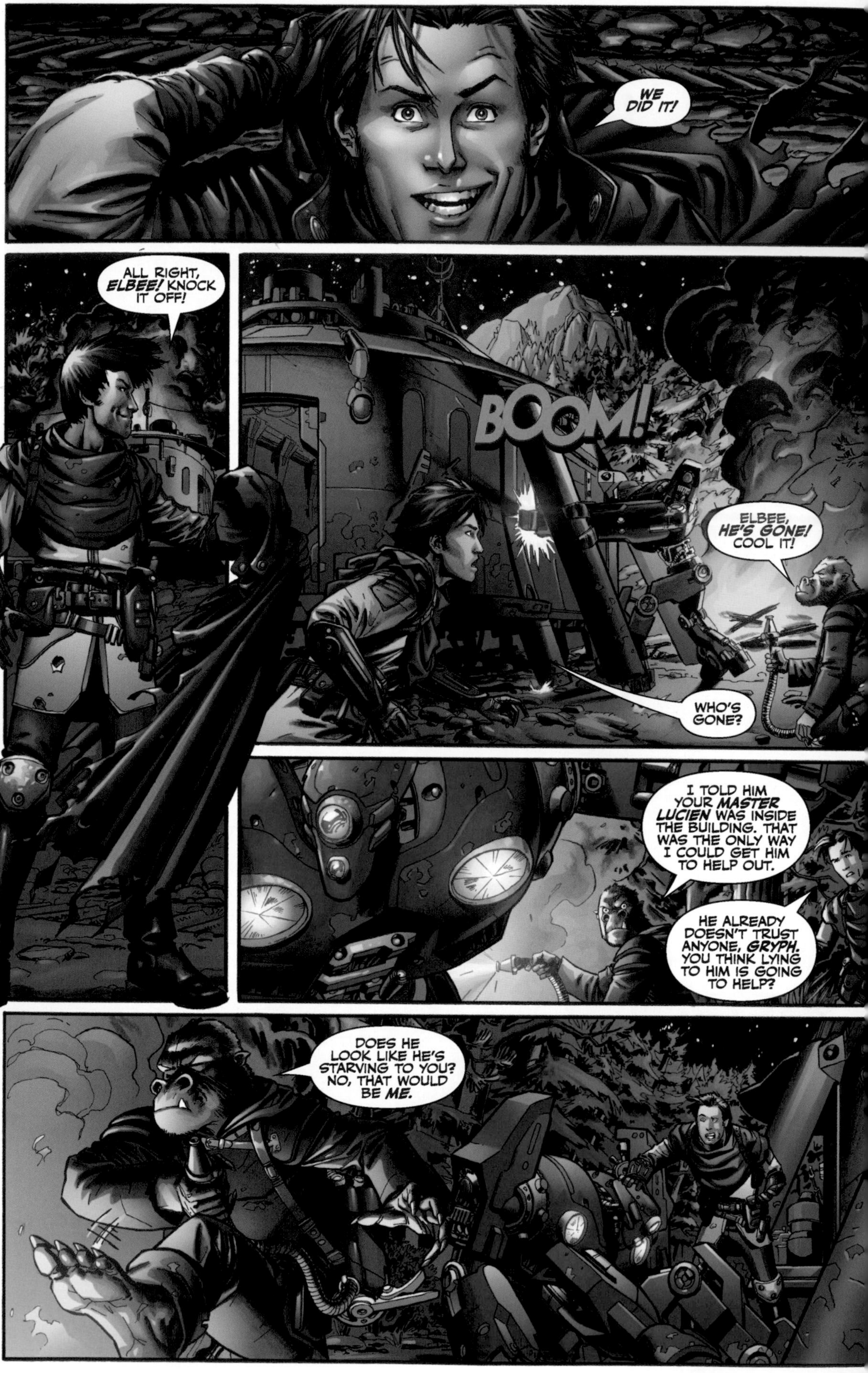
WE DID IT!
ALL RIGHT, ELBEE! KNOCK IT OFF!
BOOM!
ELBEE, HE'S GONE! COOL IT!
WHO'S GONE?
I TOLD HIM YOUR MASTER LUCIEN WAS INSIDE THE BUILDING. THAT WAS THE ONLY WAY I COULD GET HIM TO HELP OUT.
HE ALREADY DOESN'T TRUST ANYONE, GRYPH. YOU THINK LYING TO HIM IS GOING TO HELP?
DOES HE LOOK LIKE HE'S STARVING TO YOU? NO, THAT WOULD BE ME.

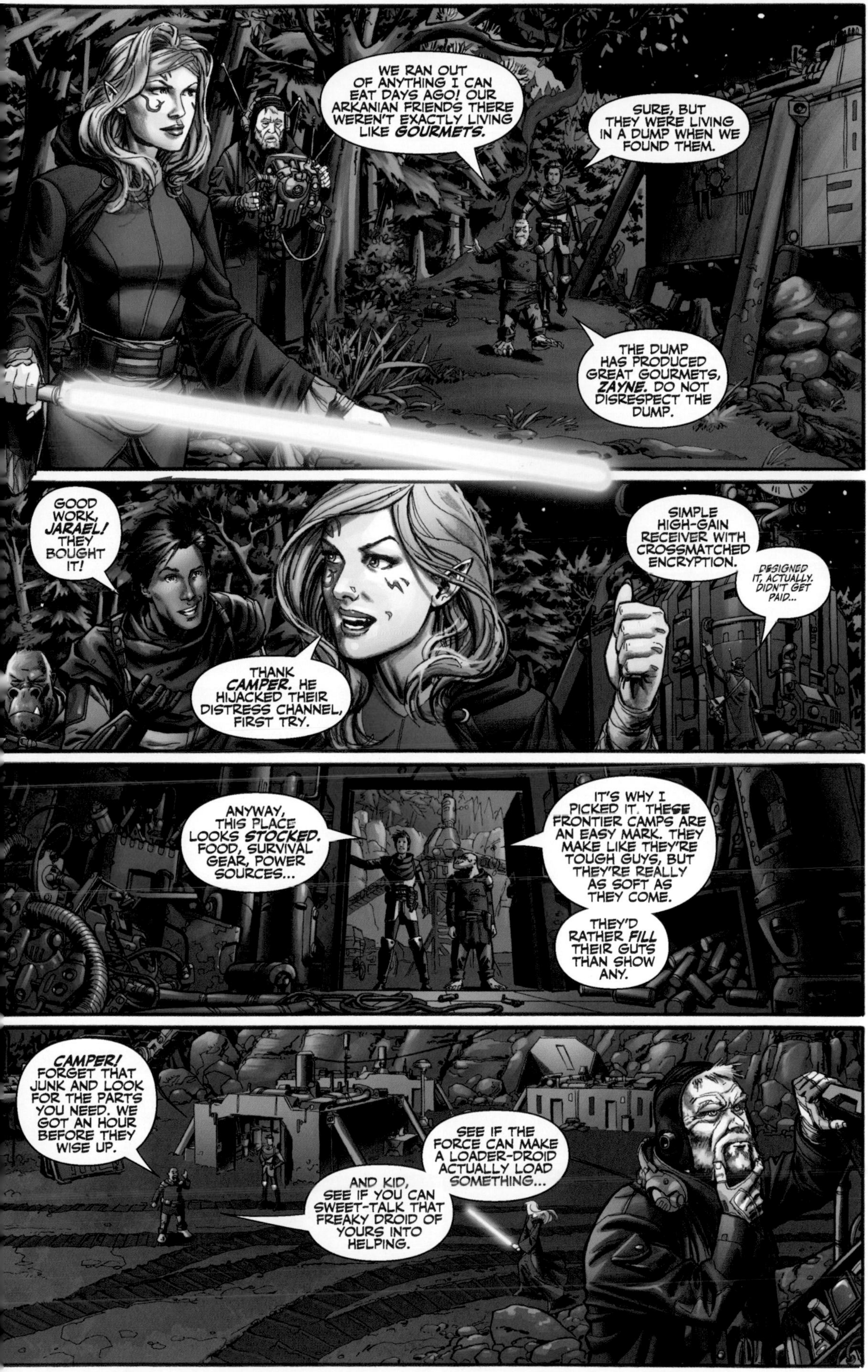
WE RAN OUT OF ANYTHING I CAN EAT DAYS AGO! OUR ARKANIAN FRIENDS THERE WEREN'T EXACTLY LIVING LIKE GOURMETS.
SURE, BUT THEY WERE LIVING IN A DUMP WHEN WE FOUND THEM.
THE DUMP HAS PRODUCED GREAT GOURMETS, ZAYNE. DO NOT DISRESPECT THE DUMP.
GOOD WORK, JARAEL! THEY BOUGHT IT!
THANK CAMPER. HE HIJACKED THEIR DISTRESS CHANNEL, FIRST TRY.
SIMPLE HIGH-GAIN RECEIVER WITH CROSSMATCHED ENCRYPTION.
DESIGNED IT, ACTUALLY. DIDN'T GET PAID...
ANYWAY, THIS PLACE LOOKS STOCKED. FOOD, SURVIVAL GEAR, POWER SOURCES...
IT'S WHY I PICKED IT. THESE FRONTIER CAMPS ARE AN EASY MARK. THEY MAKE LIKE THEY'RE TOUGH GUYS, BUT THEY'RE REALLY AS SOFT AS THEY COME.
THEY'D RATHER FILL THEIR GUTS THAN SHOW ANY.
CAMPER! FORGET THAT JUNK AND LOOK FOR THE PARTS YOU NEED. WE GOT AN HOUR BEFORE THEY WISE UP.
AND KID, SEE IF YOU CAN SWEET-TALK THAT FREAKY DROID OF YOURS INTO HELPING.
SEE IF THE FORCE CAN MAKE A LOADER-DROID ACTUALLY LOAD SOMETHING...

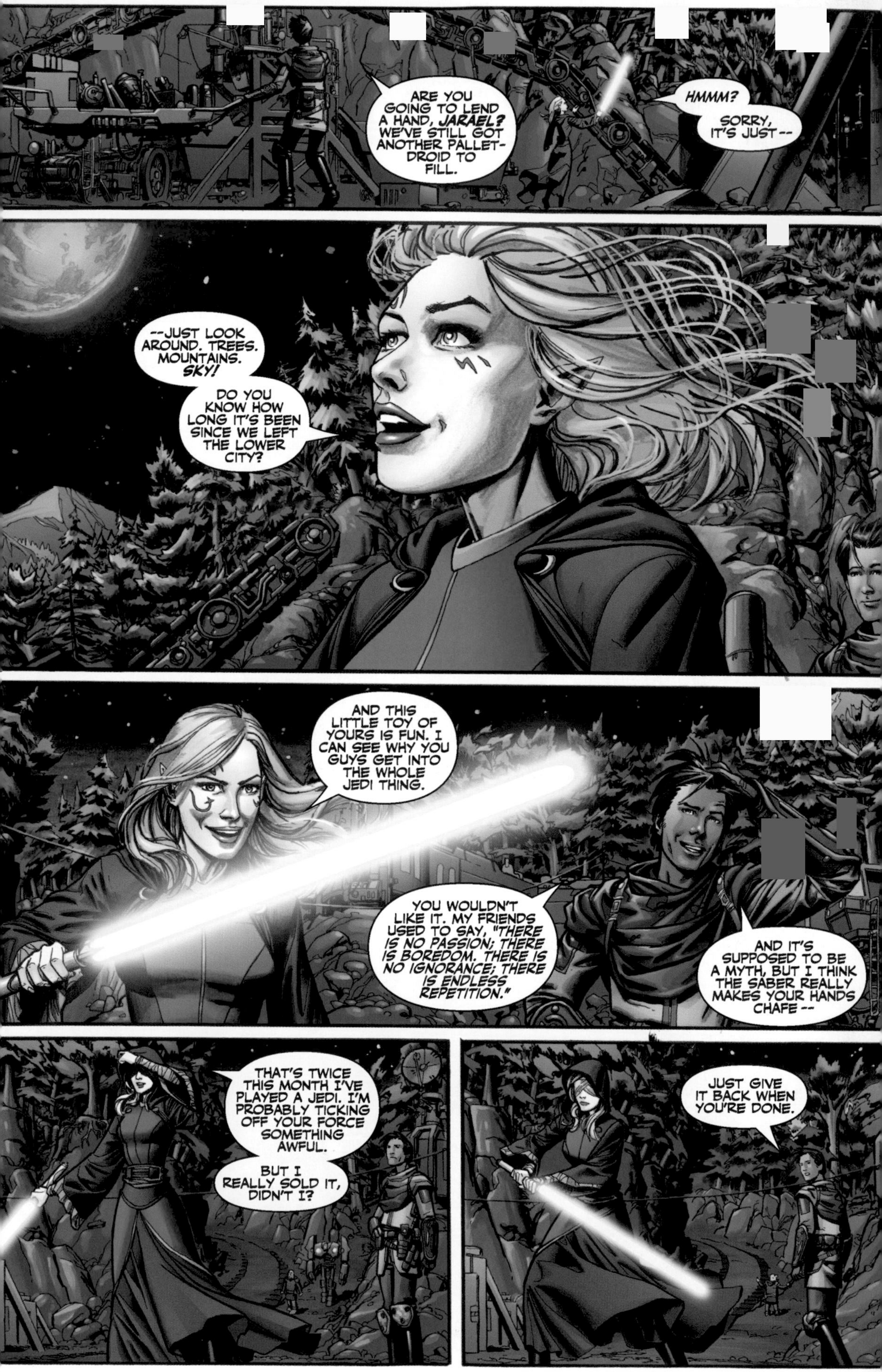
ARE YOU GOING TO LEND A HAND, JARAEL? WE'VE STILL GOT ANOTHER PALLET-DROID TO FILL.
HMMM?
SORRY, IT'S JUST --
--JUST LOOK AROUND. TREES. MOUNTAINS. SKY!
DO YOU KNOW HOW LONG IT'S BEEN SINCE WE LEFT THE LOWER CITY?
AND THIS LITTLE TOY OF YOURS IS FUN. I CAN SEE WHY YOU GUYS GET INTO THE WHOLE JEDI THING.
YOU WOULDN'T LIKE IT. MY FRIENDS USED TO SAY, "THERE IS NO PASSION; THERE IS BOREDOM. THERE IS NO IGNORANCE; THERE IS ENDLESS REPETITION."
AND IT'S SUPPOSED TO BE A MYTH, BUT I THINK THE SABER REALLY MAKES YOUR HANDS CHAFE --
THAT'S TWICE THIS MONTH I'VE PLAYED A JEDI. I'M PROBABLY TICKING OFF YOUR FORCE SOMETHING AWFUL.
BUT I REALLY SOLD IT, DIDN'T I?
JUST GIVE IT BACK WHEN YOU'RE DONE.

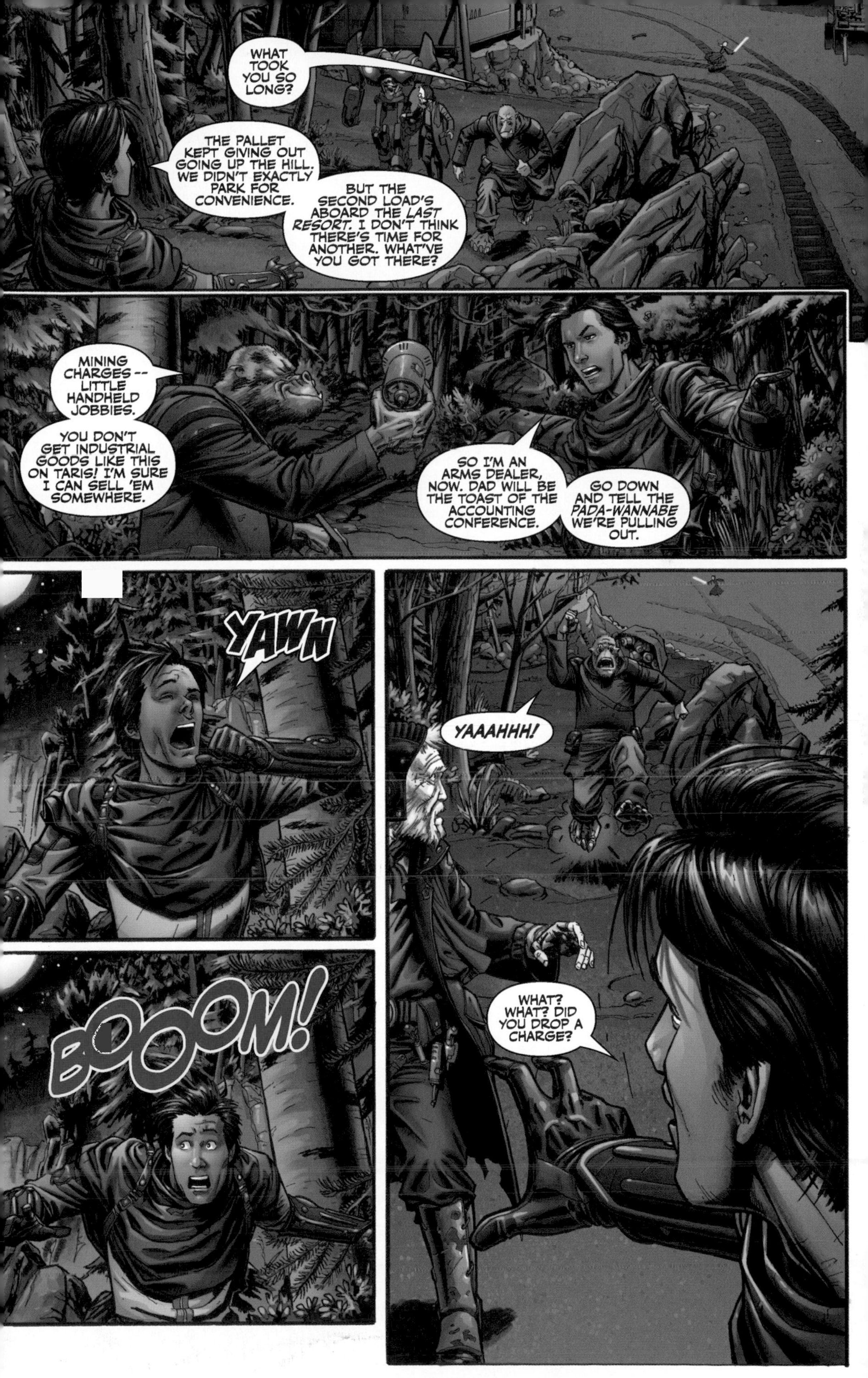
WHAT TOOK YOU SO LONG?
THE PALLET KEPT GIVING OUT GOING UP THE HILL. WE DIDN'T EXACTLY PARK FOR CONVENIENCE.
BUT THE SECOND LOAD'S ABOARD THE *LAST RESORT*. I DON'T THINK THERE'S TIME FOR ANOTHER. WHAT'VE YOU GOT THERE?
MINING CHARGES -- LITTLE HANDHELD JOBBIES.
YOU DON'T GET INDUSTRIAL GOODS LIKE THIS ON TARIS! I'M SURE I CAN SELL 'EM SOMEWHERE.
SO I'M AN ARMS DEALER, NOW. DAD WILL BE THE TOAST OF THE ACCOUNTING CONFERENCE.
GO DOWN AND TELL THE *PADA-WANNABE* WE'RE PULLING OUT.
YAWN
BOOOM!
YAAAHHH!
WHAT? WHAT? DID YOU DROP A CHARGE?

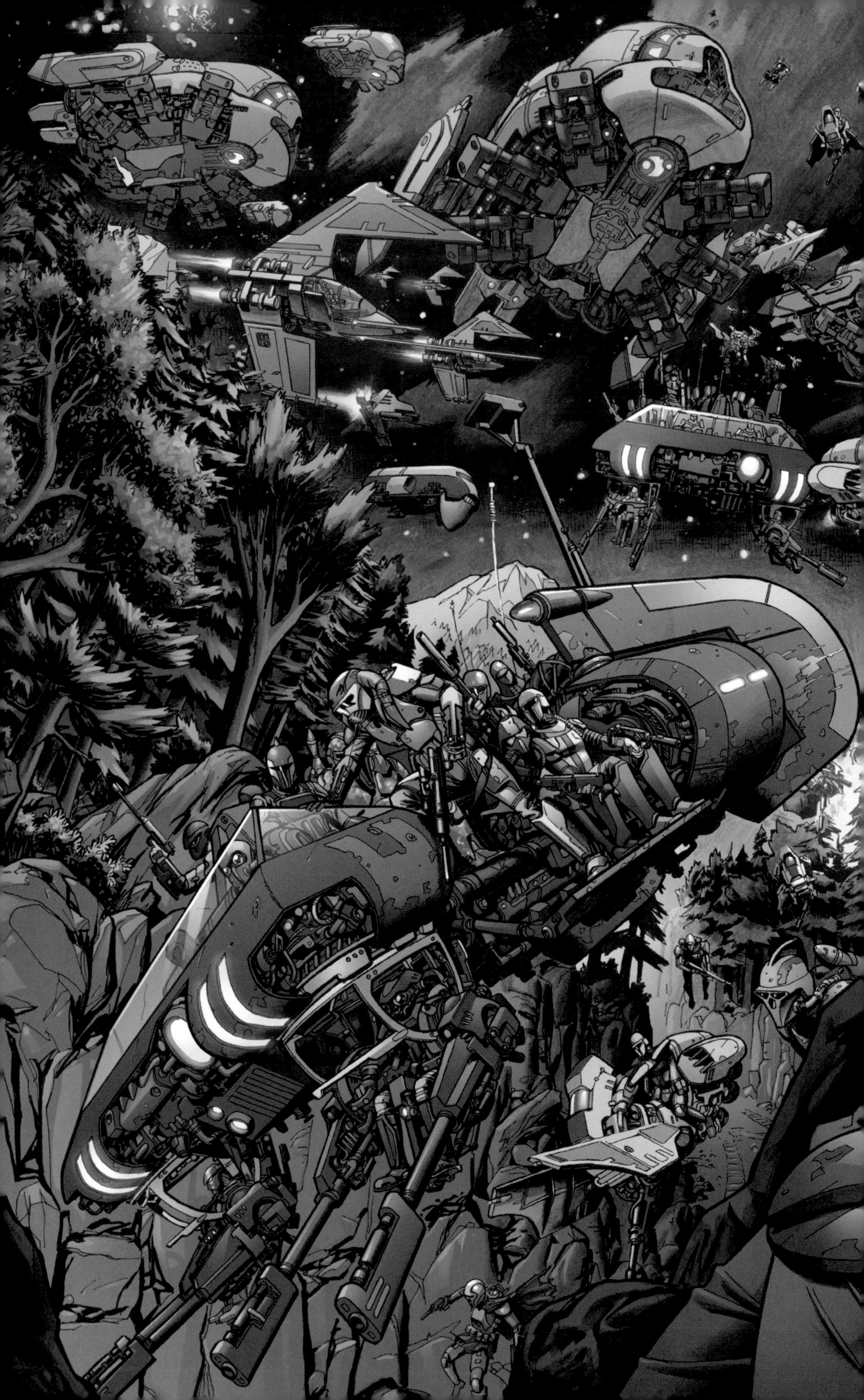

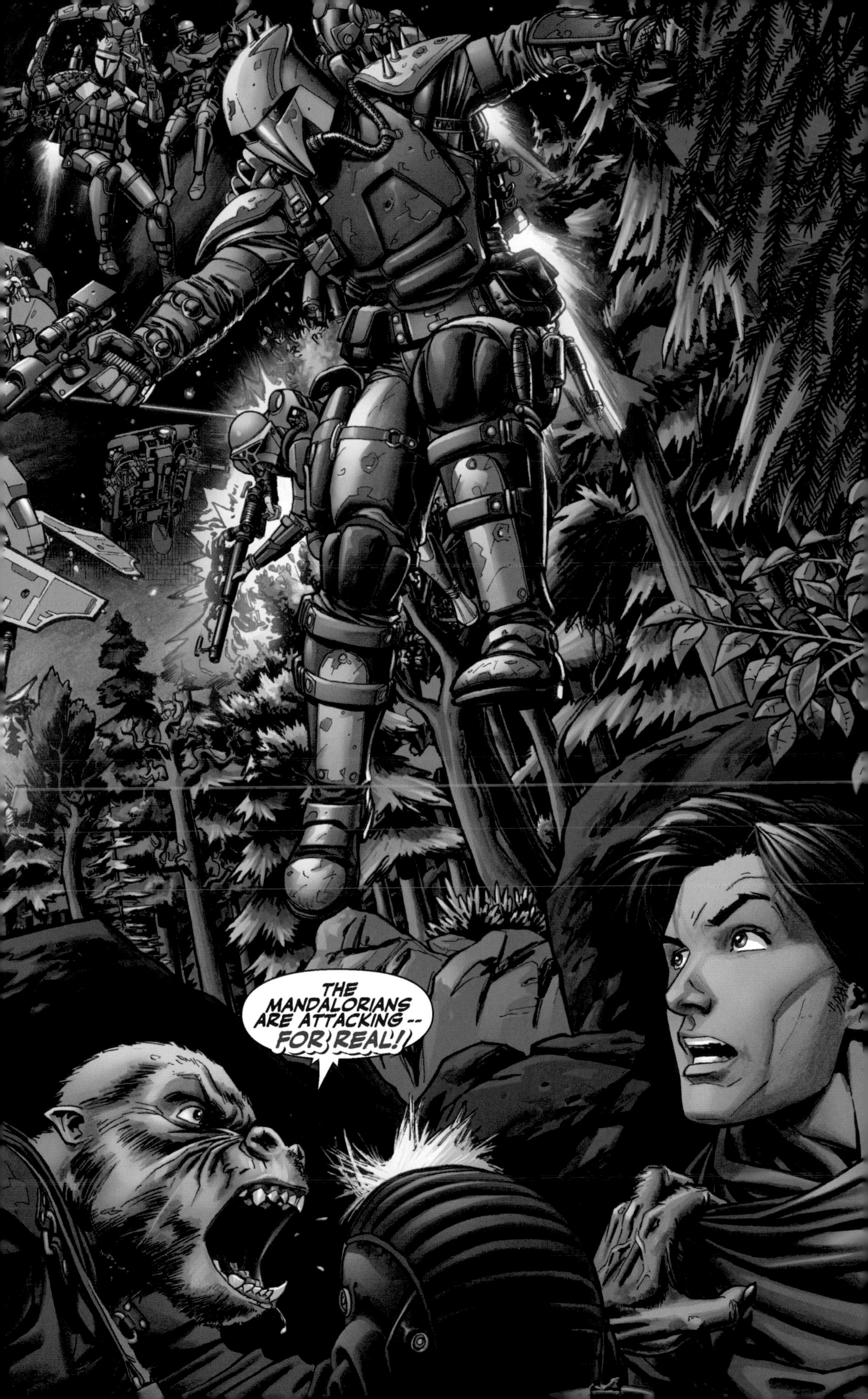
THE MANDALORIANS ARE ATTACKING -- FOR REAL!

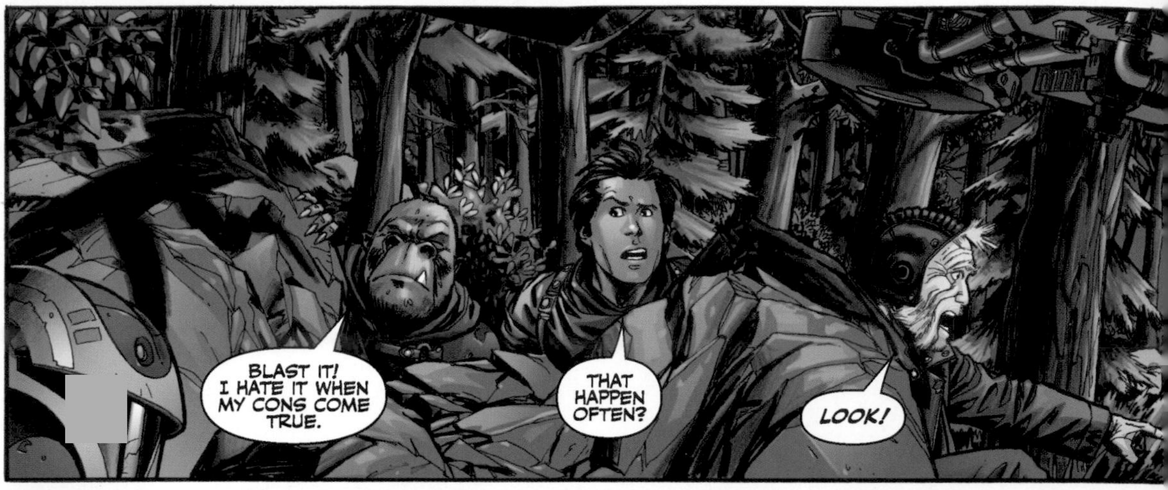
BLAST IT! I HATE IT WHEN MY CONS COME TRUE.
THAT HAPPEN OFTEN?
LOOK!

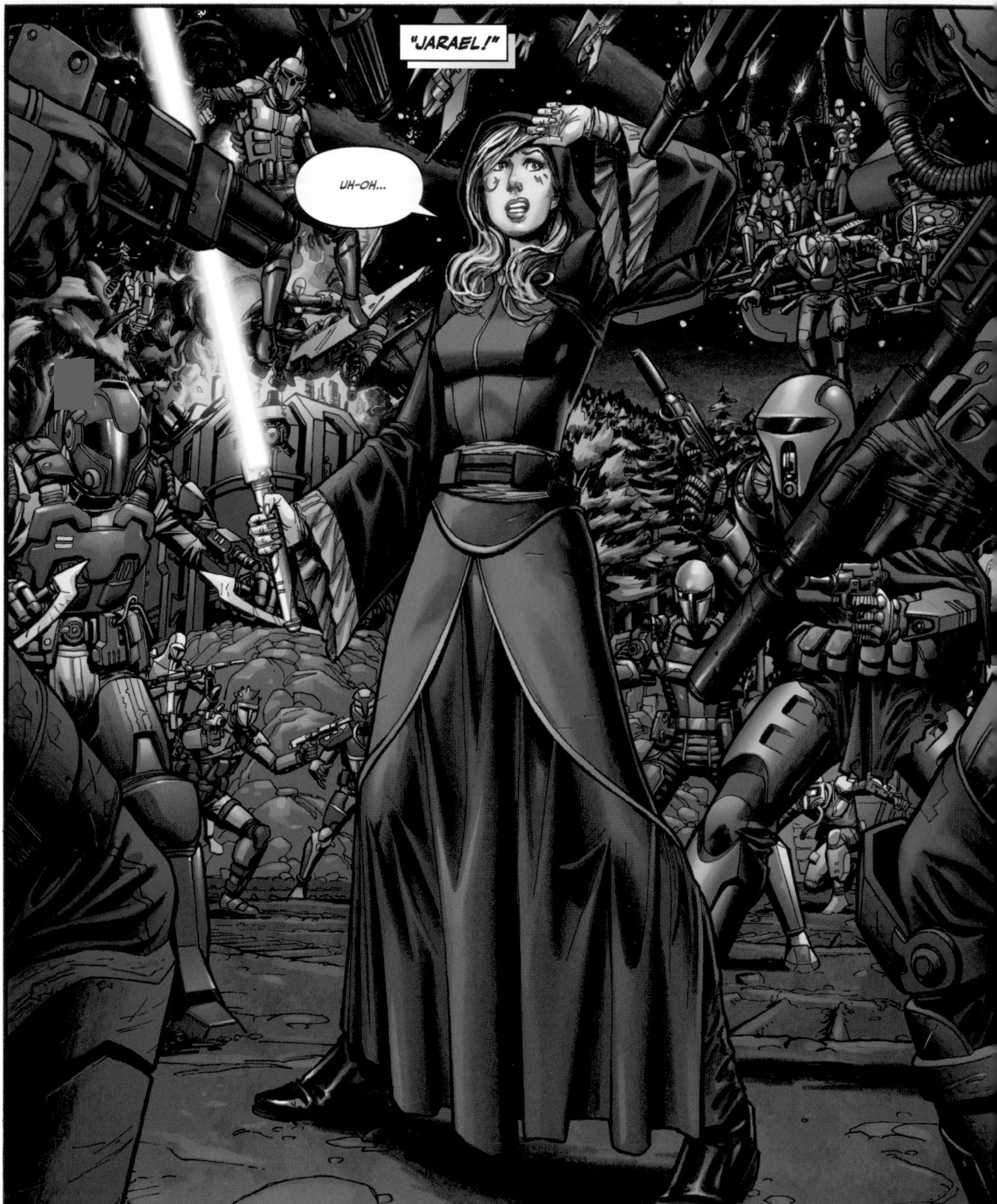
"JARAEL!"
UH-OH...

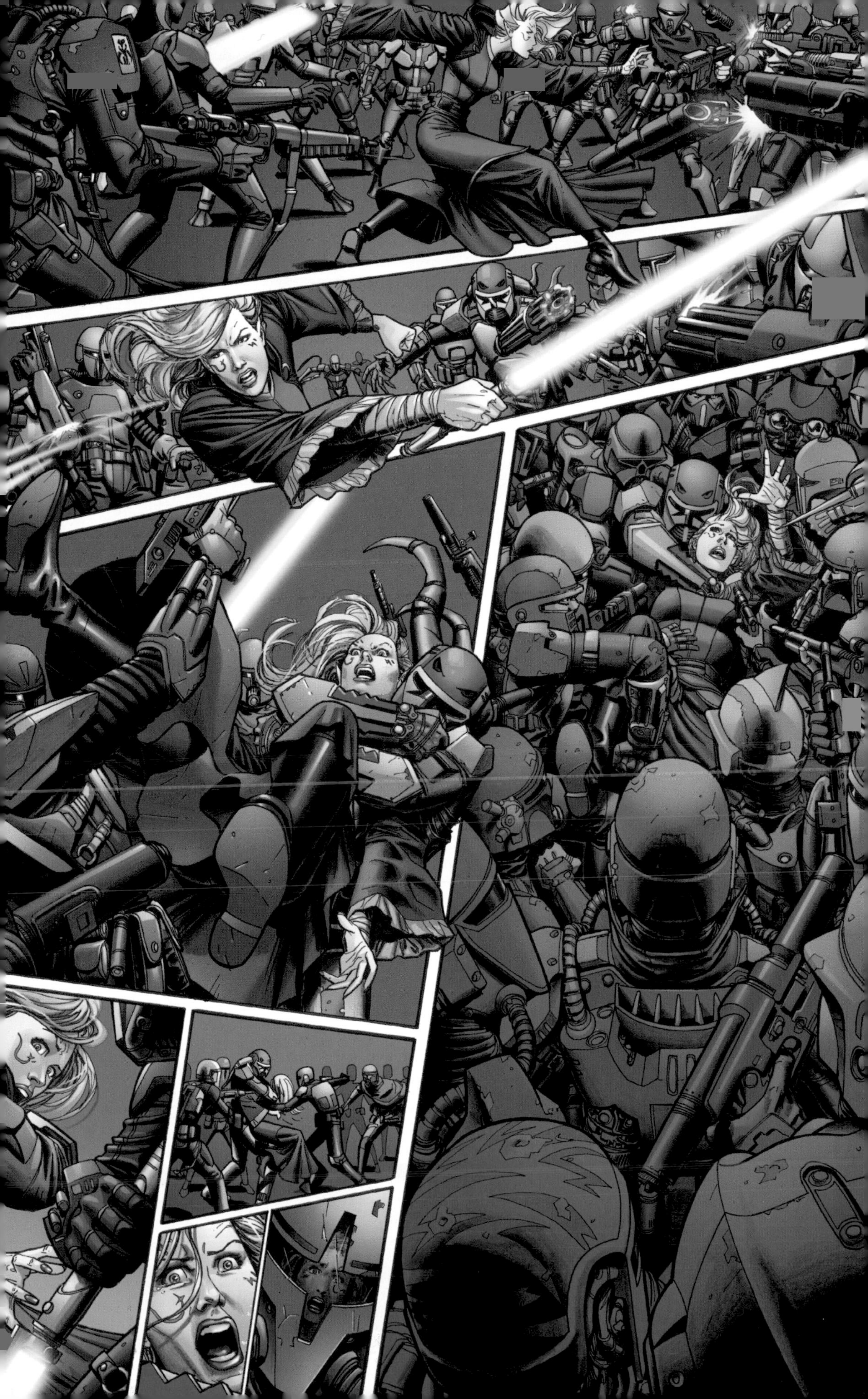

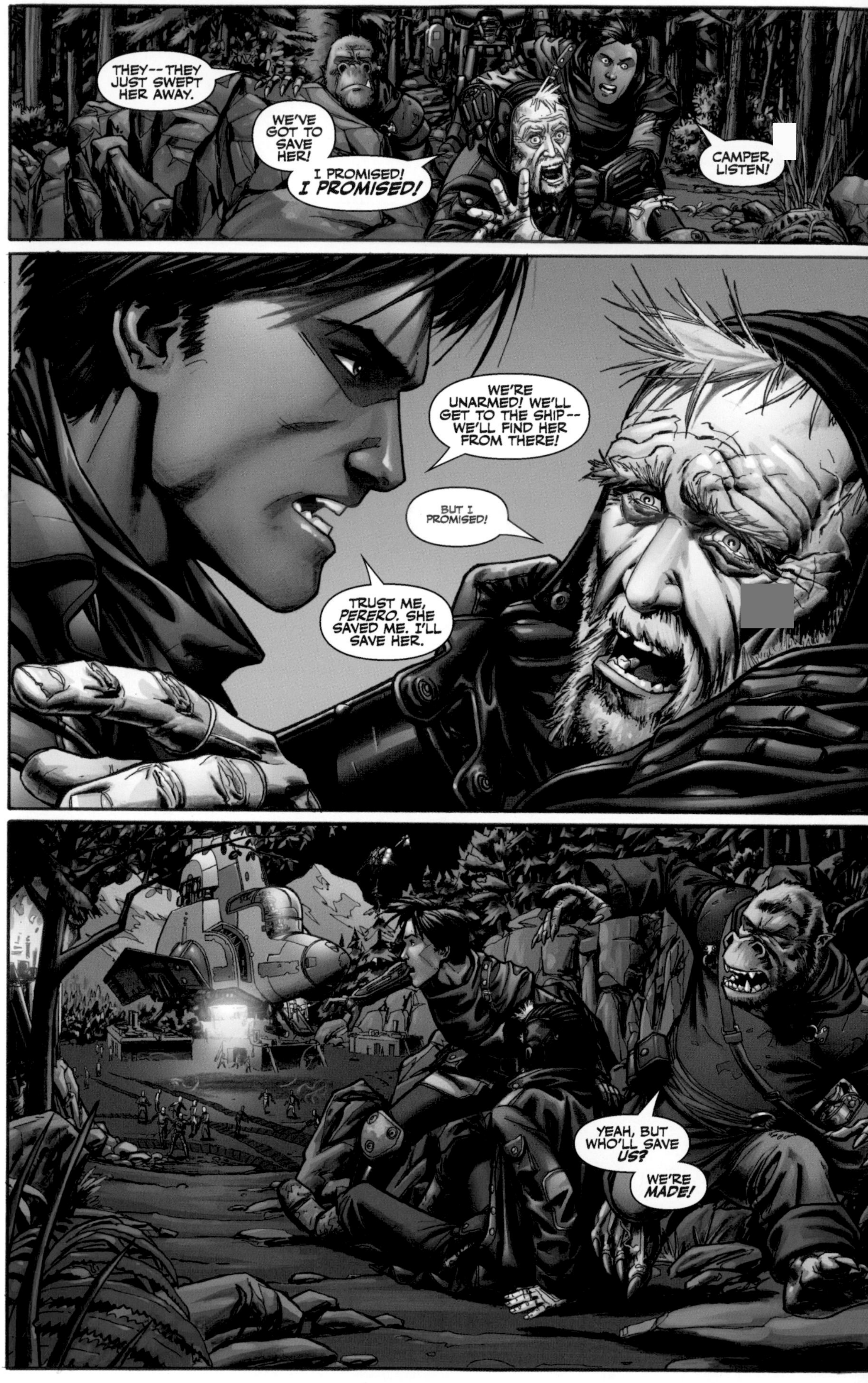
THEY--THEY JUST SWEPT HER AWAY.
WE'VE GOT TO SAVE HER!
I PROMISED! *I PROMISED!*
CAMPER, LISTEN!
WE'RE UNARMED! WE'LL GET TO THE SHIP-- WE'LL FIND HER FROM THERE!
BUT I PROMISED!
TRUST ME, *PERERO.* SHE SAVED ME. I'LL SAVE HER.
YEAH, BUT WHO'LL SAVE *US?*
WE'RE *MADE!*

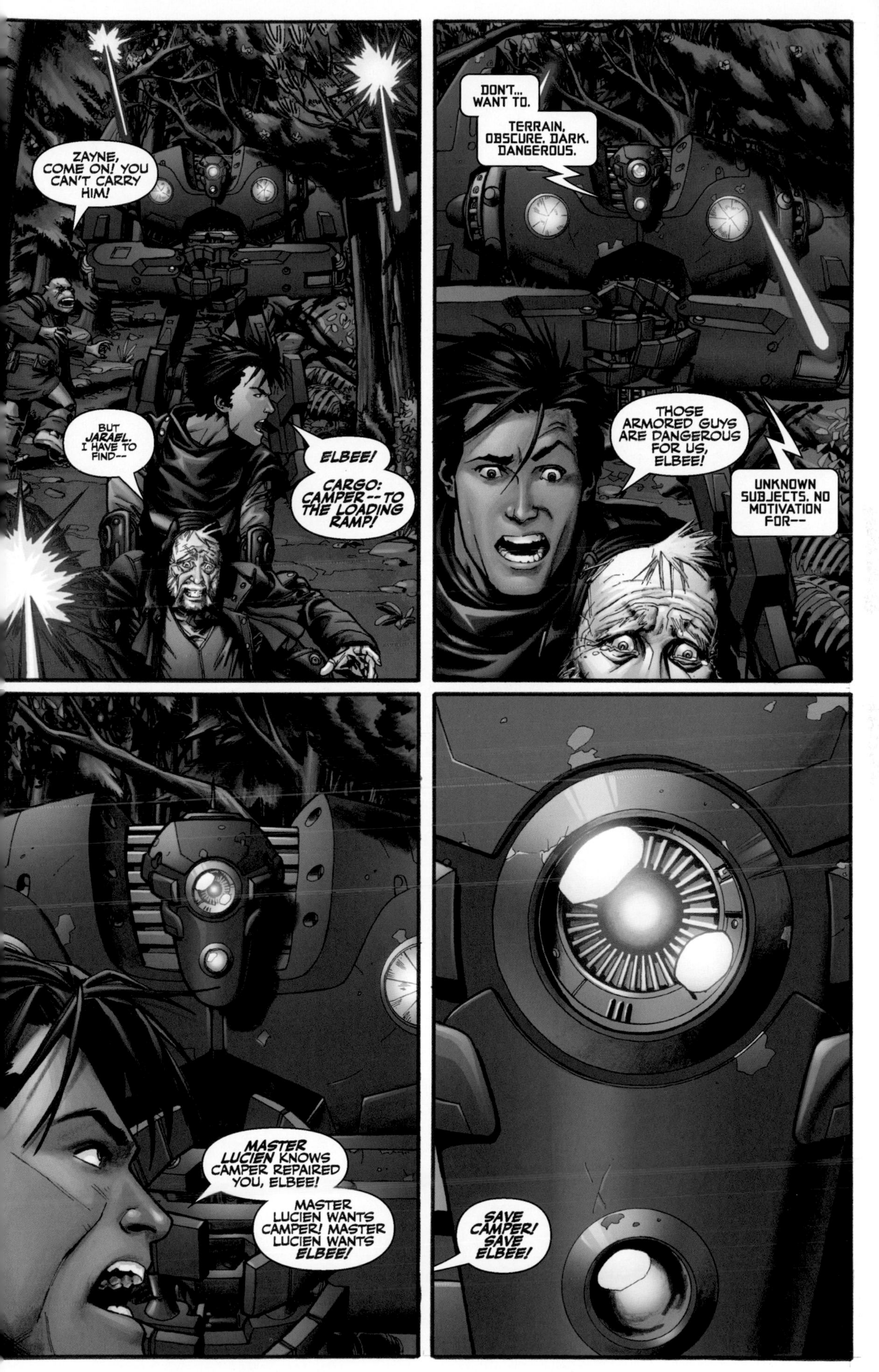
ZAYNE, COME ON! YOU CAN'T CARRY HIM!
BUT JARAEL. I HAVE TO FIND--
ELBEE!
CARGO: CAMPER--TO THE LOADING RAMP!
DON'T... WANT TO.
TERRAIN, OBSCURE. DARK. DANGEROUS.
THOSE ARMORED GUYS ARE DANGEROUS FOR US, ELBEE!
UNKNOWN SUBJECTS. NO MOTIVATION FOR--
MASTER LUCIEN KNOWS CAMPER REPAIRED YOU, ELBEE!
MASTER LUCIEN WANTS CAMPER! MASTER LUCIEN WANTS ELBEE!
SAVE CAMPER! SAVE ELBEE!

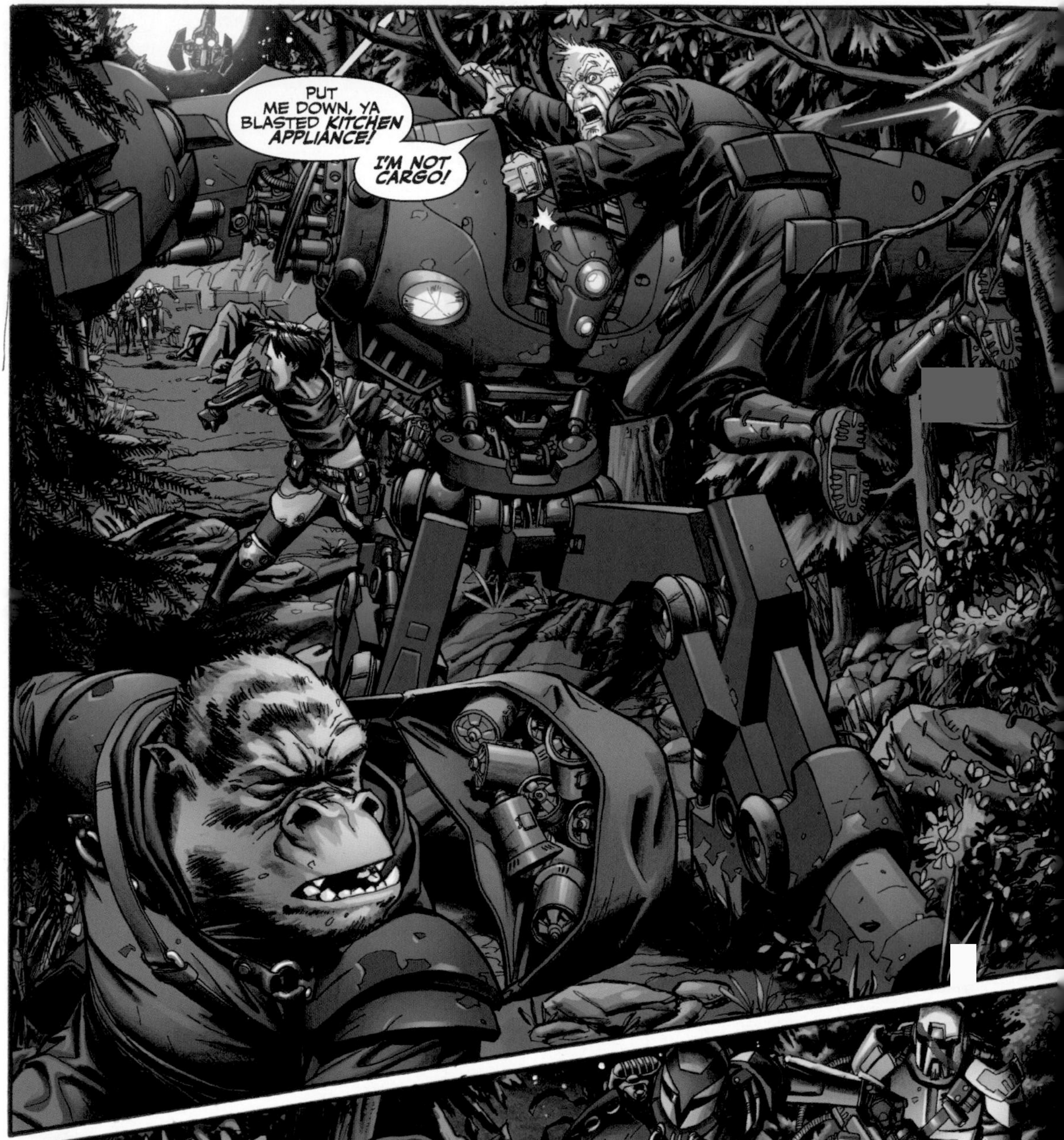
PUT ME DOWN, YA BLASTED KITCHEN APPLIANCE!
I'M NOT CARGO!

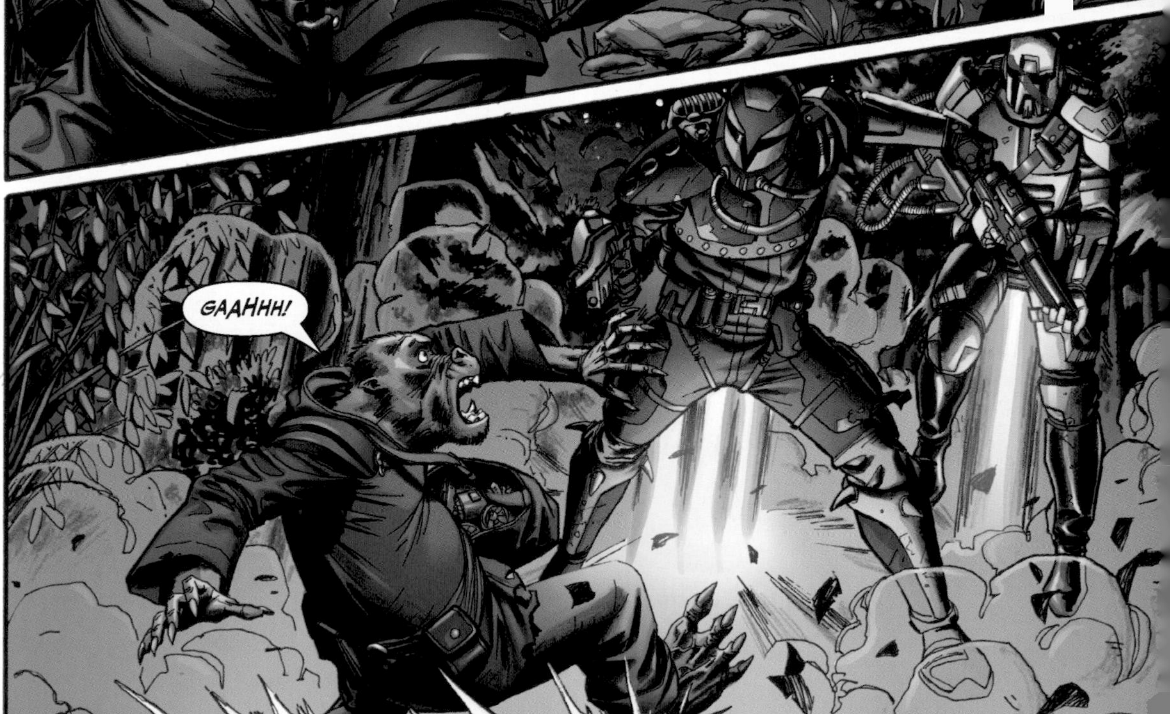
GAAHHH!

GRYPH, GET DOWN!
KRAK!
WHACK!
OOOF!
ELBEE! CARGO: MANDALORIAN--
--TO ORBIT!

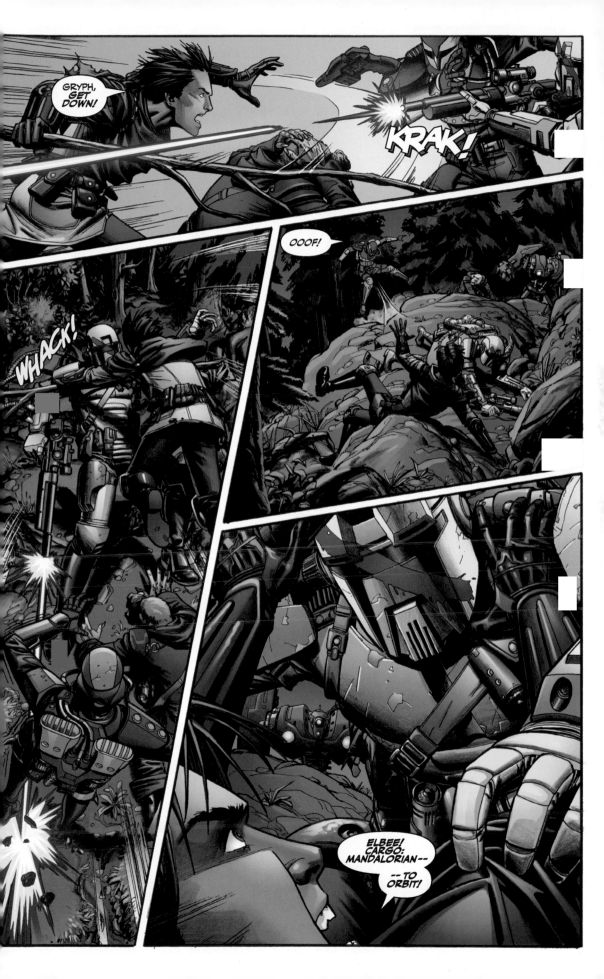

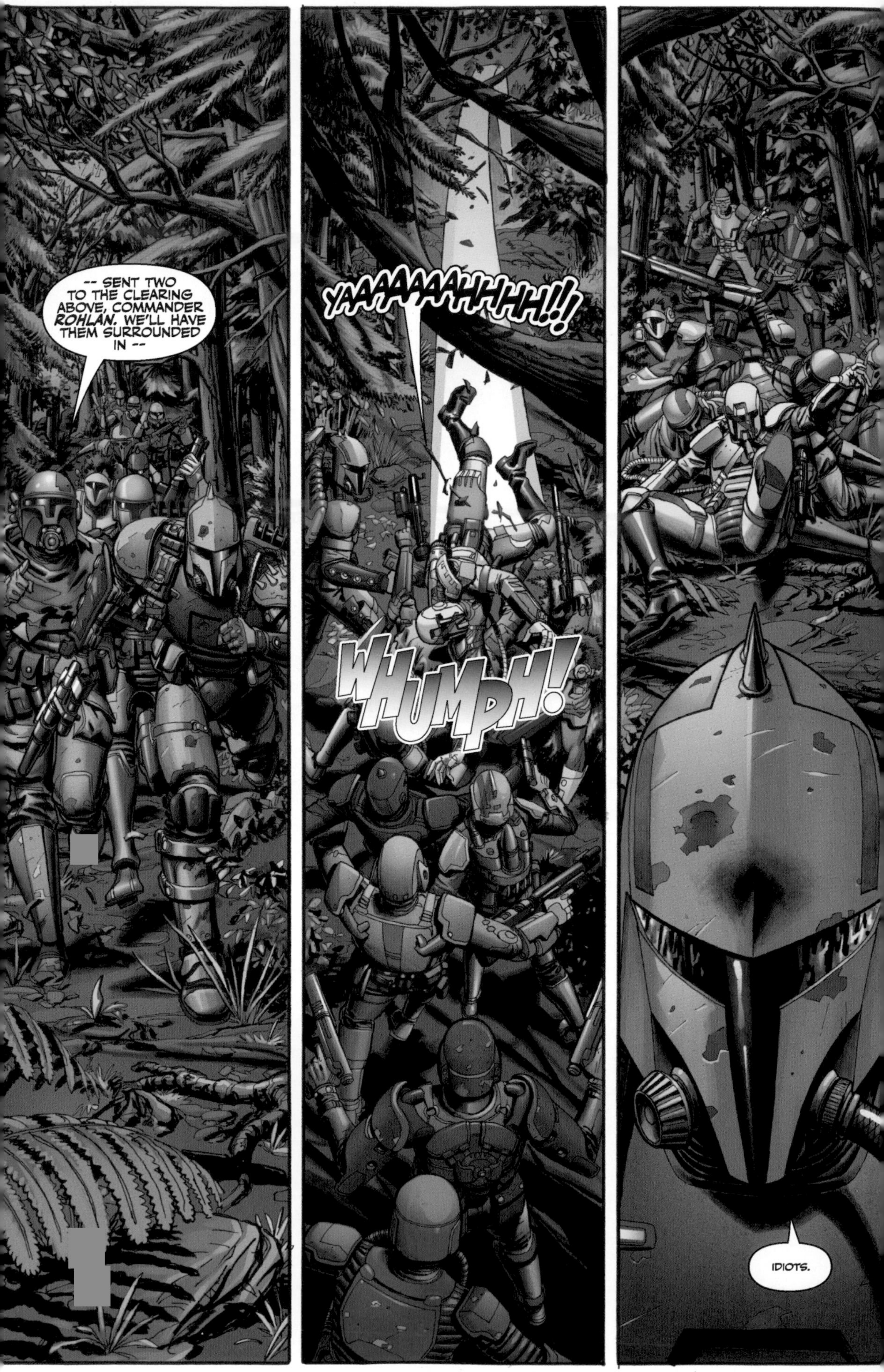
-- SENT TWO TO THE CLEARING ABOVE, COMMANDER ROHLAN. WE'LL HAVE THEM SURROUNDED IN --
YAAAAAHHHH!!!
WHUMPH!
IDIOTS.

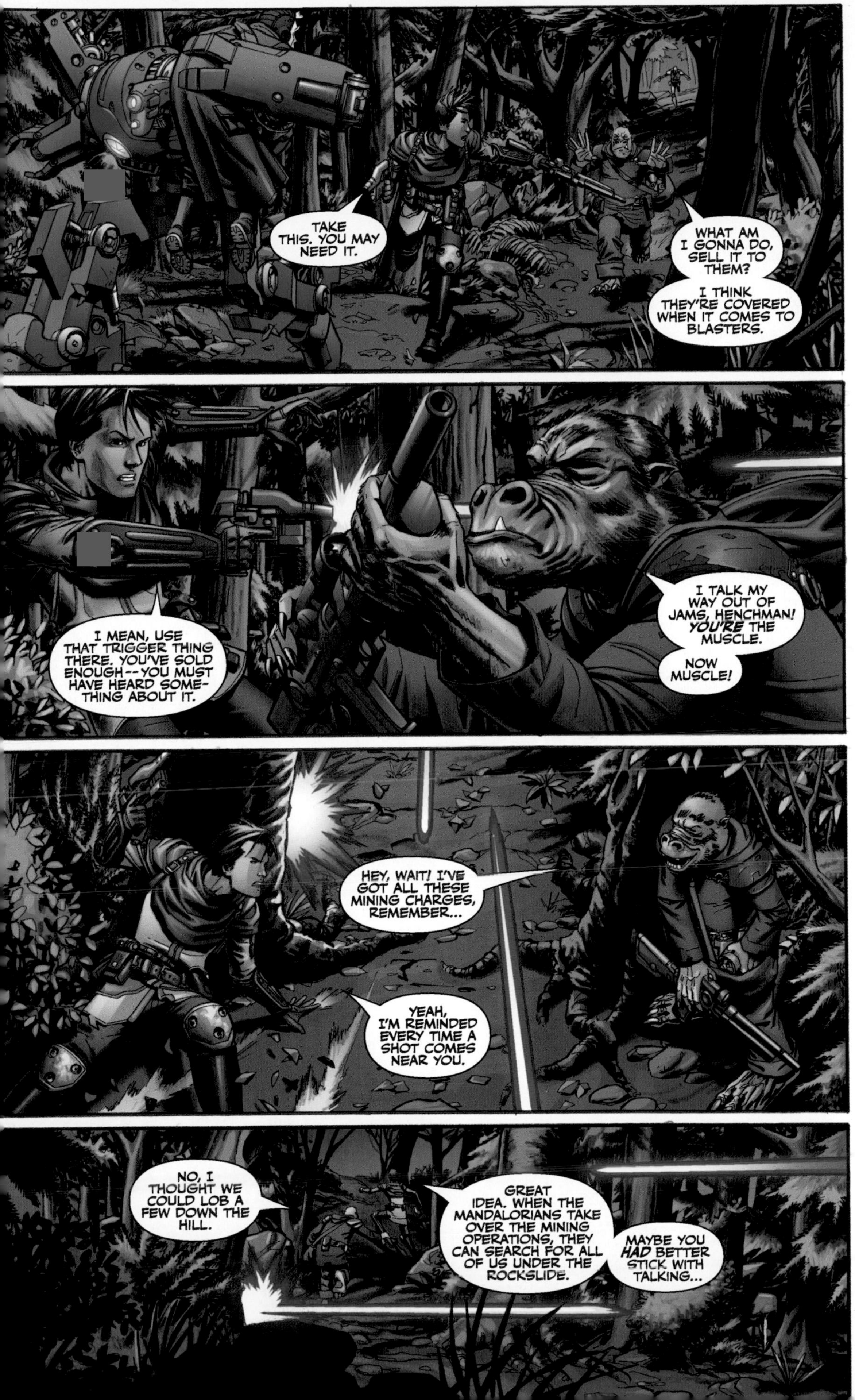
TAKE THIS. YOU MAY NEED IT.
WHAT AM I GONNA DO, SELL IT TO THEM?
I THINK THEY'RE COVERED WHEN IT COMES TO BLASTERS.
I MEAN, USE THAT TRIGGER THING THERE. YOU'VE SOLD ENOUGH--YOU MUST HAVE HEARD SOME-THING ABOUT IT.
I TALK MY WAY OUT OF JAMS, HENCHMAN! *YOU'RE* THE MUSCLE.
NOW MUSCLE!
HEY, WAIT! I'VE GOT ALL THESE MINING CHARGES, REMEMBER...
YEAH, I'M REMINDED EVERY TIME A SHOT COMES NEAR YOU.
NO, I THOUGHT WE COULD LOB A FEW DOWN THE HILL.
GREAT IDEA. WHEN THE MANDALORIANS TAKE OVER THE MINING OPERATIONS, THEY CAN SEARCH FOR ALL OF US UNDER THE ROCKSLIDE.
MAYBE YOU *HAD* BETTER STICK WITH TALKING...

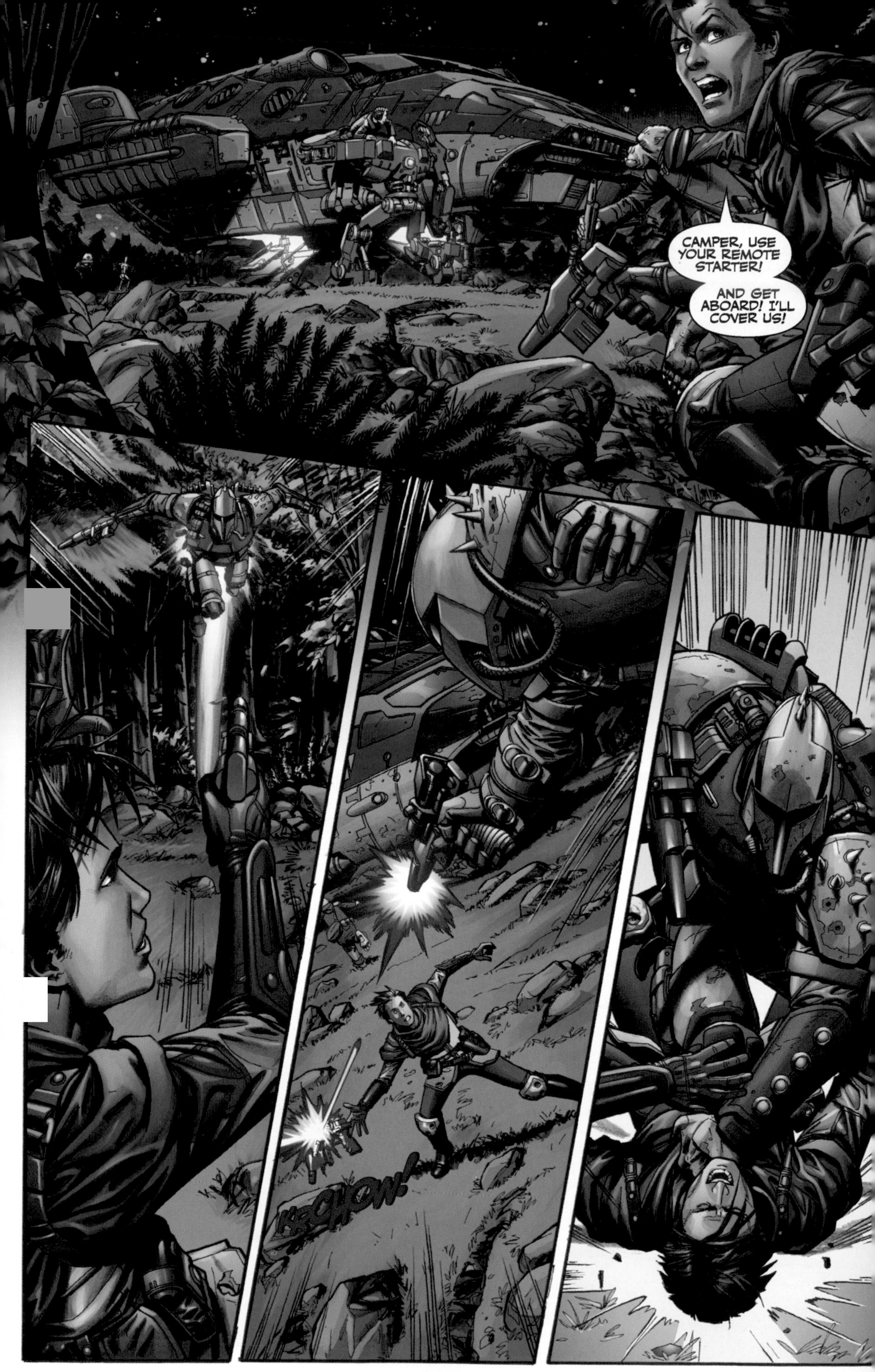
CAMPER, USE YOUR REMOTE STARTER!
AND GET ABOARD! I'LL COVER US!
KRCHOW!

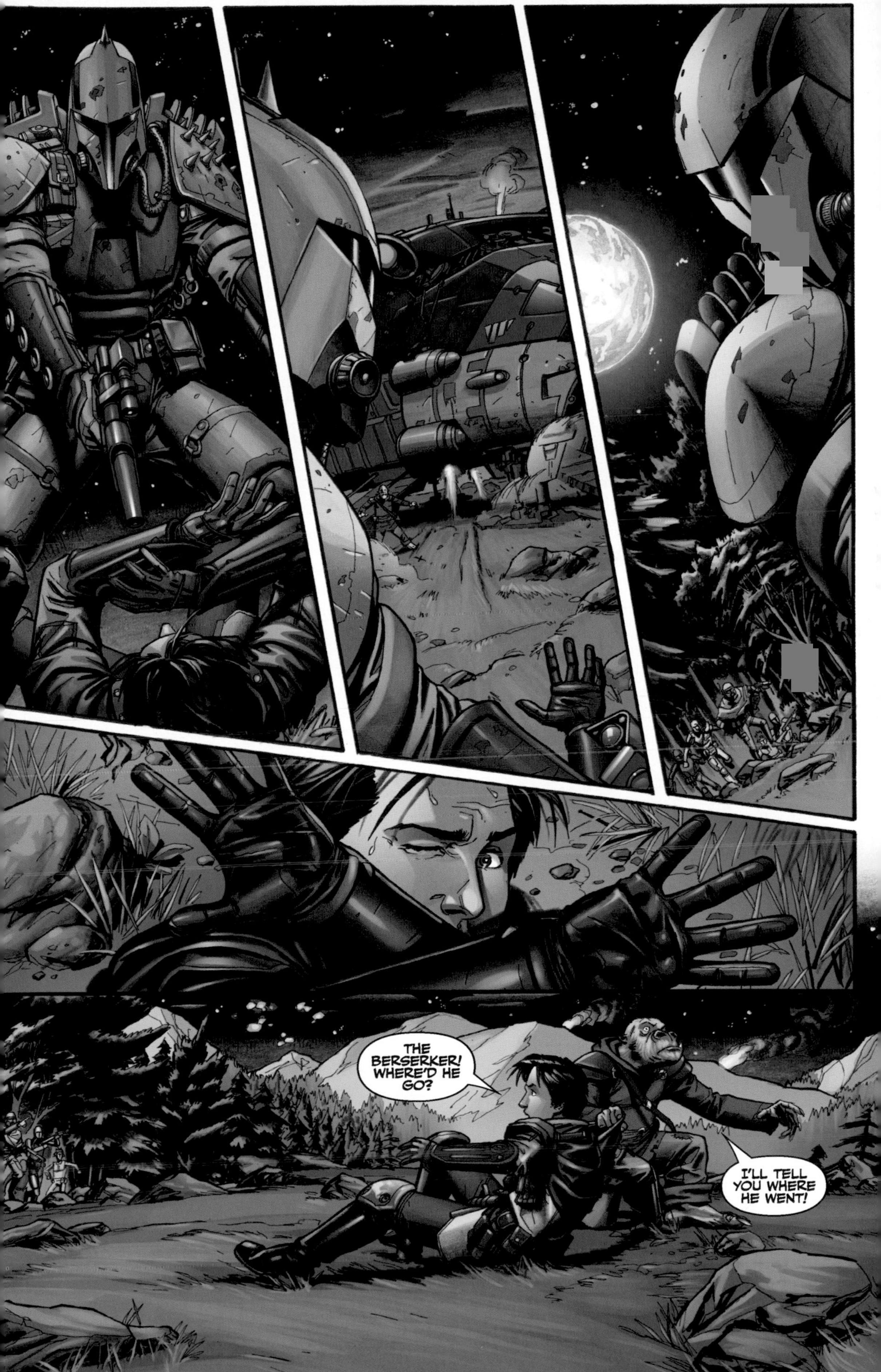
THE BERSERKER! WHERE'D HE GO?
I'LL TELL YOU WHERE HE WENT!

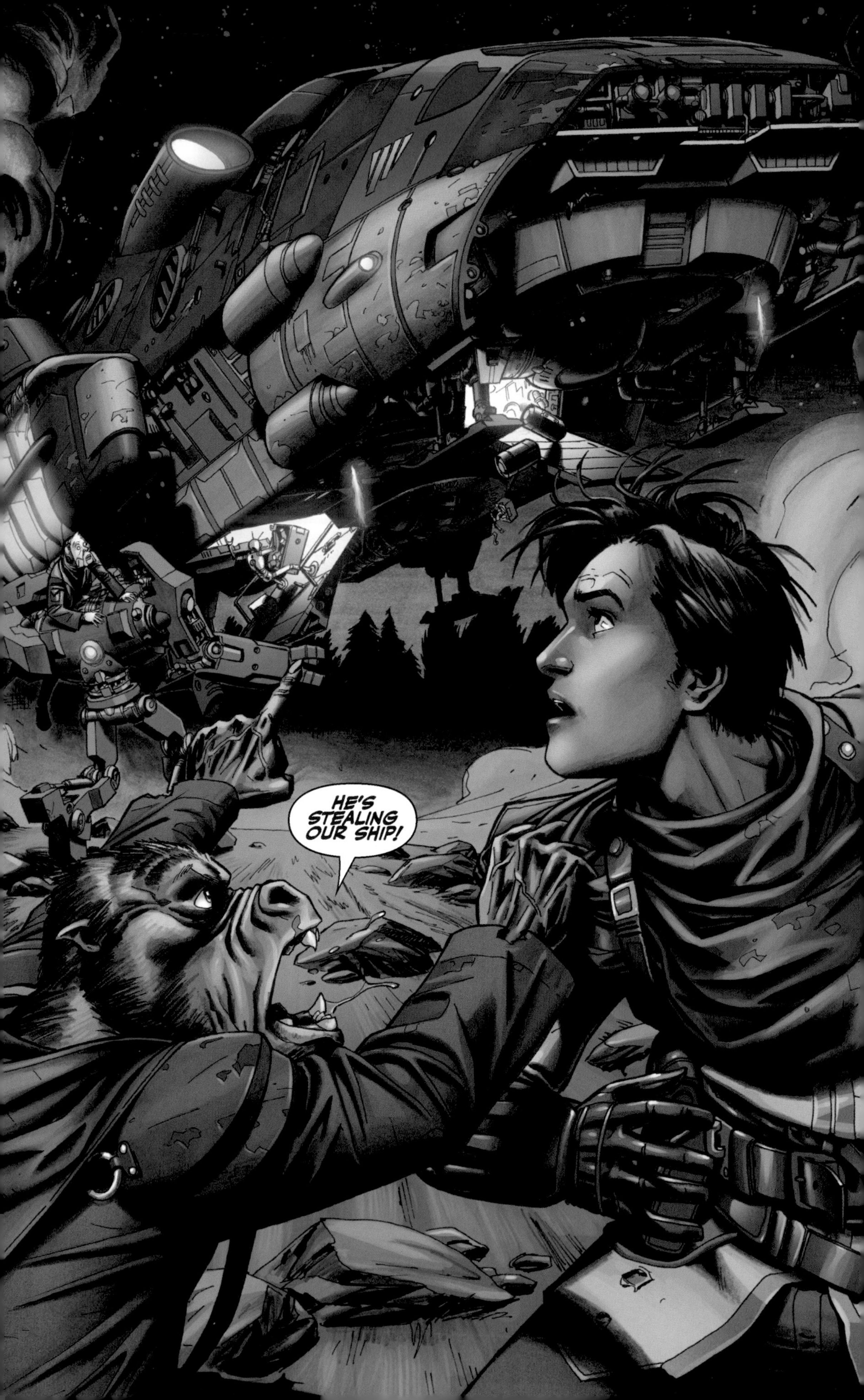
HE'S STEALING OUR SHIP!

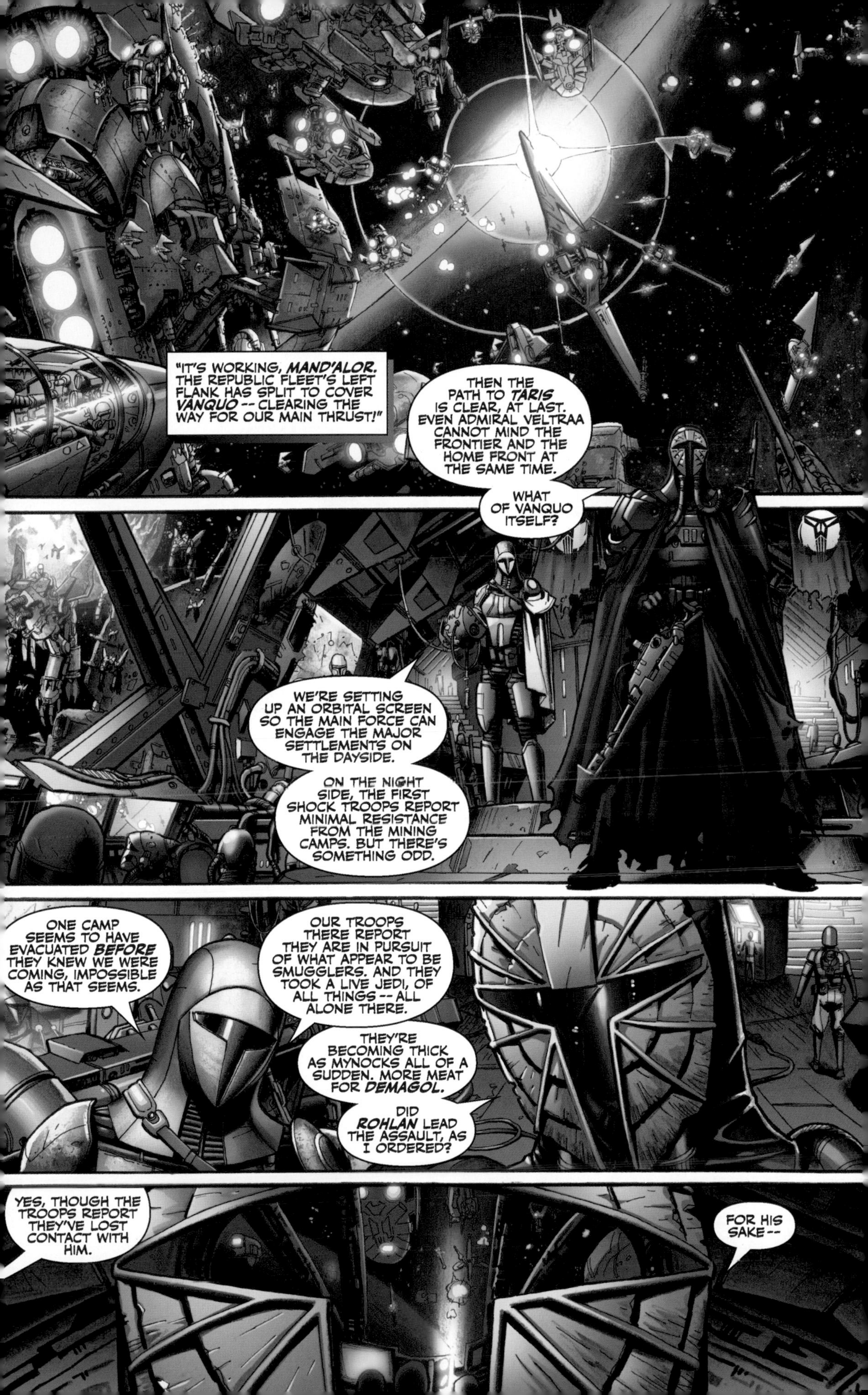
"IT'S WORKING, MAND'ALOR. THE REPUBLIC FLEET'S LEFT FLANK HAS SPLIT TO COVER VANQUO -- CLEARING THE WAY FOR OUR MAIN THRUST!"
THEN THE PATH TO TARIS IS CLEAR, AT LAST. EVEN ADMIRAL VELTRAA CANNOT MIND THE FRONTIER AND THE HOME FRONT AT THE SAME TIME.
WHAT OF VANQUO ITSELF?
WE'RE SETTING UP AN ORBITAL SCREEN SO THE MAIN FORCE CAN ENGAGE THE MAJOR SETTLEMENTS ON THE DAYSIDE.
ON THE NIGHT SIDE, THE FIRST SHOCK TROOPS REPORT MINIMAL RESISTANCE FROM THE MINING CAMPS. BUT THERE'S SOMETHING ODD.
ONE CAMP SEEMS TO HAVE EVACUATED BEFORE THEY KNEW WE WERE COMING, IMPOSSIBLE AS THAT SEEMS.
OUR TROOPS THERE REPORT THEY ARE IN PURSUIT OF WHAT APPEAR TO BE SMUGGLERS. AND THEY TOOK A LIVE JEDI, OF ALL THINGS -- ALL ALONE THERE.
THEY'RE BECOMING THICK AS MYNOCKS ALL OF A SUDDEN. MORE MEAT FOR DEMAGOL.
DID ROHLAN LEAD THE ASSAULT, AS I ORDERED?
YES, THOUGH THE TROOPS REPORT THEY'VE LOST CONTACT WITH HIM.
FOR HIS SAKE --

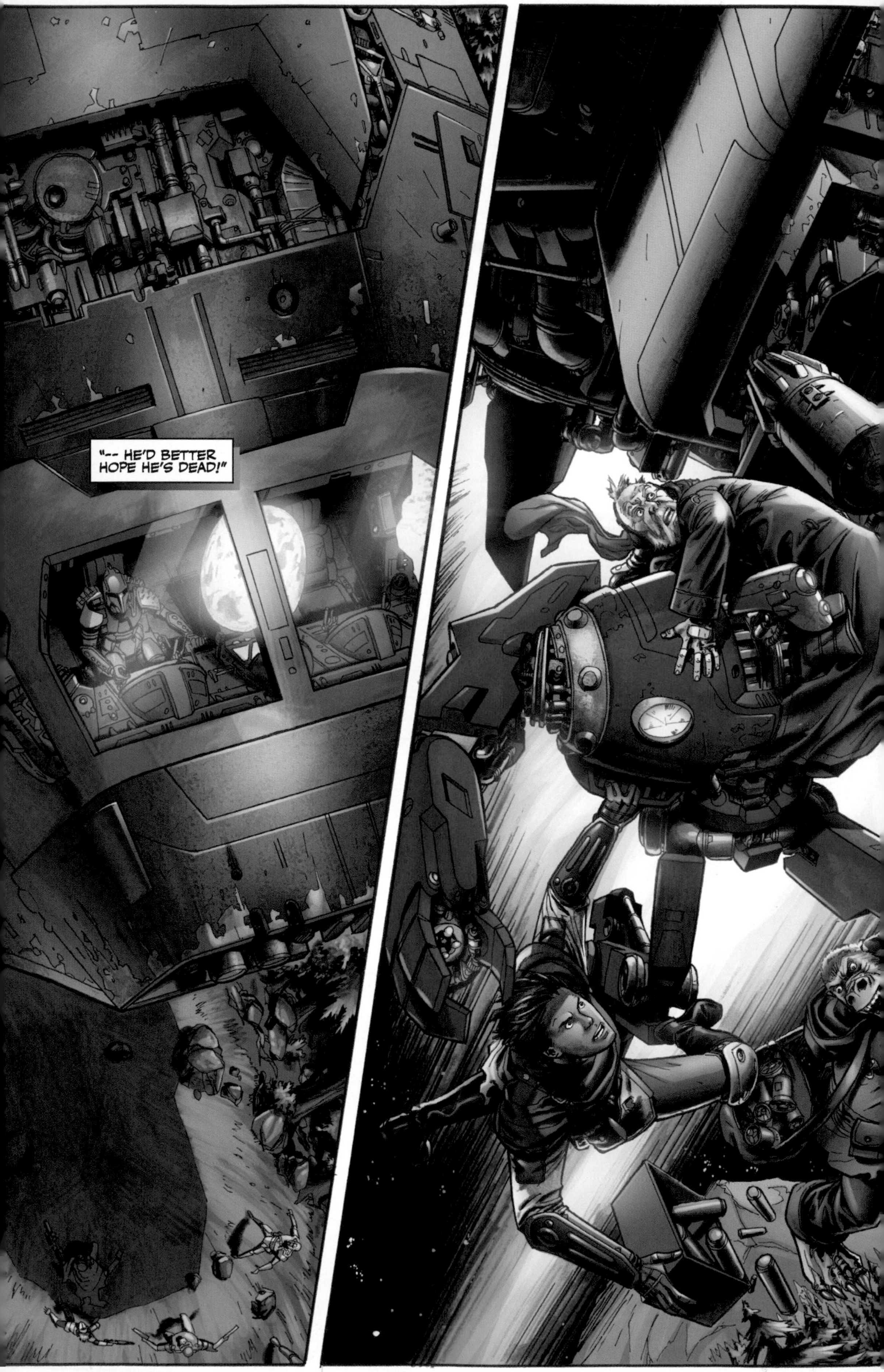
"-- HE'D BETTER HOPE HE'S DEAD!"

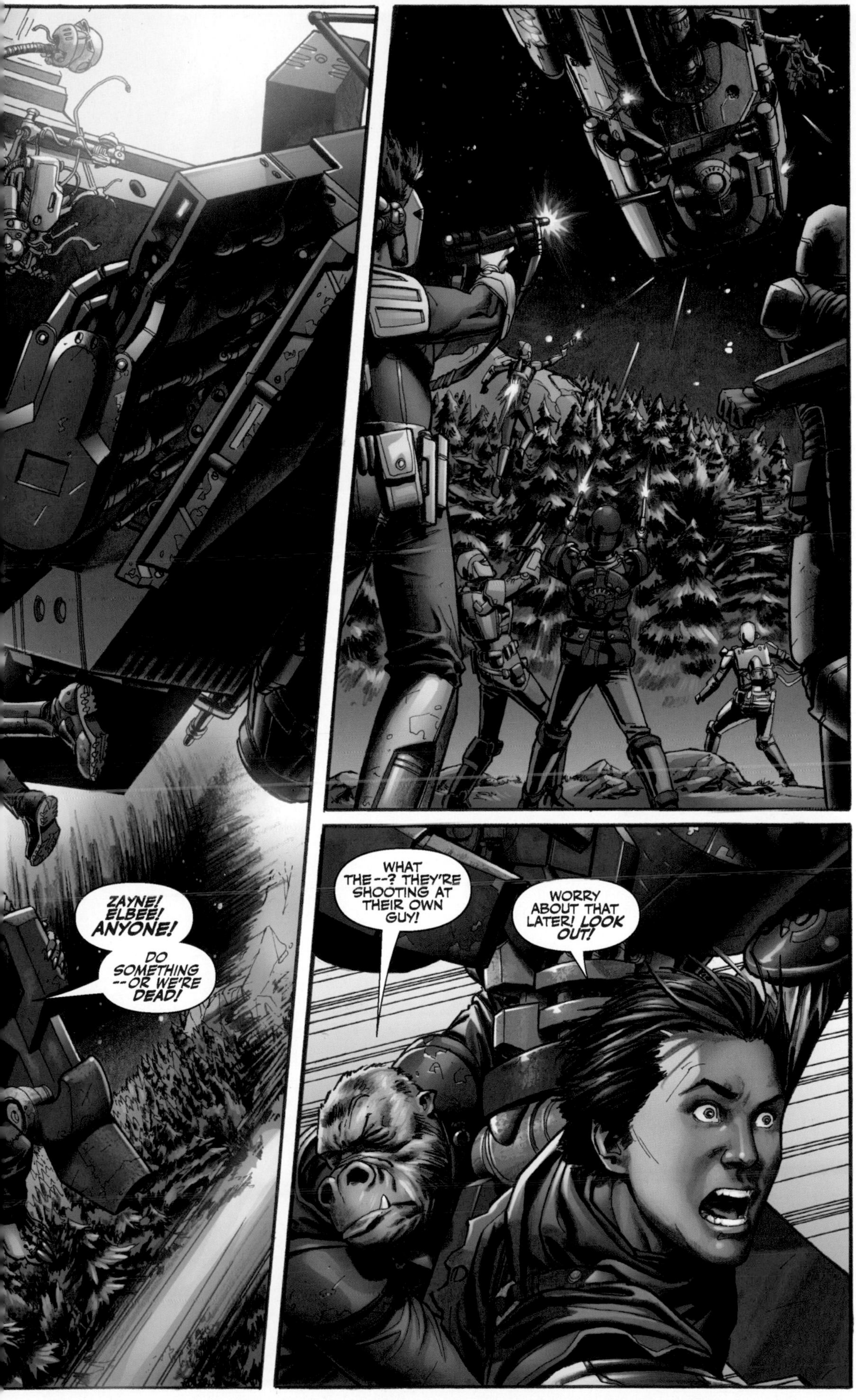
ZAYNE! ELBEE! ANYONE!
DO SOMETHING --OR WE'RE DEAD!
WHAT THE--? THEY'RE SHOOTING AT THEIR OWN GUY!
WORRY ABOUT THAT LATER! LOOK OUT!

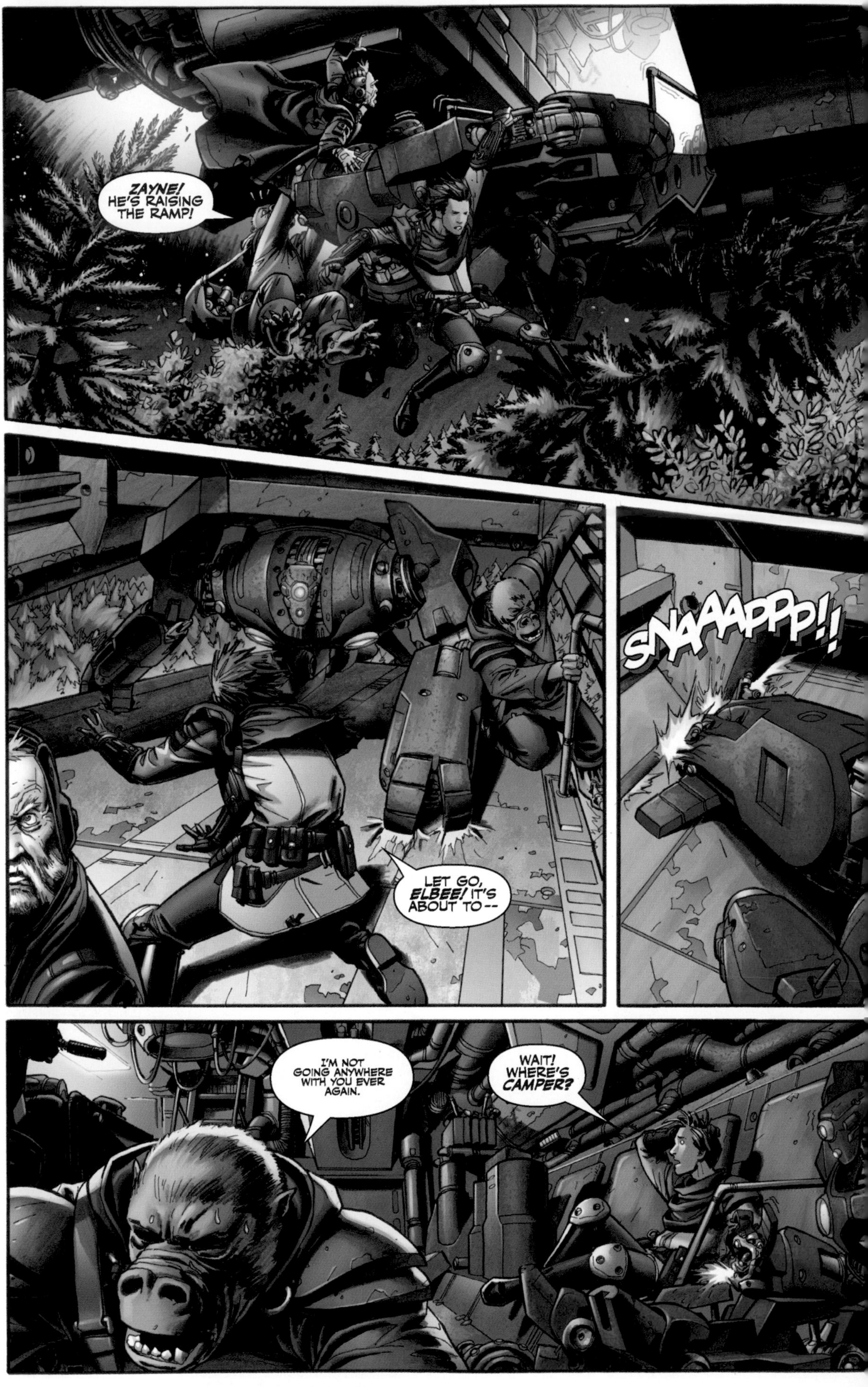
ZAYNE! HE'S RAISING THE RAMP!
LET GO, ELBEE! IT'S ABOUT TO--
SNAAAPPPP!!
I'M NOT GOING ANYWHERE WITH YOU EVER AGAIN.
WAIT! WHERE'S CAMPER?

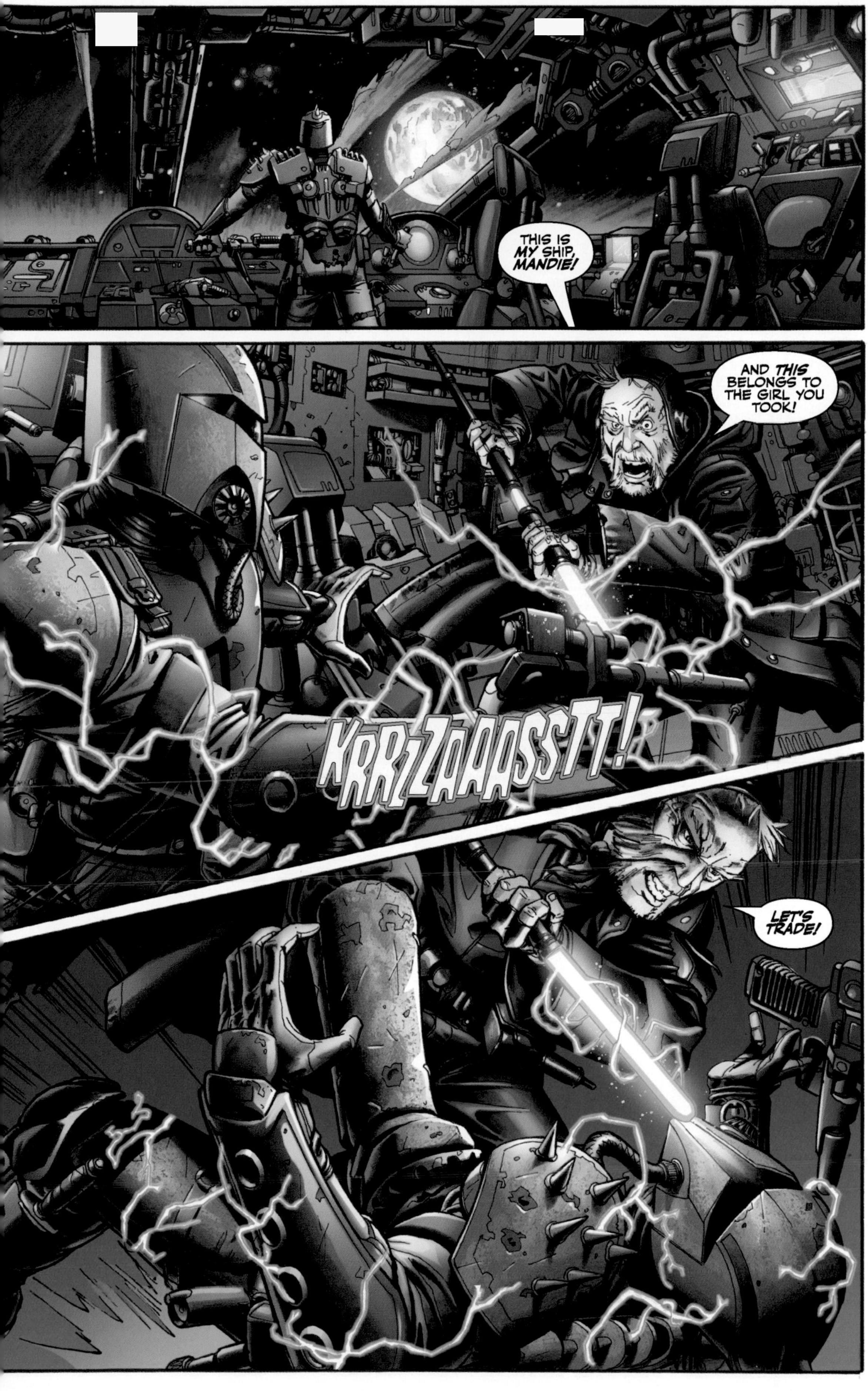
THIS IS MY SHIP, MANDIE!
AND THIS BELONGS TO THE GIRL YOU TOOK!
KRRZAAAASSTT!
LET'S TRADE!

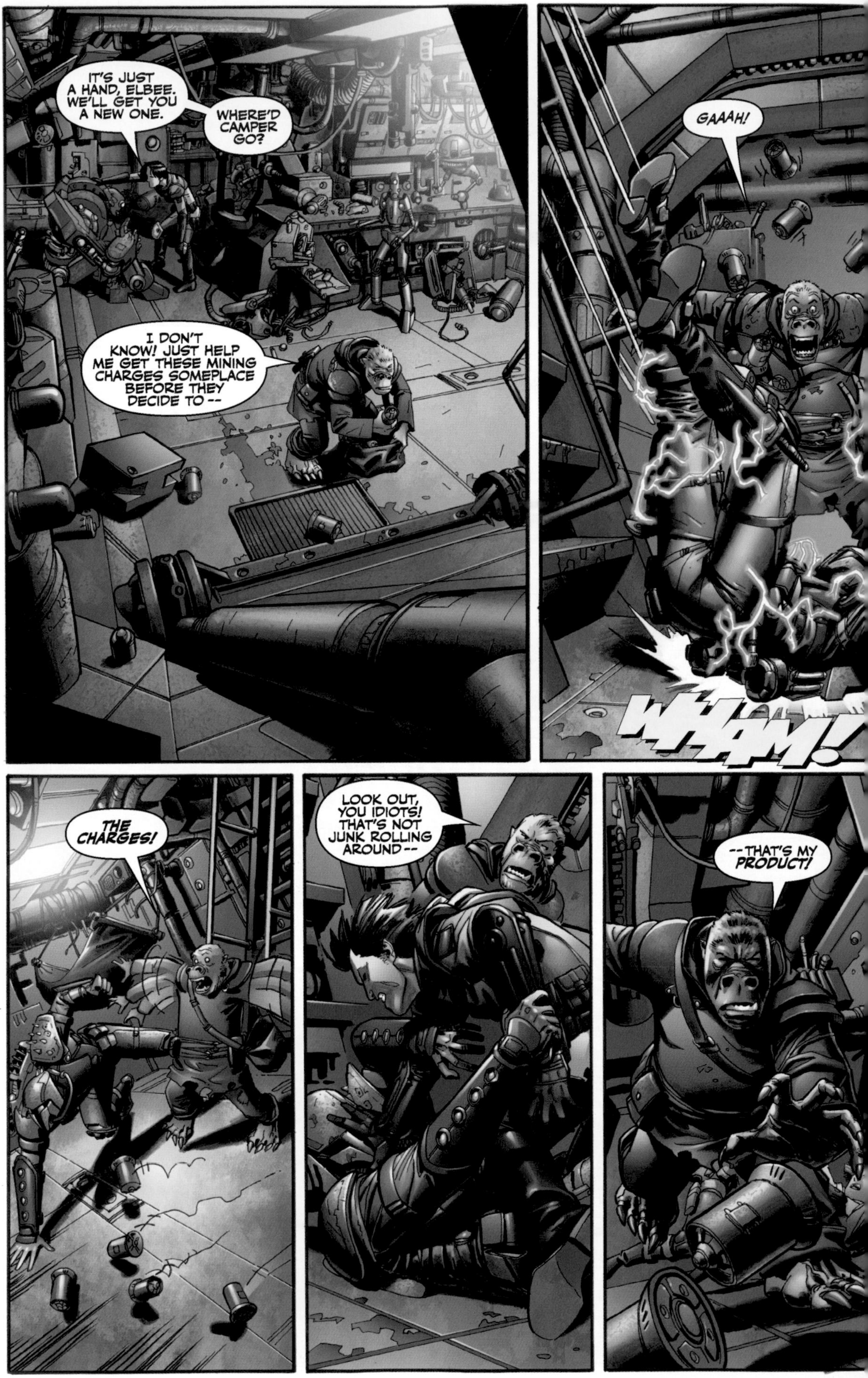
IT'S JUST A HAND, ELBEE. WE'LL GET YOU A NEW ONE.
WHERE'D CAMPER GO?
I DON'T KNOW! JUST HELP ME GET THESE MINING CHARGES SOMEPLACE BEFORE THEY DECIDE TO --
GAAAH!
WHAM!
THE CHARGES!
LOOK OUT, YOU IDIOTS! THAT'S NOT JUNK ROLLING AROUND --
-- THAT'S MY PRODUCT!

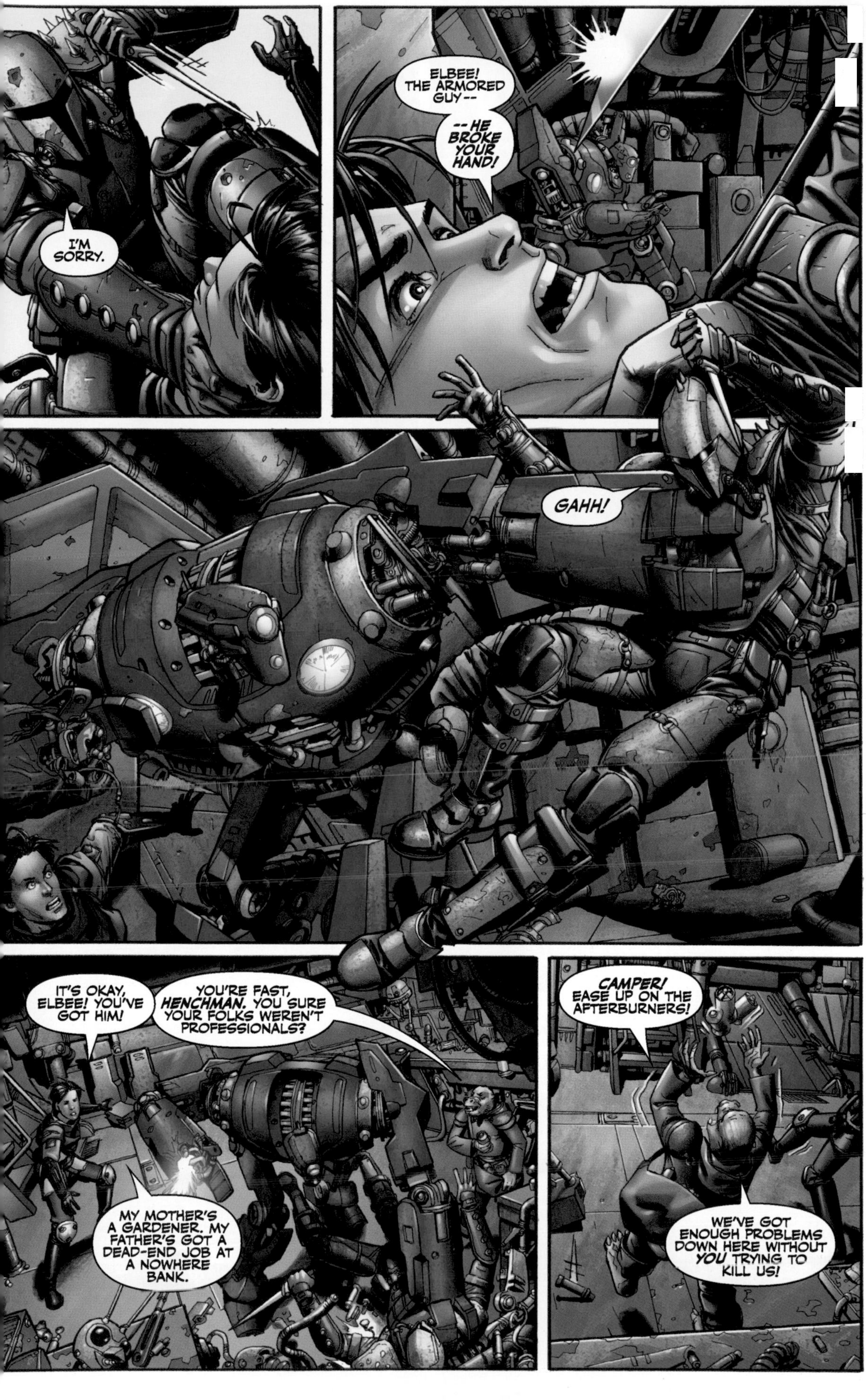
I'M SORRY.
ELBEE! THE ARMORED GUY--
--HE BROKE YOUR HAND!
GAHH!
IT'S OKAY, ELBEE! YOU'VE GOT HIM!
YOU'RE FAST, HENCHMAN. YOU SURE YOUR FOLKS WEREN'T PROFESSIONALS?
MY MOTHER'S A GARDENER. MY FATHER'S GOT A DEAD-END JOB AT A NOWHERE BANK.
CAMPER! EASE UP ON THE AFTERBURNERS!
WE'VE GOT ENOUGH PROBLEMS DOWN HERE WITHOUT YOU TRYING TO KILL US!

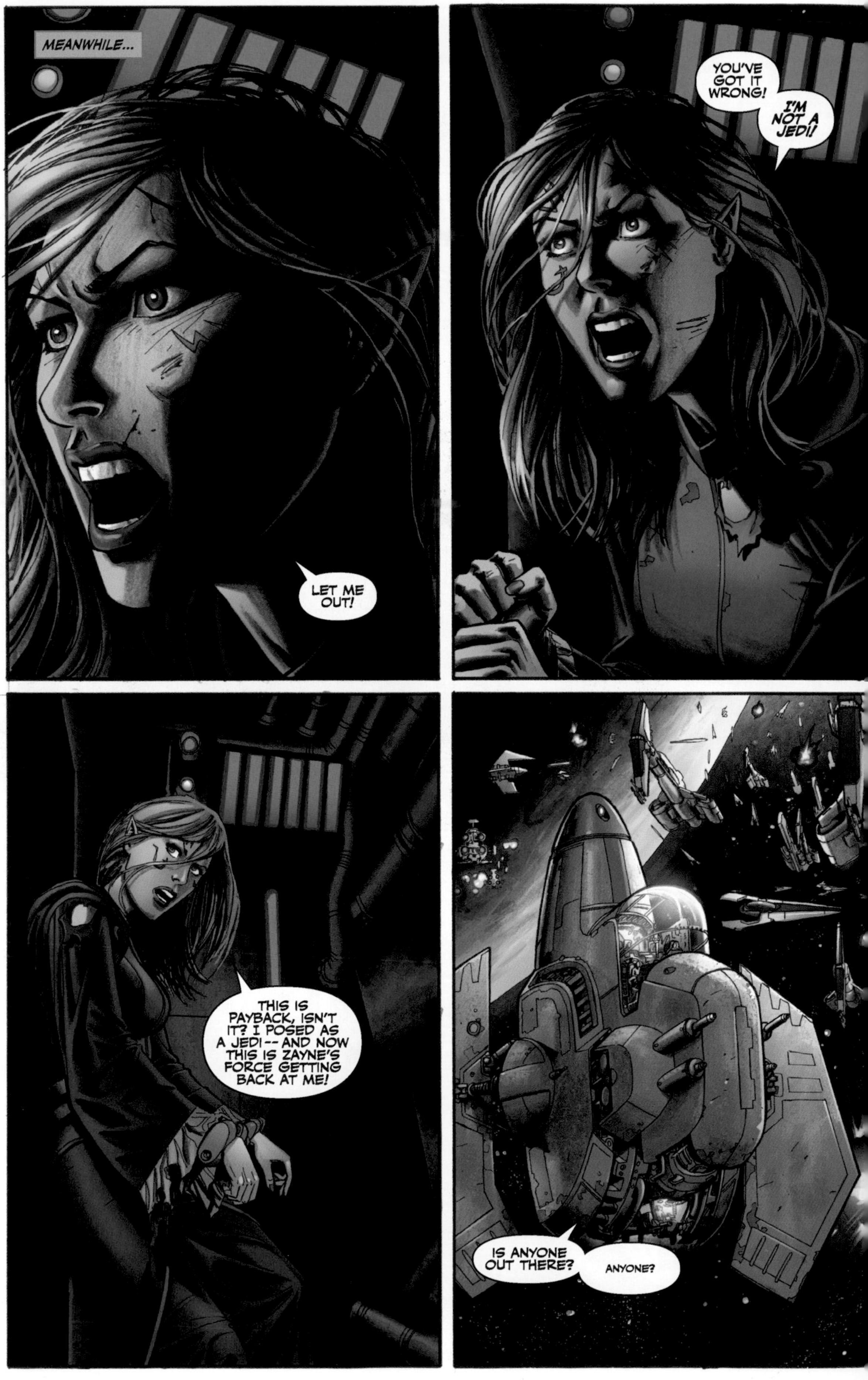
MEANWHILE...
LET ME OUT!
YOU'VE GOT IT WRONG!
I'M NOT A JEDI!
THIS IS PAYBACK, ISN'T IT? I POSED AS A JEDI--AND NOW THIS IS ZAYNE'S FORCE GETTING BACK AT ME!
IS ANYONE OUT THERE?
ANYONE?

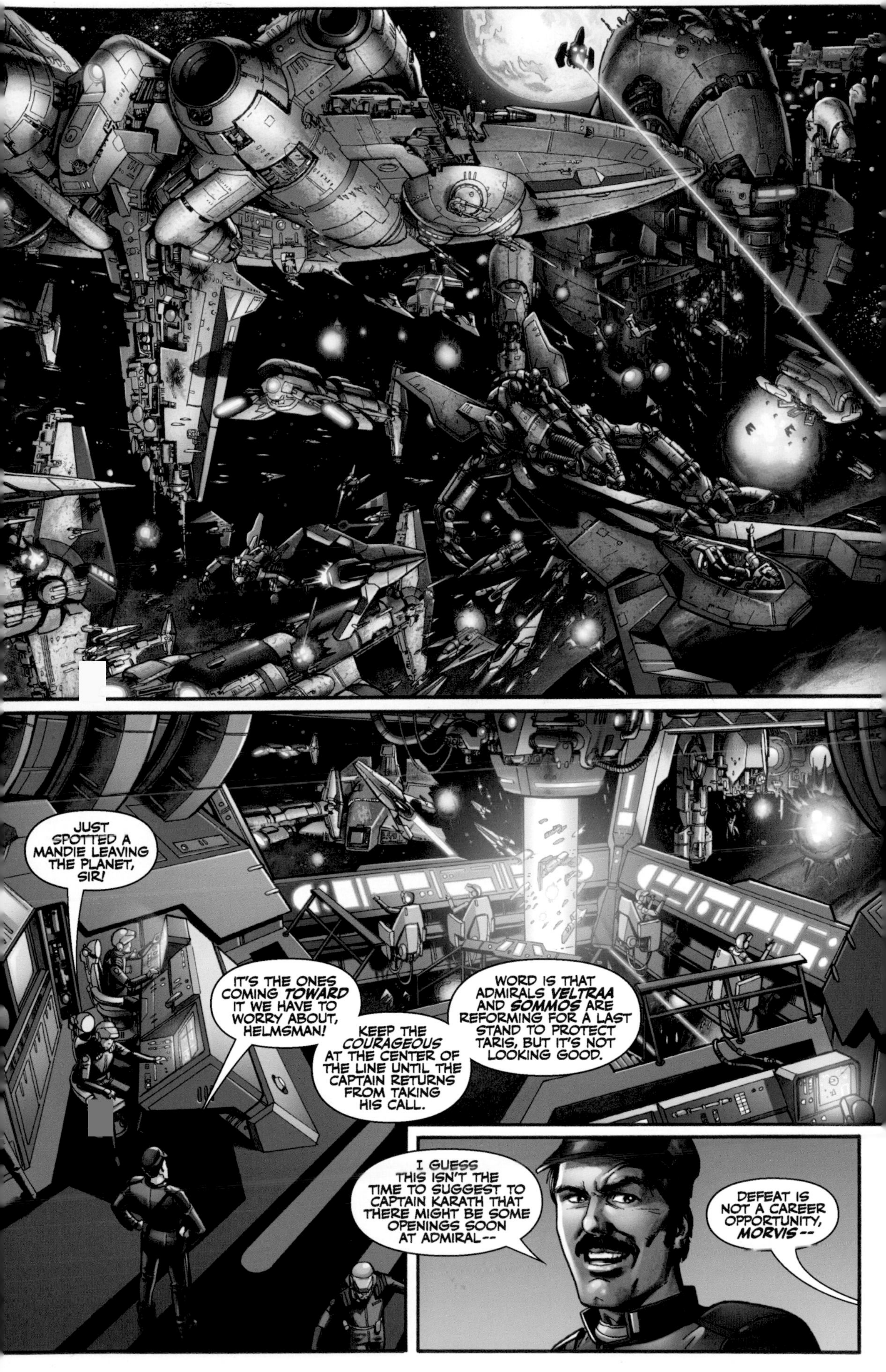
JUST SPOTTED A MANDIE LEAVING THE PLANET, SIR!
IT'S THE ONES COMING TOWARD IT WE HAVE TO WORRY ABOUT, HELMSMAN!
KEEP THE COURAGEOUS AT THE CENTER OF THE LINE UNTIL THE CAPTAIN RETURNS FROM TAKING HIS CALL.
WORD IS THAT ADMIRALS VELTRAA AND SOMMOS ARE REFORMING FOR A LAST STAND TO PROTECT TARIS, BUT IT'S NOT LOOKING GOOD.
I GUESS THIS ISN'T THE TIME TO SUGGEST TO CAPTAIN KARATH THAT THERE MIGHT BE SOME OPENINGS SOON AT ADMIRAL--
DEFEAT IS NOT A CAREER OPPORTUNITY, MORVIS--

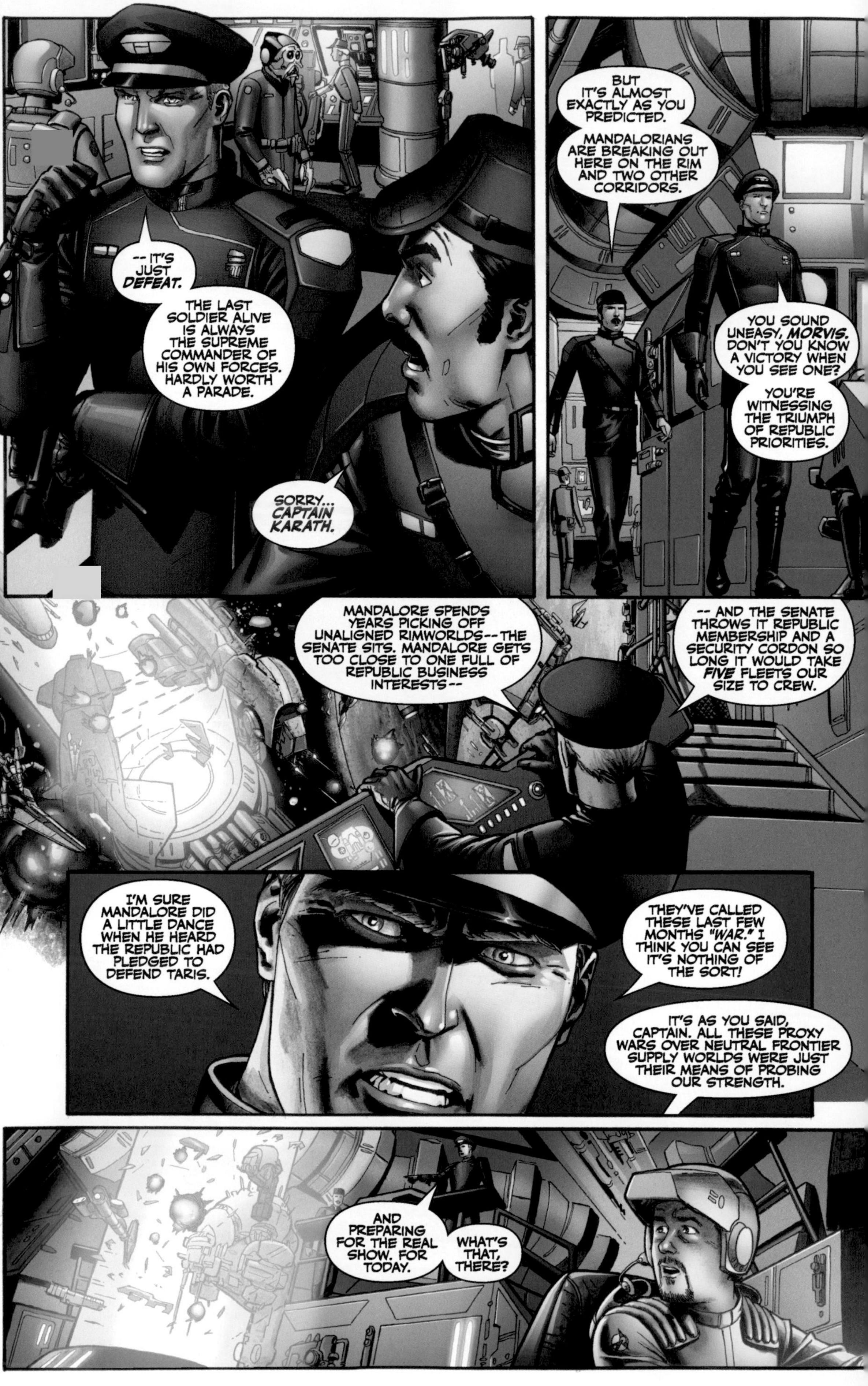
-- IT'S JUST DEFEAT.
THE LAST SOLDIER ALIVE IS ALWAYS THE SUPREME COMMANDER OF HIS OWN FORCES. HARDLY WORTH A PARADE.
SORRY... CAPTAIN KARATH.
BUT IT'S ALMOST EXACTLY AS YOU PREDICTED.
MANDALORIANS ARE BREAKING OUT HERE ON THE RIM AND TWO OTHER CORRIDORS.
YOU SOUND UNEASY, MORVIS. DON'T YOU KNOW A VICTORY WHEN YOU SEE ONE?
YOU'RE WITNESSING THE TRIUMPH OF REPUBLIC PRIORITIES.
MANDALORE SPENDS YEARS PICKING OFF UNALIGNED RIMWORLDS--THE SENATE SITS. MANDALORE GETS TOO CLOSE TO ONE FULL OF REPUBLIC BUSINESS INTERESTS--
-- AND THE SENATE THROWS IT REPUBLIC MEMBERSHIP AND A SECURITY CORDON SO LONG IT WOULD TAKE FIVE FLEETS OUR SIZE TO CREW.
I'M SURE MANDALORE DID A LITTLE DANCE WHEN HE HEARD THE REPUBLIC HAD PLEDGED TO DEFEND TARIS.
THEY'VE CALLED THESE LAST FEW MONTHS "WAR." I THINK YOU CAN SEE IT'S NOTHING OF THE SORT!
IT'S AS YOU SAID, CAPTAIN. ALL THESE PROXY WARS OVER NEUTRAL FRONTIER SUPPLY WORLDS WERE JUST THEIR MEANS OF PROBING OUR STRENGTH.
AND PREPARING FOR THE REAL SHOW. FOR TODAY.
WHAT'S THAT, THERE?

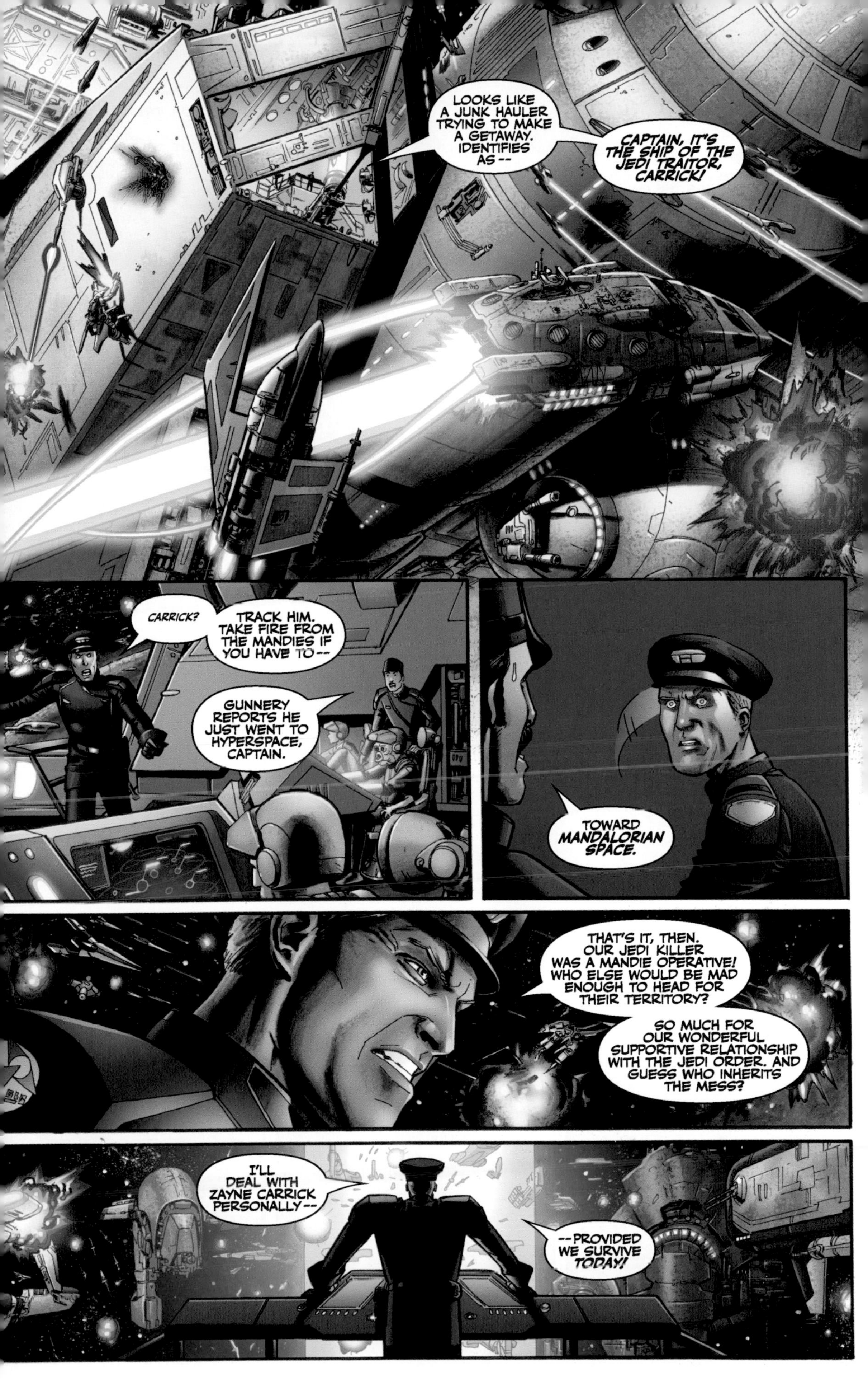
LOOKS LIKE A JUNK HAULER TRYING TO MAKE A GETAWAY. IDENTIFIES AS--
CAPTAIN, IT'S THE SHIP OF THE JEDI TRAITOR, CARRICK!
CARRICK?
TRACK HIM. TAKE FIRE FROM THE MANDIES IF YOU HAVE TO--
GUNNERY REPORTS HE JUST WENT TO HYPERSPACE, CAPTAIN.
TOWARD MANDALORIAN SPACE.
THAT'S IT, THEN. OUR JEDI KILLER WAS A MANDIE OPERATIVE! WHO ELSE WOULD BE MAD ENOUGH TO HEAD FOR THEIR TERRITORY?
SO MUCH FOR OUR WONDERFUL SUPPORTIVE RELATIONSHIP WITH THE JEDI ORDER. AND GUESS WHO INHERITS THE MESS?
I'LL DEAL WITH ZAYNE CARRICK PERSONALLY--
--PROVIDED WE SURVIVE TODAY!

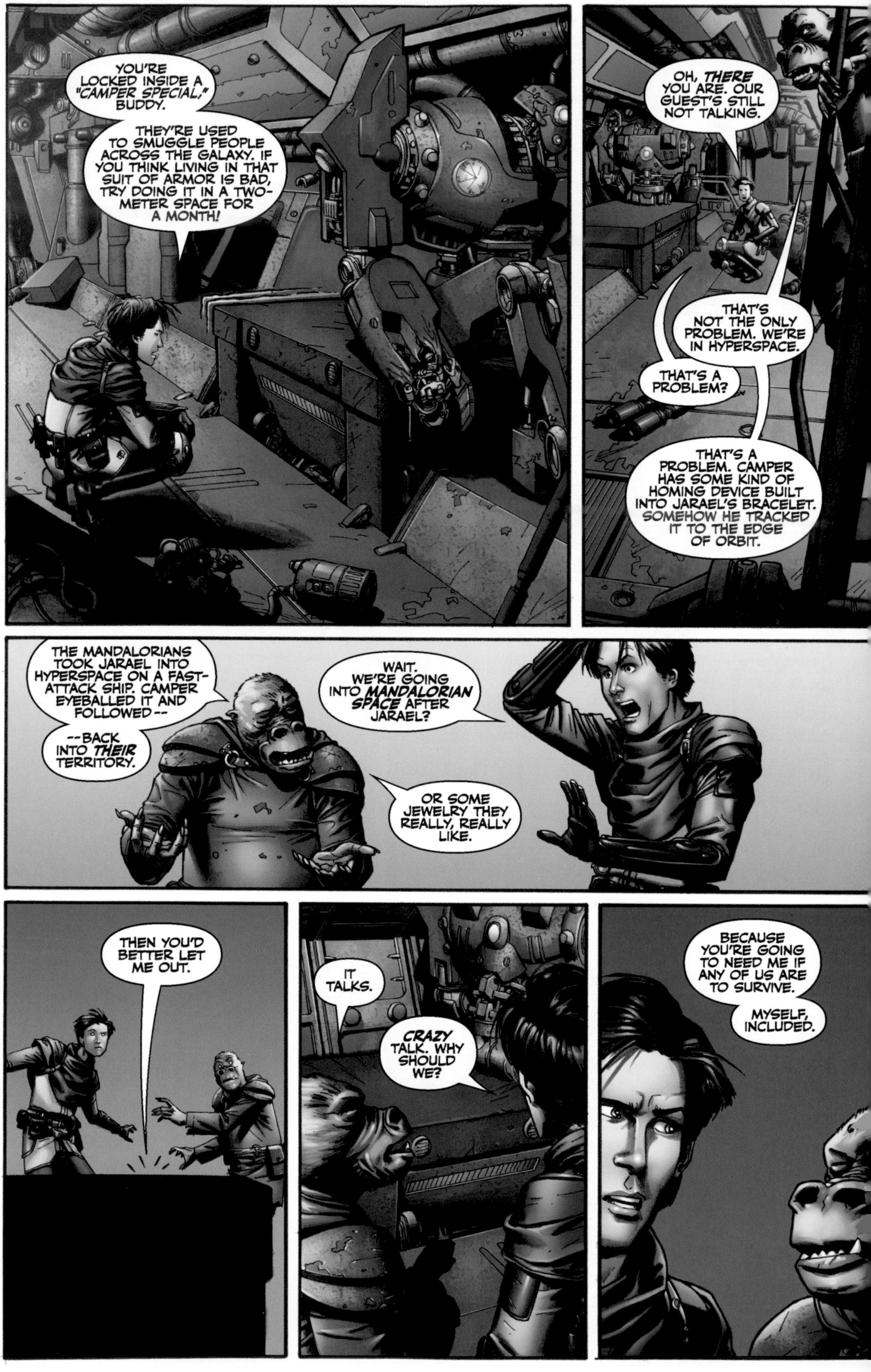
YOU'RE LOCKED INSIDE A "CAMPER SPECIAL," BUDDY.
THEY'RE USED TO SMUGGLE PEOPLE ACROSS THE GALAXY. IF YOU THINK LIVING IN THAT SUIT OF ARMOR IS BAD, TRY DOING IT IN A TWO-METER SPACE FOR A MONTH!
OH, THERE YOU ARE. OUR GUEST'S STILL NOT TALKING.
THAT'S NOT THE ONLY PROBLEM. WE'RE IN HYPERSPACE.
THAT'S A PROBLEM?
THAT'S A PROBLEM. CAMPER HAS SOME KIND OF HOMING DEVICE BUILT INTO JARAEL'S BRACELET. SOMEHOW HE TRACKED IT TO THE EDGE OF ORBIT.
THE MANDALORIANS TOOK JARAEL INTO HYPERSPACE ON A FAST-ATTACK SHIP. CAMPER EYEBALLED IT AND FOLLOWED--
--BACK INTO THEIR TERRITORY.
WAIT. WE'RE GOING INTO MANDALORIAN SPACE AFTER JARAEL?
OR SOME JEWELRY THEY REALLY, REALLY LIKE.
THEN YOU'D BETTER LET ME OUT.
IT TALKS.
CRAZY TALK. WHY SHOULD WE?
BECAUSE YOU'RE GOING TO NEED ME IF ANY OF US ARE TO SURVIVE.
MYSELF, INCLUDED.

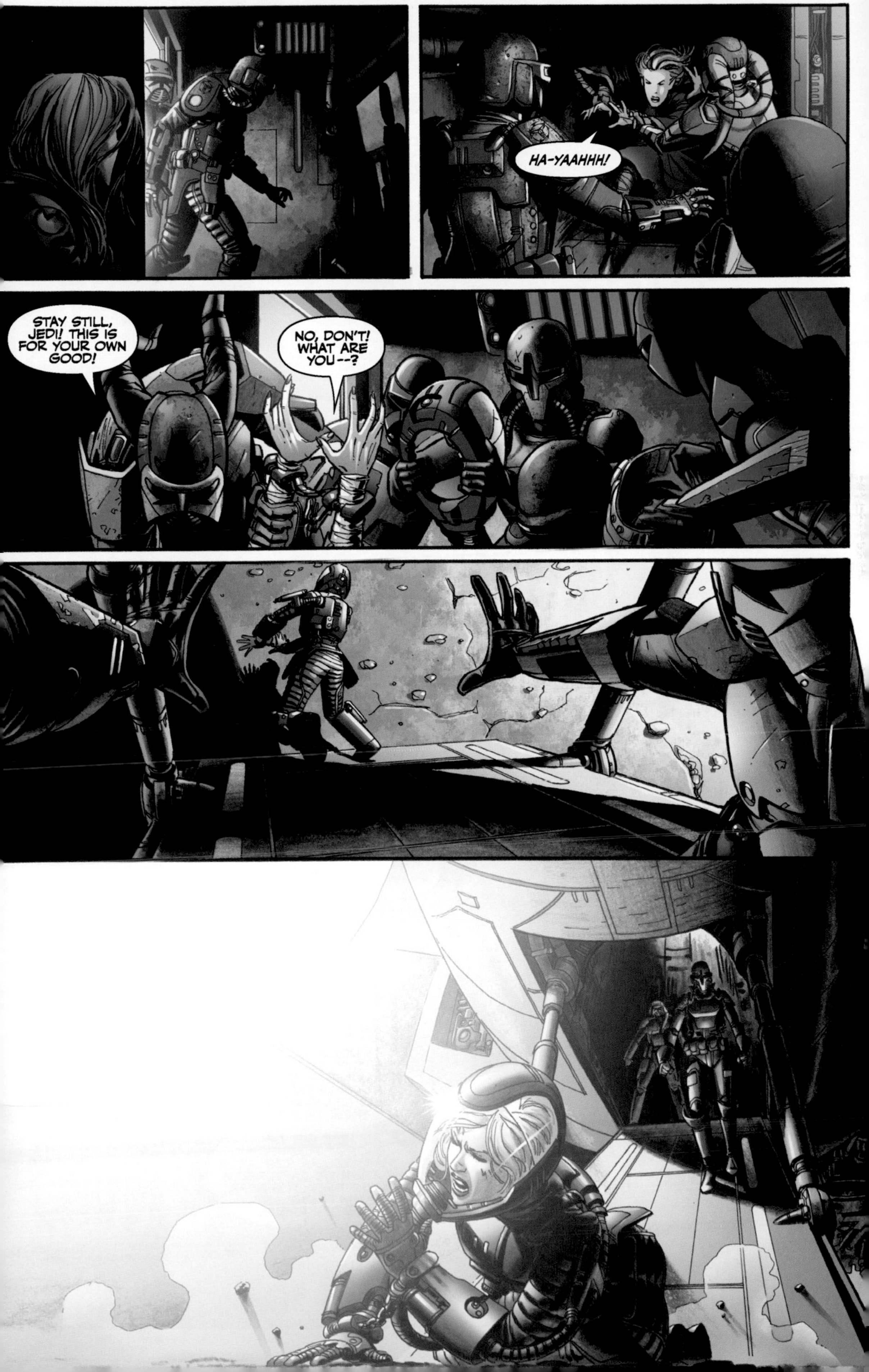
HA-YAAHHH!
STAY STILL, JEDI! THIS IS FOR YOUR OWN GOOD!
NO, DON'T! WHAT ARE YOU--?

KEEP AN EYE ON HIM, KID.

DON'T BOTHER. YOU'RE AS TRAPPED AS I AM. THEY'RE GOING TO *FLASHPOINT*.

WAS YOUR FRIEND A JEDI?

NO. I AM.

...MORE OR LESS.

WELL, THE TROOPS MUST THINK YOUR FRIEND'S A JEDI, BECAUSE *FLASHPOINT* IS WHERE WE'VE BEEN TAKING THE CATCH.

THE CATCH? *THE CATCH?*

SHE HAD MY LIGHTSABER. MAYBE THEY THOUGHT--

THEY WOULDN'T HAVE TAKEN TIME TO THINK. SINCE YOUR JEDI SCOUTS STARTED NOSING AROUND THE FRONTIER, WE'VE GOT A STANDING ORDER--

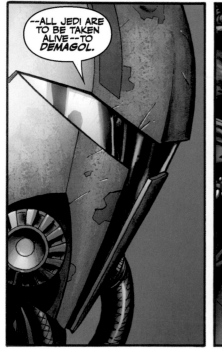

--ALL JEDI ARE TO BE TAKEN ALIVE--TO DEMAGOL.

WHAT'S A DEMAGOL?

DEMAGOL IS THE TOP MANDALORIAN BIOLOGIST--AND HE'S STUDYING CAPTURED JEDI TO UNDERSTAND THEIR TALENTS.

HE'S SET UP SHOP AT FLASHPOINT, THAT STELLAR RESEARCH STATION WE CAPTURED A WHILE BACK. IT'S NEAR THE FRONT, YET INACCESSIBLE.

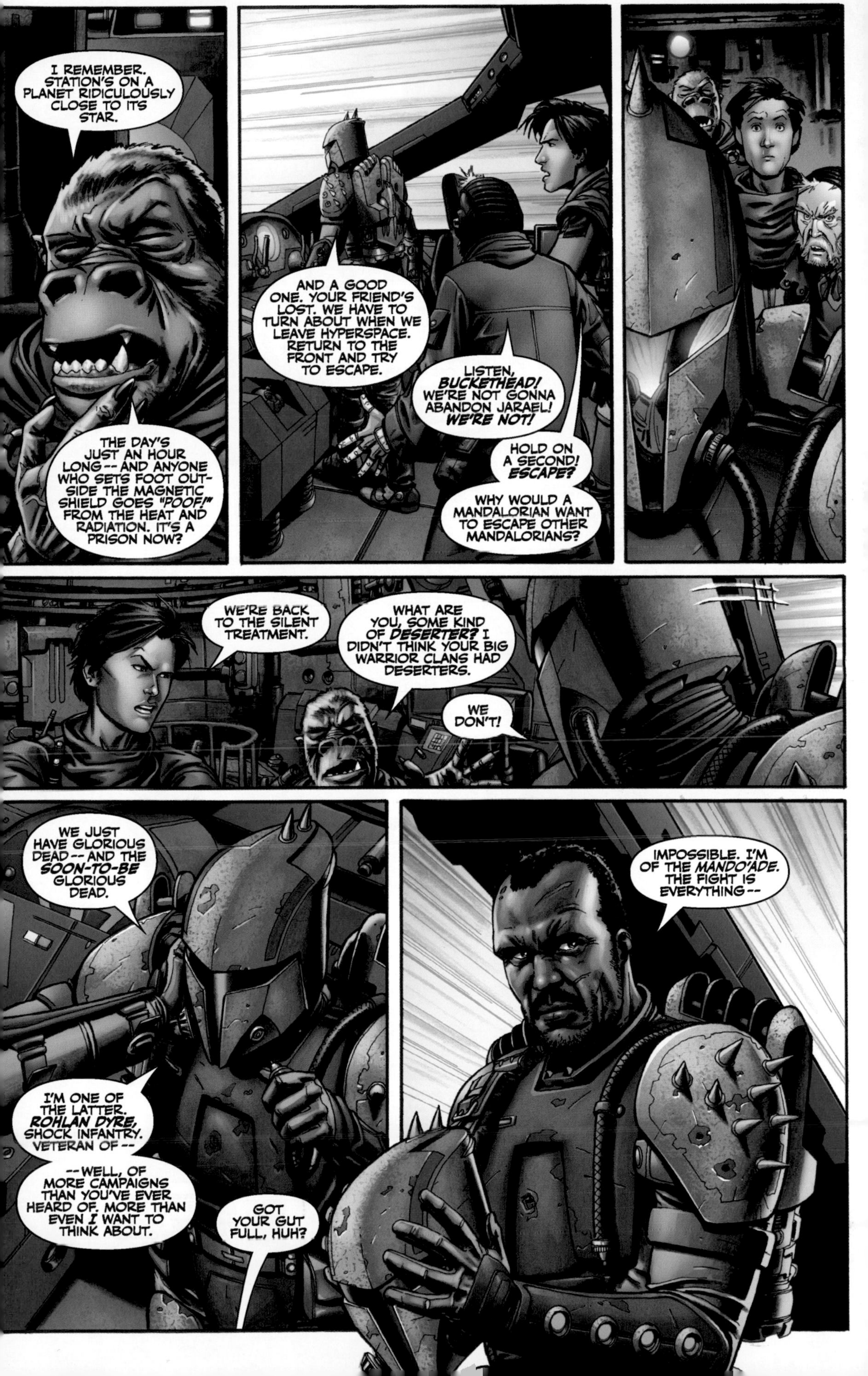

I REMEMBER. STATION'S ON A PLANET RIDICULOUSLY CLOSE TO ITS STAR.
THE DAY'S JUST AN HOUR LONG--AND ANYONE WHO SETS FOOT OUT-SIDE THE MAGNETIC SHIELD GOES "POOF!" FROM THE HEAT AND RADIATION. IT'S A PRISON NOW?
AND A GOOD ONE. YOUR FRIEND'S LOST. WE HAVE TO TURN ABOUT WHEN WE LEAVE HYPERSPACE. RETURN TO THE FRONT AND TRY TO ESCAPE.
LISTEN, BUCKETHEAD! WE'RE NOT GONNA ABANDON JARAEL! WE'RE NOT!
HOLD ON A SECOND! ESCAPE?
WHY WOULD A MANDALORIAN WANT TO ESCAPE OTHER MANDALORIANS?
WE'RE BACK TO THE SILENT TREATMENT.
WHAT ARE YOU, SOME KIND OF DESERTER? I DIDN'T THINK YOUR BIG WARRIOR CLANS HAD DESERTERS.
WE DON'T!
WE JUST HAVE GLORIOUS DEAD--AND THE SOON-TO-BE GLORIOUS DEAD.
I'M ONE OF THE LATTER. ROHLAN DYRE, SHOCK INFANTRY. VETERAN OF--
--WELL, OF MORE CAMPAIGNS THAN YOU'VE EVER HEARD OF. MORE THAN EVEN I WANT TO THINK ABOUT.
GOT YOUR GUT FULL, HUH?
IMPOSSIBLE. I'M OF THE MANDO'ADE. THE FIGHT IS EVERYTHING--

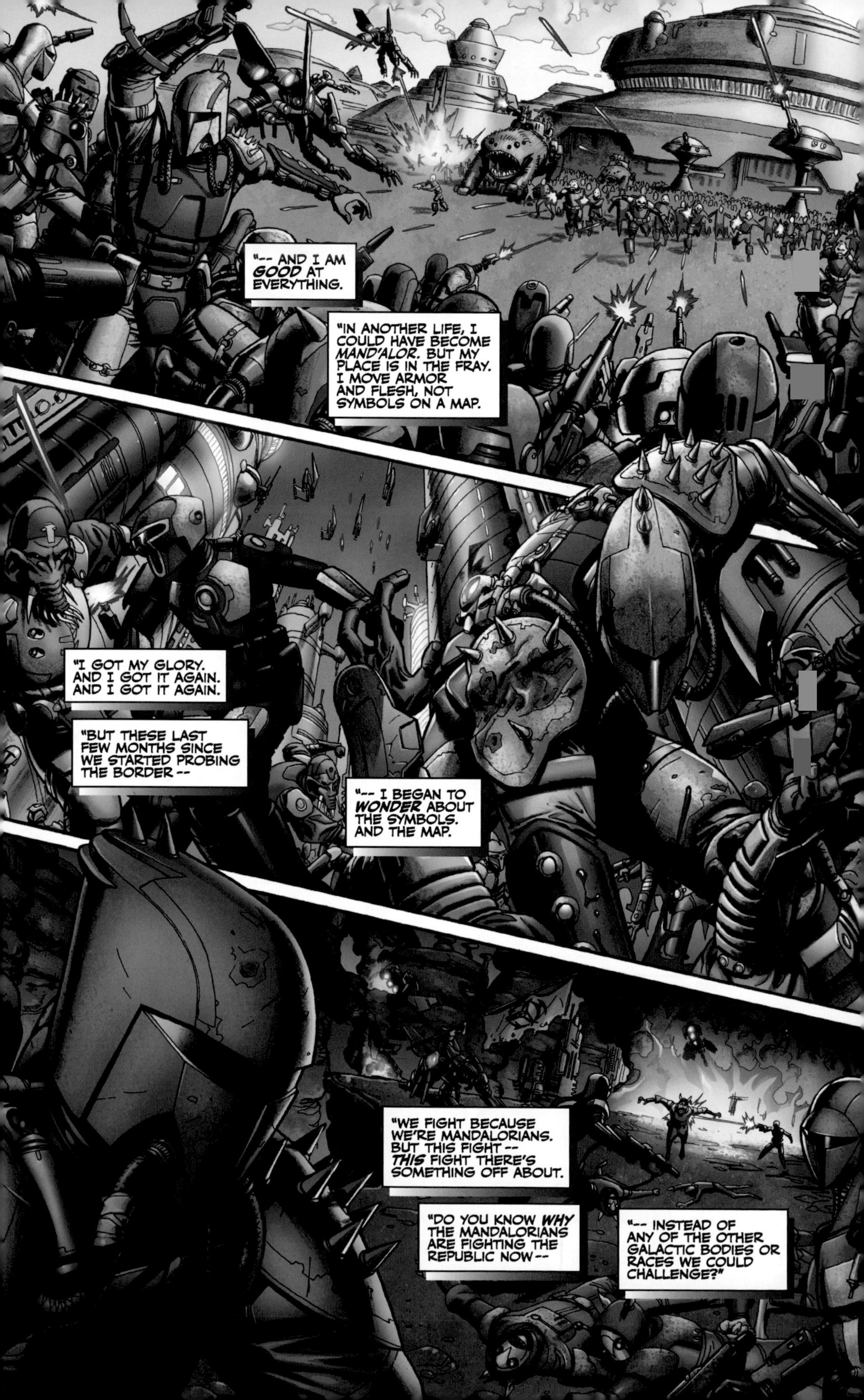
"-- AND I AM GOOD AT EVERYTHING.
"IN ANOTHER LIFE, I COULD HAVE BECOME MAND'ALOR. BUT MY PLACE IS IN THE FRAY. I MOVE ARMOR AND FLESH, NOT SYMBOLS ON A MAP.
"I GOT MY GLORY. AND I GOT IT AGAIN. AND I GOT IT AGAIN.
"BUT THESE LAST FEW MONTHS SINCE WE STARTED PROBING THE BORDER --
"-- I BEGAN TO WONDER ABOUT THE SYMBOLS. AND THE MAP.
"WE FIGHT BECAUSE WE'RE MANDALORIANS. BUT THIS FIGHT -- THIS FIGHT THERE'S SOMETHING OFF ABOUT.
"DO YOU KNOW WHY THE MANDALORIANS ARE FIGHTING THE REPUBLIC NOW --
"-- INSTEAD OF ANY OF THE OTHER GALACTIC BODIES OR RACES WE COULD CHALLENGE?"

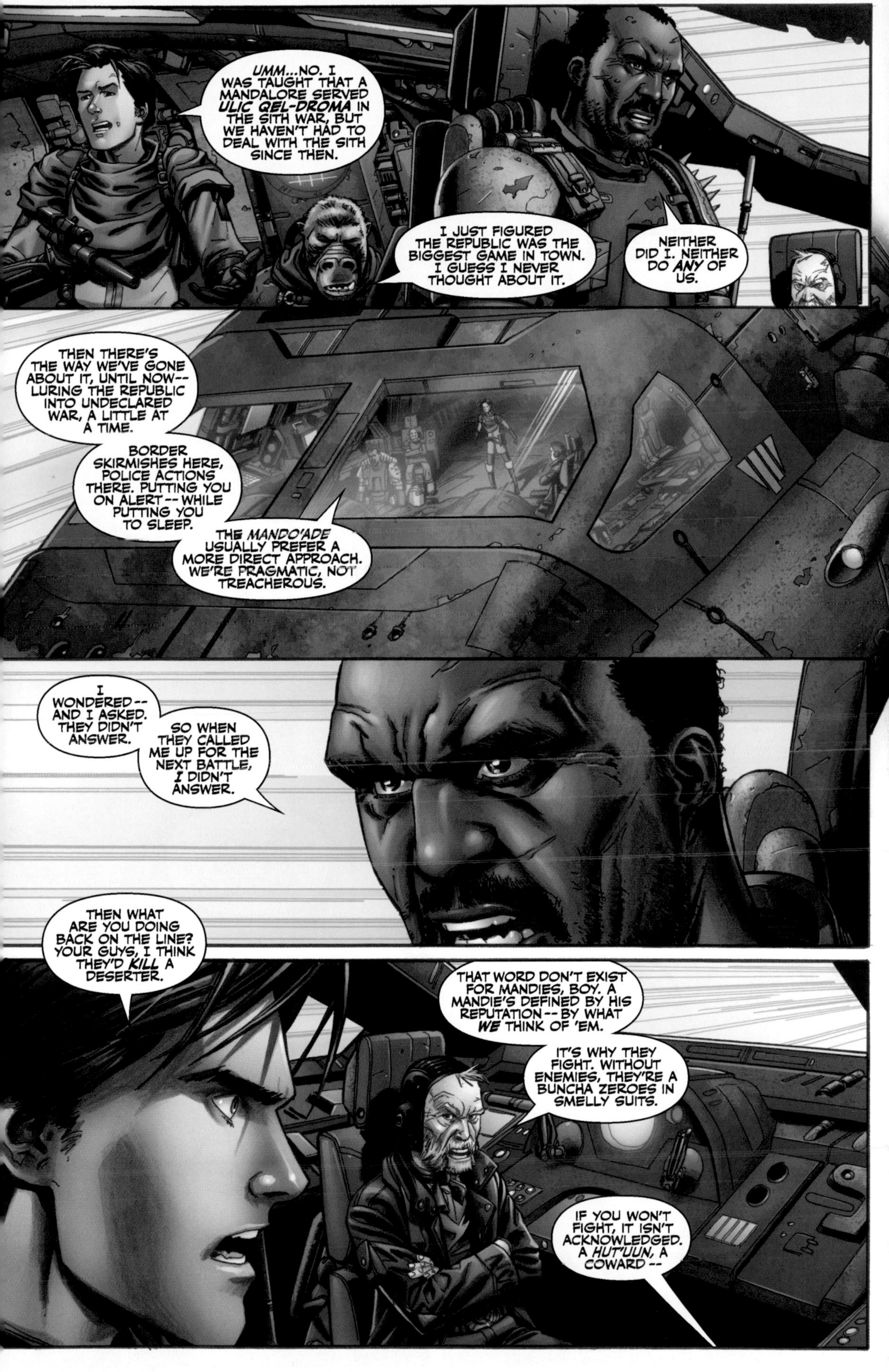

UMM...NO. I WAS TAUGHT THAT A MANDALORE SERVED ULIC QEL-DROMA IN THE SITH WAR, BUT WE HAVEN'T HAD TO DEAL WITH THE SITH SINCE THEN.
I JUST FIGURED THE REPUBLIC WAS THE BIGGEST GAME IN TOWN. I GUESS I NEVER THOUGHT ABOUT IT.
NEITHER DID I. NEITHER DO ANY OF US.
THEN THERE'S THE WAY WE'VE GONE ABOUT IT, UNTIL NOW-- LURING THE REPUBLIC INTO UNDECLARED WAR, A LITTLE AT A TIME.
BORDER SKIRMISHES HERE, POLICE ACTIONS THERE. PUTTING YOU ON ALERT--WHILE PUTTING YOU TO SLEEP.
THE MANDO'ADE USUALLY PREFER A MORE DIRECT APPROACH. WE'RE PRAGMATIC, NOT TREACHEROUS.
I WONDERED-- AND I ASKED. THEY DIDN'T ANSWER.
SO WHEN THEY CALLED ME UP FOR THE NEXT BATTLE, I DIDN'T ANSWER.
THEN WHAT ARE YOU DOING BACK ON THE LINE? YOUR GUYS, I THINK THEY'D KILL A DESERTER.
THAT WORD DON'T EXIST FOR MANDIES, BOY. A MANDIE'S DEFINED BY HIS REPUTATION--BY WHAT WE THINK OF 'EM.
IT'S WHY THEY FIGHT. WITHOUT ENEMIES, THEY'RE A BUNCHA ZEROES IN SMELLY SUITS.
IF YOU WON'T FIGHT, IT ISN'T ACKNOWLEDGED. A HUT'UUN, A COWARD--

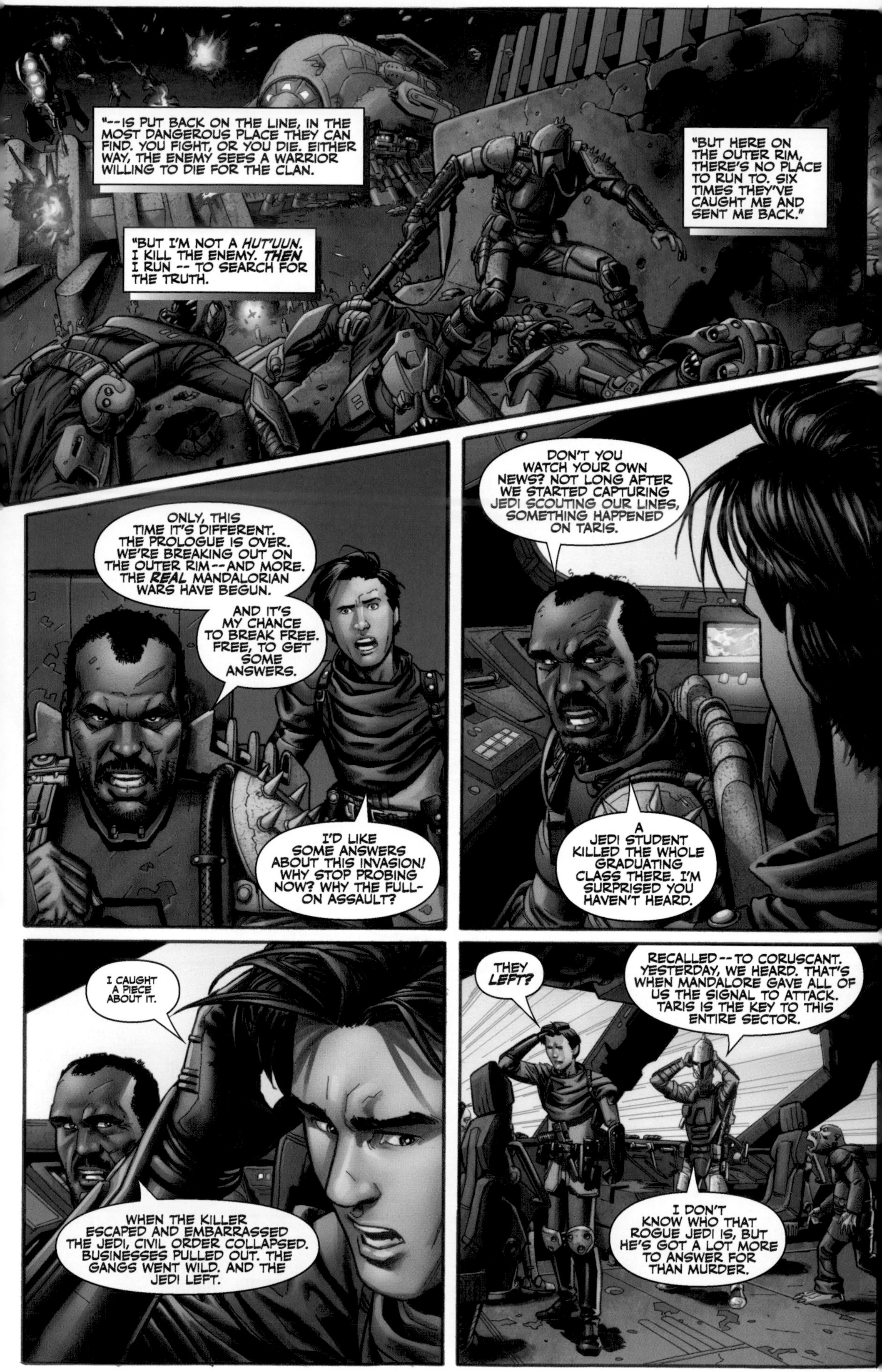
"--IS PUT BACK ON THE LINE, IN THE MOST DANGEROUS PLACE THEY CAN FIND. YOU FIGHT, OR YOU DIE. EITHER WAY, THE ENEMY SEES A WARRIOR WILLING TO DIE FOR THE CLAN.
"BUT I'M NOT A *HUT'UUN*. I KILL THE ENEMY. *THEN* I RUN -- TO SEARCH FOR THE TRUTH.
"BUT HERE ON THE OUTER RIM, THERE'S NO PLACE TO RUN TO. SIX TIMES THEY'VE CAUGHT ME AND SENT ME BACK."
ONLY, THIS TIME IT'S DIFFERENT. THE PROLOGUE IS OVER. WE'RE BREAKING OUT ON THE OUTER RIM--AND MORE. THE *REAL* MANDALORIAN WARS HAVE BEGUN.
AND IT'S MY CHANCE TO BREAK FREE. FREE, TO GET SOME ANSWERS.
I'D LIKE SOME ANSWERS ABOUT THIS INVASION! WHY STOP PROBING NOW? WHY THE FULL-ON ASSAULT?
DON'T YOU WATCH YOUR OWN NEWS? NOT LONG AFTER WE STARTED CAPTURING JEDI SCOUTING OUR LINES, SOMETHING HAPPENED ON TARIS.
A JEDI STUDENT KILLED THE WHOLE GRADUATING CLASS THERE. I'M SURPRISED YOU HAVEN'T HEARD.
I CAUGHT A PIECE ABOUT IT.
WHEN THE KILLER ESCAPED AND EMBARRASSED THE JEDI, CIVIL ORDER COLLAPSED. BUSINESSES PULLED OUT. THE GANGS WENT WILD. AND THE JEDI LEFT.
THEY *LEFT?*
RECALLED--TO CORUSCANT. YESTERDAY, WE HEARD. THAT'S WHEN MANDALORE GAVE ALL OF US THE SIGNAL TO ATTACK. TARIS IS THE KEY TO THIS ENTIRE SECTOR.
I DON'T KNOW WHO THAT ROGUE JEDI IS, BUT HE'S GOT A LOT MORE TO ANSWER FOR THAN MURDER.

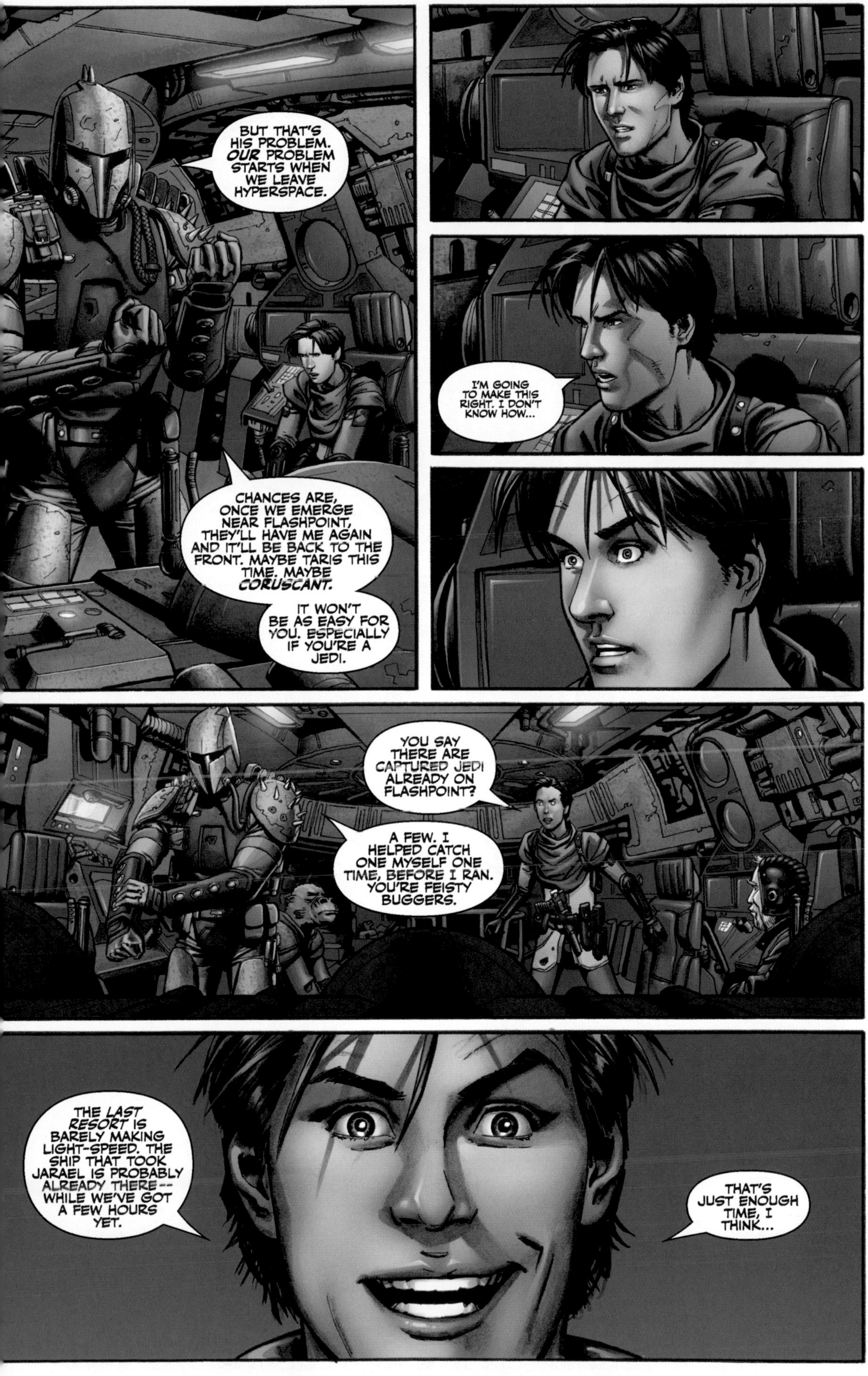
BUT THAT'S HIS PROBLEM. OUR PROBLEM STARTS WHEN WE LEAVE HYPERSPACE.
CHANCES ARE, ONCE WE EMERGE NEAR FLASHPOINT, THEY'LL HAVE ME AGAIN AND IT'LL BE BACK TO THE FRONT. MAYBE TARIS THIS TIME. MAYBE CORUSCANT.
IT WON'T BE AS EASY FOR YOU. ESPECIALLY IF YOU'RE A JEDI.
I'M GOING TO MAKE THIS RIGHT. I DON'T KNOW HOW...
YOU SAY THERE ARE CAPTURED JEDI ALREADY ON FLASHPOINT?
A FEW. I HELPED CATCH ONE MYSELF ONE TIME, BEFORE I RAN. YOU'RE FEISTY BUGGERS.
THE LAST RESORT IS BARELY MAKING LIGHT-SPEED. THE SHIP THAT TOOK JARAEL IS PROBABLY ALREADY THERE-- WHILE WE'VE GOT A FEW HOURS YET.
THAT'S JUST ENOUGH TIME, I THINK...

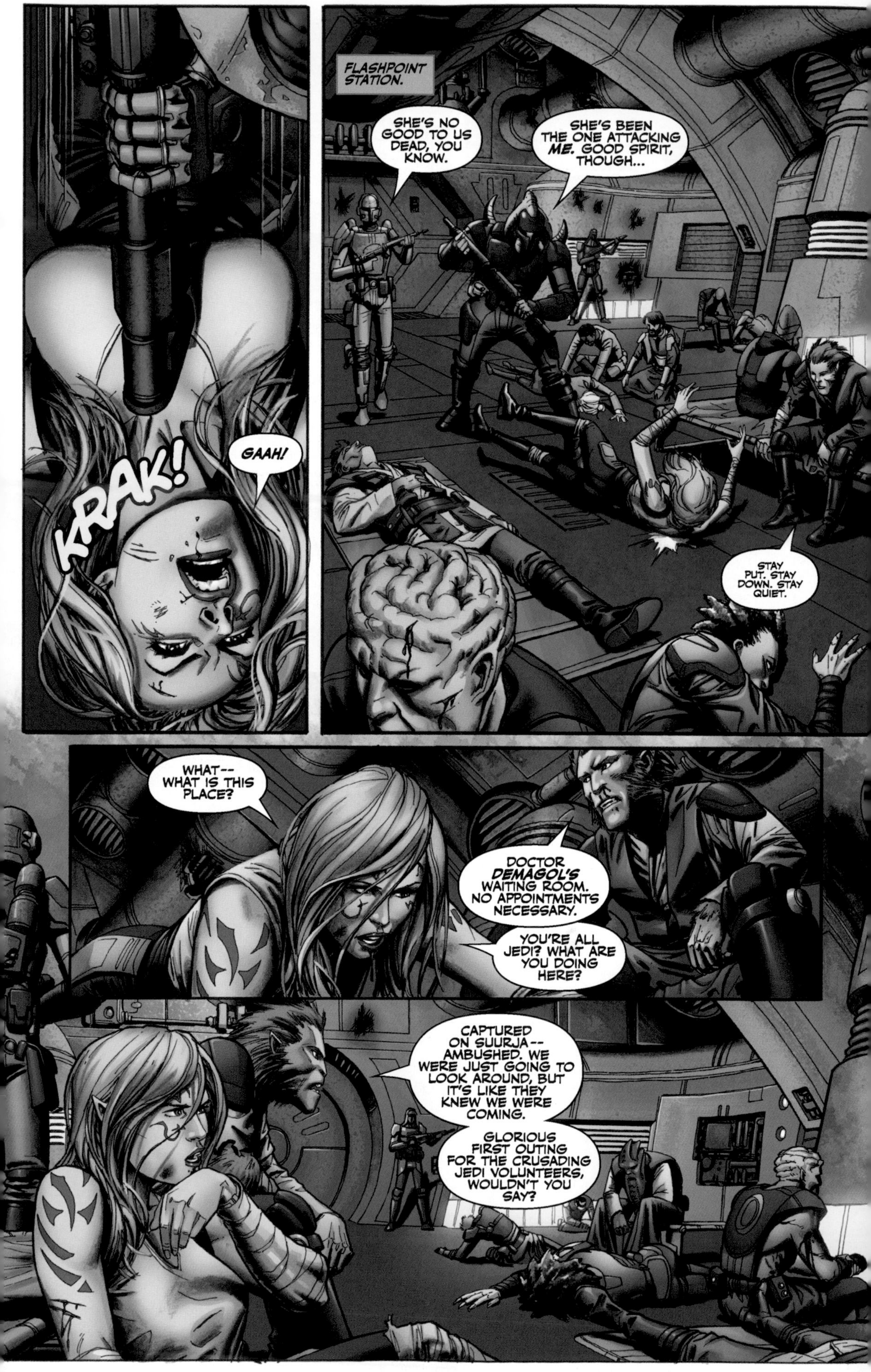
KRAK!
GAAH!
FLASHPOINT STATION.
SHE'S NO GOOD TO US DEAD, YOU KNOW.
SHE'S BEEN THE ONE ATTACKING ME. GOOD SPIRIT, THOUGH...
STAY PUT. STAY DOWN. STAY QUIET.
WHAT-- WHAT IS THIS PLACE?
DOCTOR DEMAGOL'S WAITING ROOM. NO APPOINTMENTS NECESSARY.
YOU'RE ALL JEDI? WHAT ARE YOU DOING HERE?
CAPTURED ON SUURJA-- AMBUSHED. WE WERE JUST GOING TO LOOK AROUND, BUT IT'S LIKE THEY KNEW WE WERE COMING.
GLORIOUS FIRST OUTING FOR THE CRUSADING JEDI VOLUNTEERS, WOULDN'T YOU SAY?

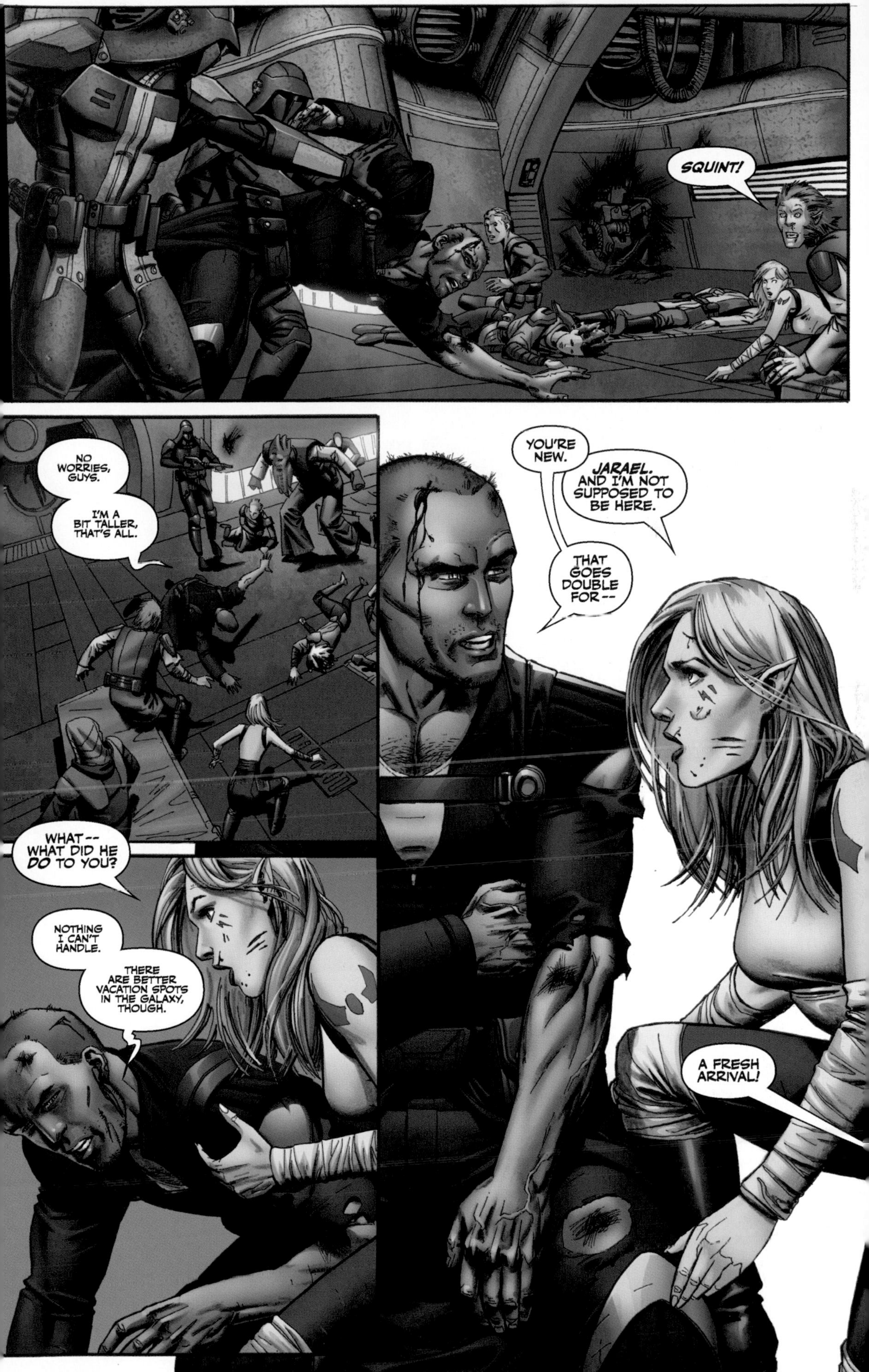
SQUINT!
NO WORRIES, GUYS.
I'M A BIT TALLER, THAT'S ALL.
YOU'RE NEW.
THAT GOES DOUBLE FOR --
JARAEL. AND I'M NOT SUPPOSED TO BE HERE.
WHAT -- WHAT DID HE DO TO YOU?
NOTHING I CAN'T HANDLE.
THERE ARE BETTER VACATION SPOTS IN THE GALAXY, THOUGH.
A FRESH ARRIVAL!

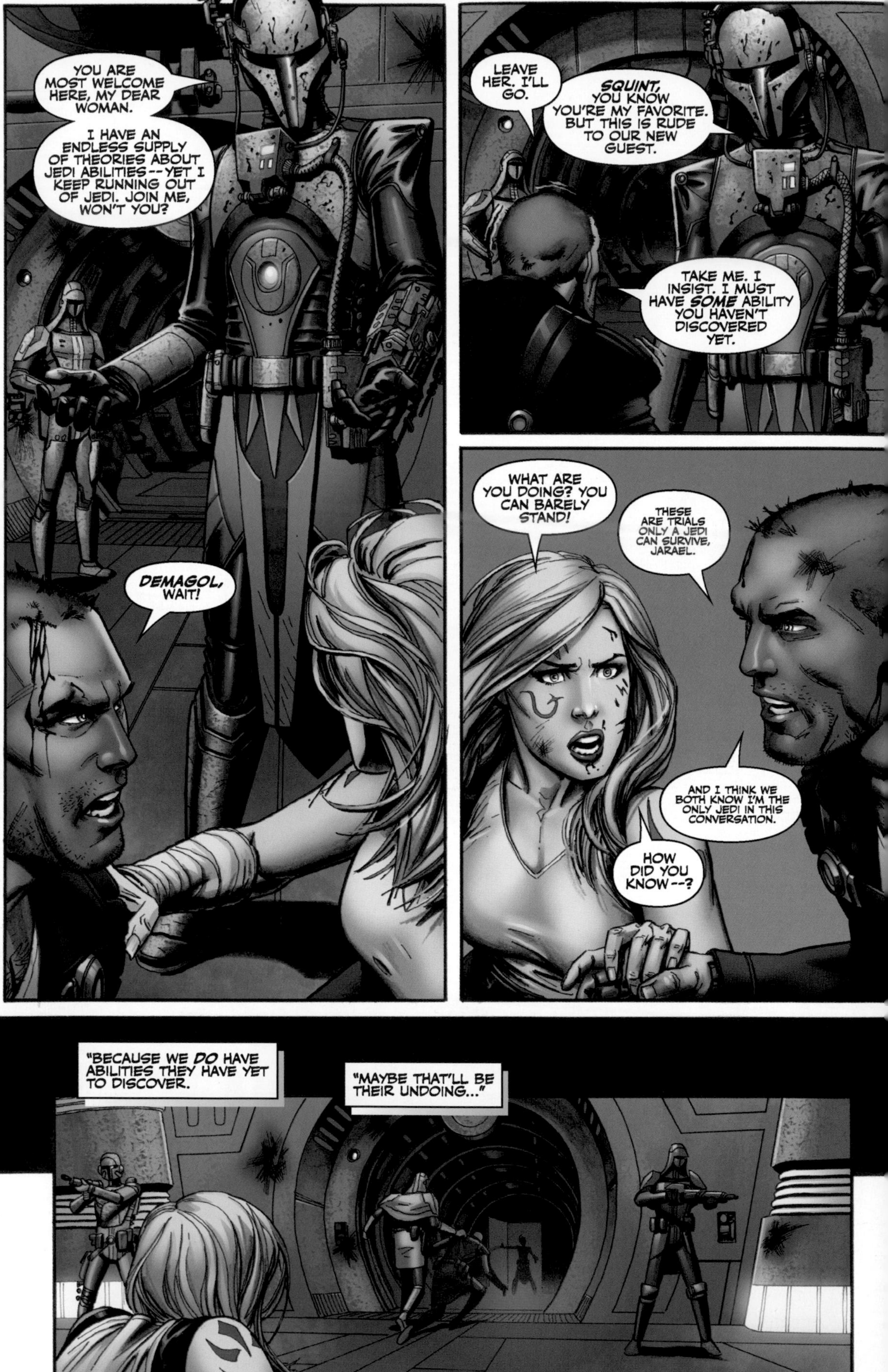

YOU ARE MOST WELCOME HERE, MY DEAR WOMAN.
I HAVE AN ENDLESS SUPPLY OF THEORIES ABOUT JEDI ABILITIES--YET I KEEP RUNNING OUT OF JEDI. JOIN ME, WON'T YOU?
DEMAGOL, WAIT!
LEAVE HER. I'LL GO.
SQUINT, YOU KNOW YOU'RE MY FAVORITE. BUT THIS IS RUDE TO OUR NEW GUEST.
TAKE ME. I INSIST. I MUST HAVE SOME ABILITY YOU HAVEN'T DISCOVERED YET.
WHAT ARE YOU DOING? YOU CAN BARELY STAND!
THESE ARE TRIALS ONLY A JEDI CAN SURVIVE, JARAEL.
AND I THINK WE BOTH KNOW I'M THE ONLY JEDI IN THIS CONVERSATION.
HOW DID YOU KNOW--?
"BECAUSE WE DO HAVE ABILITIES THEY HAVE YET TO DISCOVER.
"MAYBE THAT'LL BE THEIR UNDOING..."

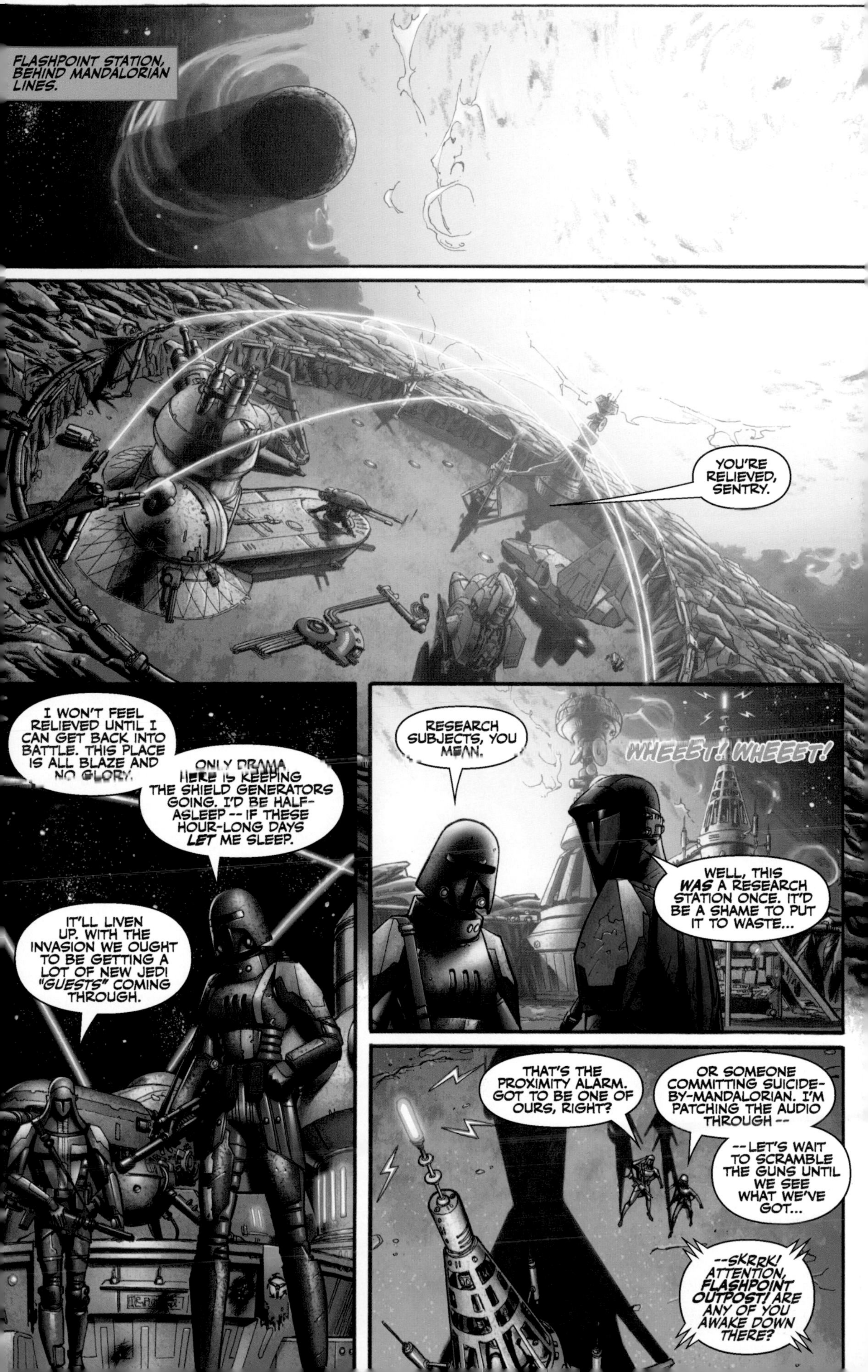
FLASHPOINT STATION, BEHIND MANDALORIAN LINES.
YOU'RE RELIEVED, SENTRY.
I WON'T FEEL RELIEVED UNTIL I CAN GET BACK INTO BATTLE. THIS PLACE IS ALL BLAZE AND NO GLORY.
ONLY DRAMA HERE IS KEEPING THE SHIELD GENERATORS GOING. I'D BE HALF-ASLEEP -- IF THESE HOUR-LONG DAYS *LET* ME SLEEP.
IT'LL LIVEN UP. WITH THE INVASION WE OUGHT TO BE GETTING A LOT OF NEW JEDI *"GUESTS"* COMING THROUGH.
RESEARCH SUBJECTS, YOU MEAN.
WHEEEET! WHEEEET!
WELL, THIS *WAS* A RESEARCH STATION ONCE. IT'D BE A SHAME TO PUT IT TO WASTE...
THAT'S THE PROXIMITY ALARM. GOT TO BE ONE OF OURS, RIGHT?
OR SOMEONE COMMITTING SUICIDE-BY-MANDALORIAN. I'M PATCHING THE AUDIO THROUGH --
--LET'S WAIT TO SCRAMBLE THE GUNS UNTIL WE SEE WHAT WE'VE GOT...
--SKRRK! ATTENTION, *FLASHPOINT OUTPOST!* ARE ANY OF YOU AWAKE DOWN THERE?

REPEAT, I NEED CLEARANCE TO LAND! I HAVE A PRISONER FROM VANQUO. OPEN THE MAGNETIC FIELD!

HOLD, WARRIOR. I'M GOING TO NEED SOME KIND OF AUTHORIZATION FROM--

DON'T GIVE ME THAT REARGUARD GARBAGE! I DON'T KNOW HOW IT IS DOWN THERE--

-- BUT ON THE FRONT WHEN A *REAL* MANDALORIAN CAPTURES A JEDI IN HIS OWN SHIP, THEY PAY HIM HEED! NOW OPEN THE FIELD!

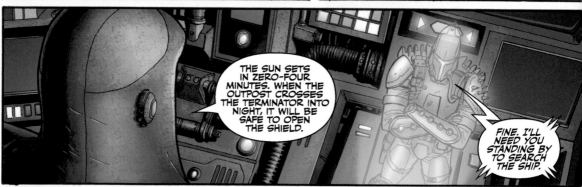

THE SUN SETS IN ZERO-FOUR MINUTES. WHEN THE OUTPOST CROSSES THE TERMINATOR INTO NIGHT, IT WILL BE SAFE TO OPEN THE SHIELD.

FINE. I'LL NEED YOU STANDING BY TO SEARCH THE SHIP.

WHAT DO YOU THINK?

LET'S SCRAMBLE THE GUNS ANYWAY. HE AS MUCH AS WAGGLES FUNNY, WE'LL BE PICKING HIM OUT OF THE WRECKAGE...

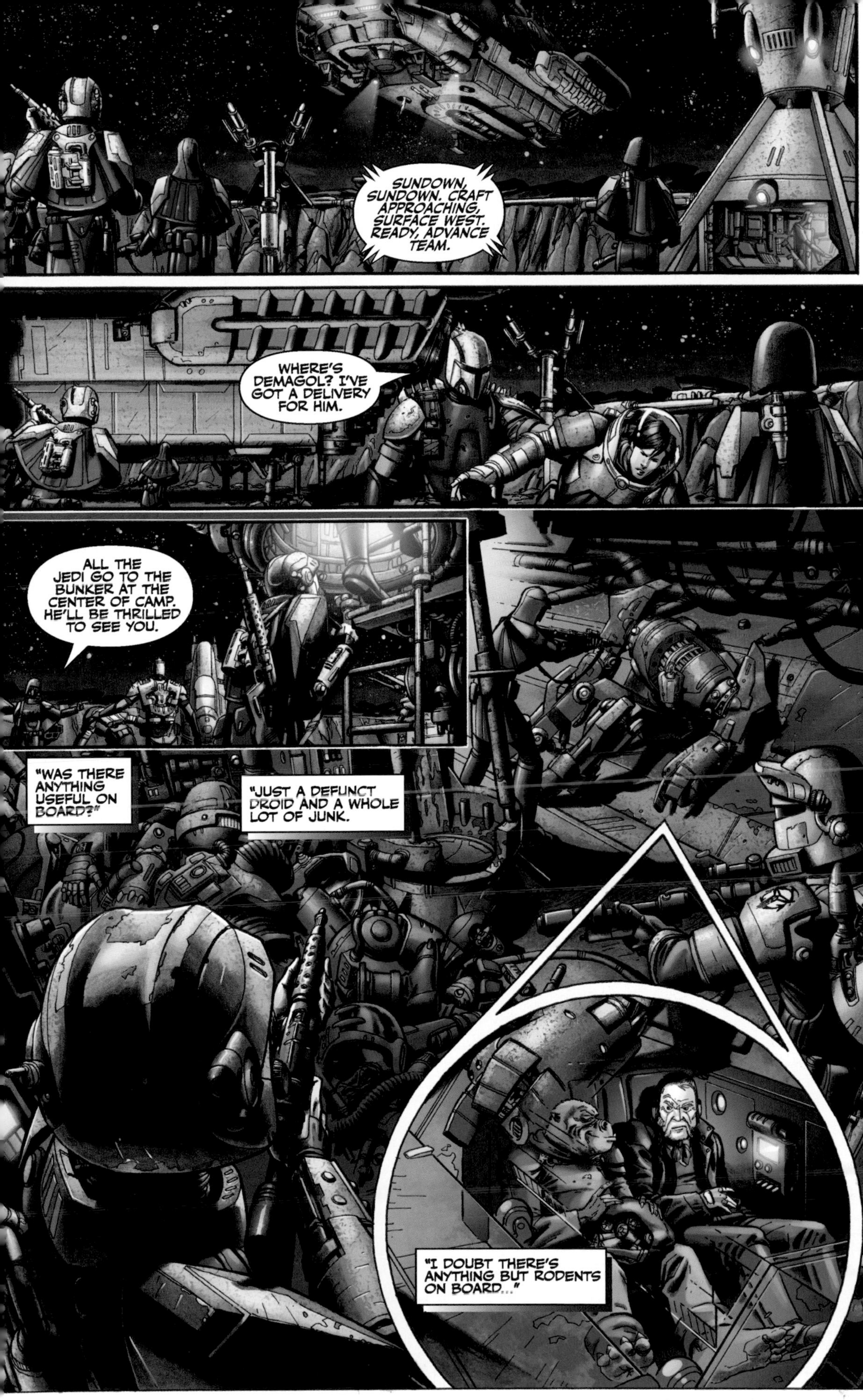
SUNDOWN, SUNDOWN. CRAFT APPROACHING, SURFACE WEST. READY, ADVANCE TEAM.
WHERE'S DEMAGOL? I'VE GOT A DELIVERY FOR HIM.
ALL THE JEDI GO TO THE BUNKER AT THE CENTER OF CAMP. HE'LL BE THRILLED TO SEE YOU.
"WAS THERE ANYTHING USEFUL ON BOARD?"
"JUST A DEFUNCT DROID AND A WHOLE LOT OF JUNK.
"I DOUBT THERE'S ANYTHING BUT RODENTS ON BOARD..."

INSIDE THE BUNKER...

MORNING, *JARAEL.* WE HAVE TO STOP MEETING LIKE THIS...

YOU CAN'T LET THEM KEEP TORTURING YOU. WE'VE GOT TO GET YOU OUT OF HERE BEFORE THEY KILL YOU!

DO ARKANIANS FASCINATE YOU, TOO, *SQUINT?* SO LOVING OF SCIENCE -- AND SO WILLING TO USE IT.

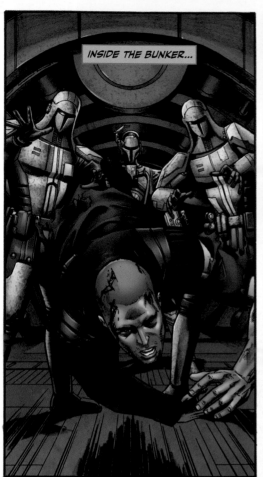

YOU MIGHT CLOSE AN UNPRODUCTIVE MINE. AN ANCIENT ARKANIAN BREEDS NEW WORKERS WITH HUMAN HANDS, TO REACH MORE GEMS.

IT'S HARD TO SAY WHAT A *TRUE* ARKANIAN IS, ANY MORE. THESE EYES -- THESE...

OSI'KYR!

THIS IS INTERESTING. YES, DEFINITELY THE GIRL NEXT, GUARD --

DEMAGOL! I'VE GOT YOUR NEXT SUBJECT.

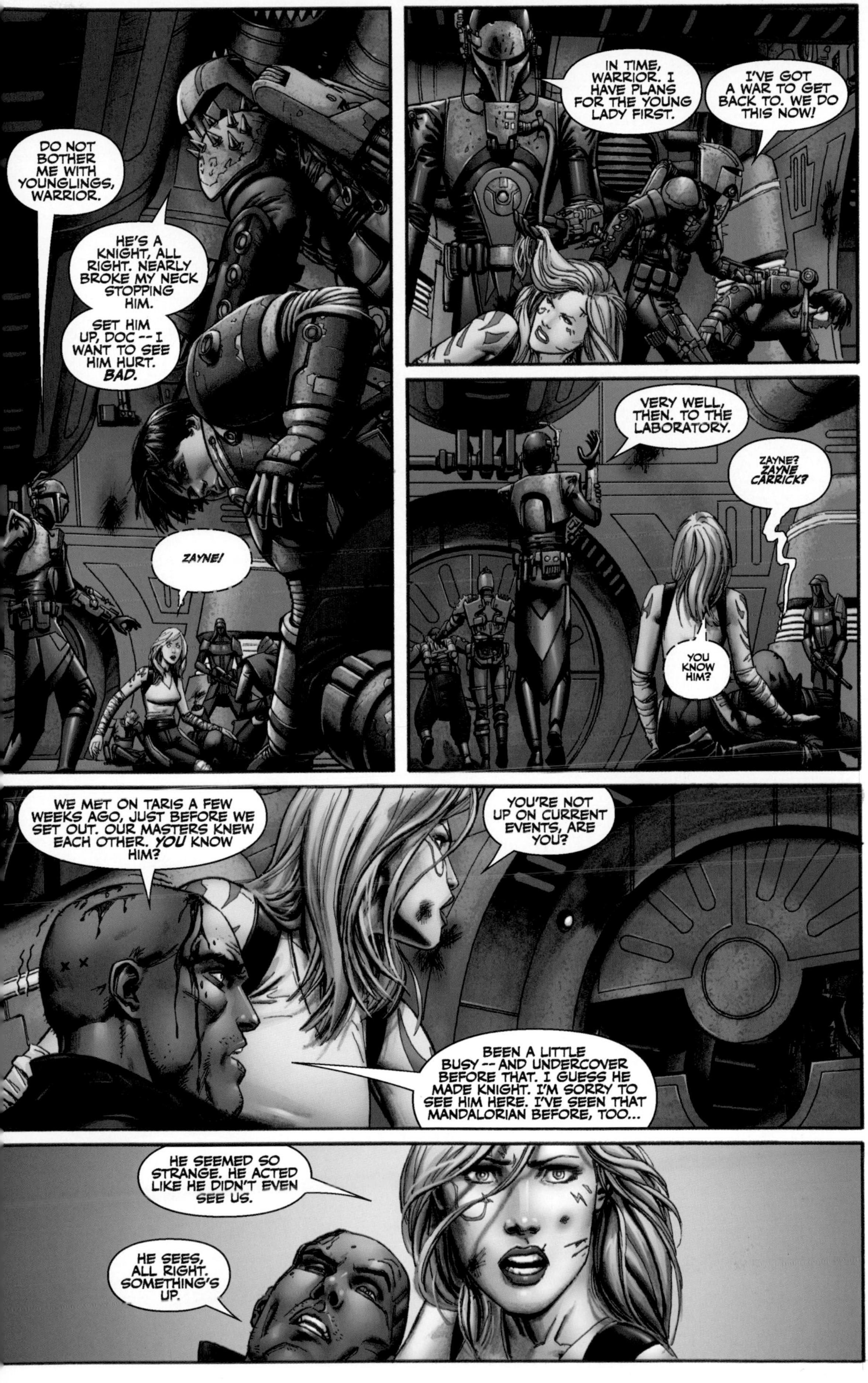
DO NOT BOTHER ME WITH YOUNGLINGS, WARRIOR.
HE'S A KNIGHT, ALL RIGHT. NEARLY BROKE MY NECK STOPPING HIM.
SET HIM UP, DOC -- I WANT TO SEE HIM HURT. *BAD.*
ZAYNE!
IN TIME, WARRIOR. I HAVE PLANS FOR THE YOUNG LADY FIRST.
I'VE GOT A WAR TO GET BACK TO. WE DO THIS NOW!
VERY WELL, THEN. TO THE LABORATORY.
ZAYNE? *ZAYNE CARRICK?*
YOU KNOW HIM?
WE MET ON TARIS A FEW WEEKS AGO, JUST BEFORE WE SET OUT. OUR MASTERS KNEW EACH OTHER. *YOU* KNOW HIM?
YOU'RE NOT UP ON CURRENT EVENTS, ARE YOU?
BEEN A LITTLE BUSY -- AND UNDERCOVER BEFORE THAT. I GUESS HE MADE KNIGHT. I'M SORRY TO SEE HIM HERE. I'VE SEEN THAT MANDALORIAN BEFORE, TOO...
HE SEEMED SO STRANGE. HE ACTED LIKE HE DIDN'T EVEN SEE US.
HE SEES, ALL RIGHT. SOMETHING'S UP.

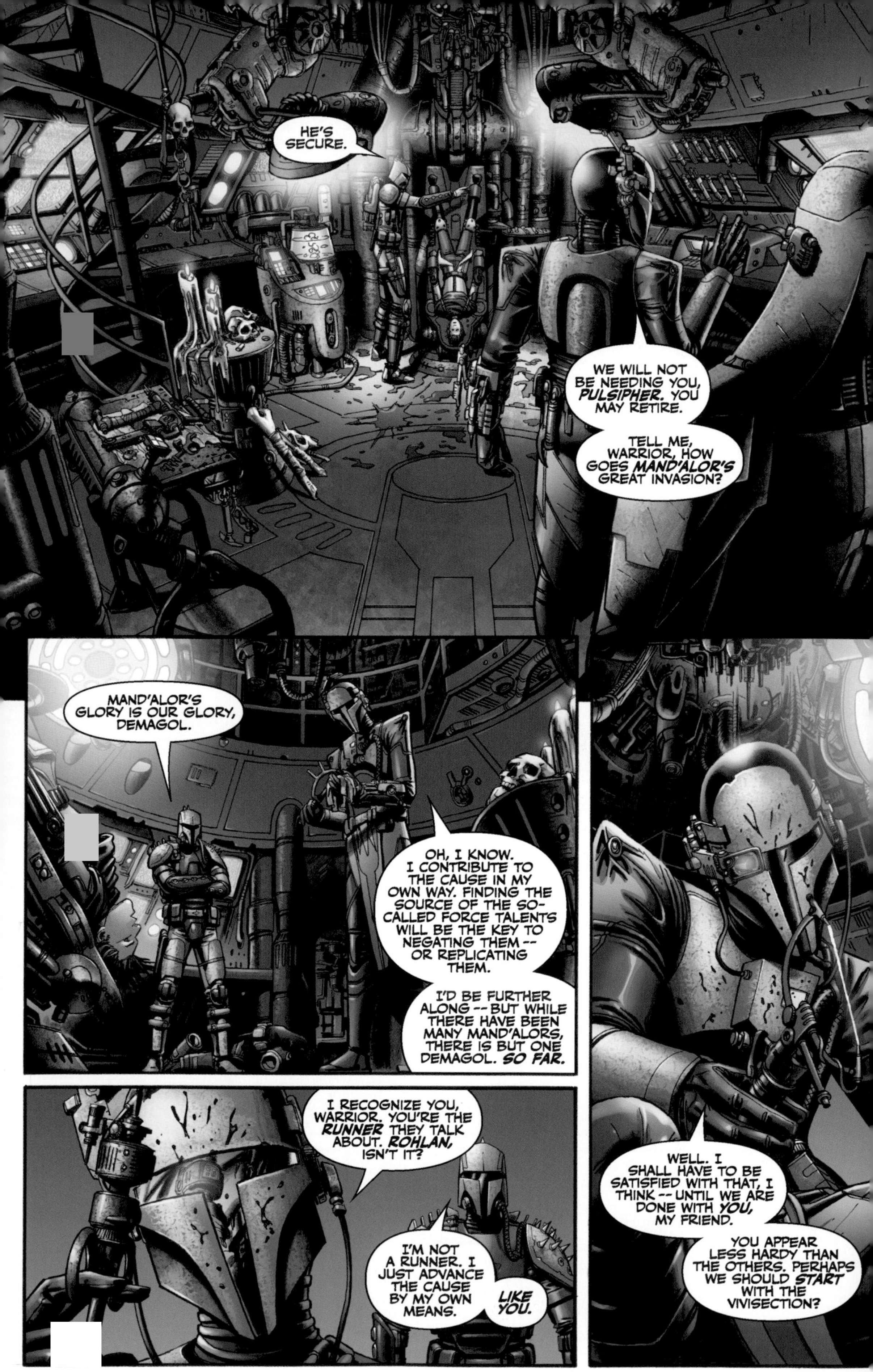
HE'S SECURE.
WE WILL NOT BE NEEDING YOU, PULSIPHER. YOU MAY RETIRE.
TELL ME, WARRIOR, HOW GOES MAND'ALOR'S GREAT INVASION?
MAND'ALOR'S GLORY IS OUR GLORY, DEMAGOL.
OH, I KNOW. I CONTRIBUTE TO THE CAUSE IN MY OWN WAY. FINDING THE SOURCE OF THE SO-CALLED FORCE TALENTS WILL BE THE KEY TO NEGATING THEM -- OR REPLICATING THEM.
I'D BE FURTHER ALONG -- BUT WHILE THERE HAVE BEEN MANY MAND'ALORS, THERE IS BUT ONE DEMAGOL. SO FAR.
I RECOGNIZE YOU, WARRIOR. YOU'RE THE RUNNER THEY TALK ABOUT. ROHLAN, ISN'T IT?
I'M NOT A RUNNER. I JUST ADVANCE THE CAUSE BY MY OWN MEANS.
LIKE YOU.
WELL. I SHALL HAVE TO BE SATISFIED WITH THAT, I THINK -- UNTIL WE ARE DONE WITH YOU, MY FRIEND.
YOU APPEAR LESS HARDY THAN THE OTHERS. PERHAPS WE SHOULD START WITH THE VIVISECTION?

I THINK YOU SHOULD LET ME GO.

I THINK YOU SHOULD LET HIM GO.

WHA--?

THAT'S QUITE ENOUGH OF *THAT!*

BETTER JEDI THAN YOU HAVE TRIED, YOUNGLING.

WHAK!

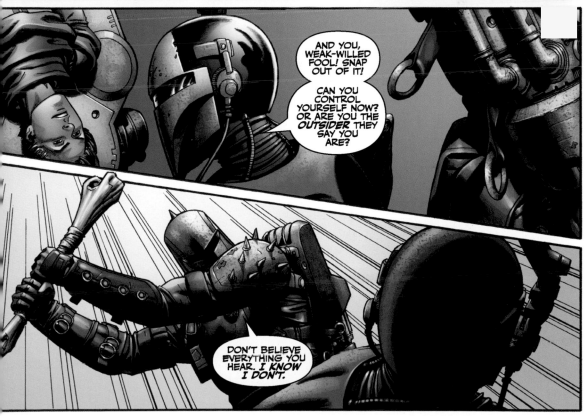

AND YOU, WEAK-WILLED *FOOL!* SNAP OUT OF IT!

CAN YOU CONTROL YOURSELF NOW? OR ARE YOU THE *OUTSIDER* THEY SAY YOU ARE?

DON'T BELIEVE EVERYTHING YOU HEAR. *I KNOW I DON'T.*

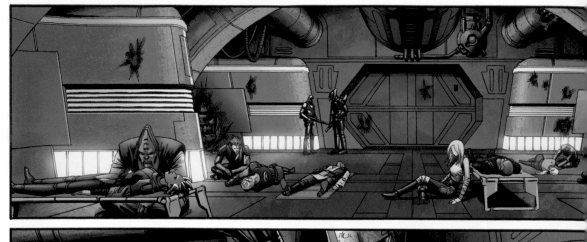

ANIMAL!

OOOF!

OOOF!

TOO BAD, DEMAGOL. I THOUGHT HE'D LIVE LONGER.

I MUST HAVE BEATEN MOST OF THE LIFE OUT OF HIM ON HIS SHIP.

NO!

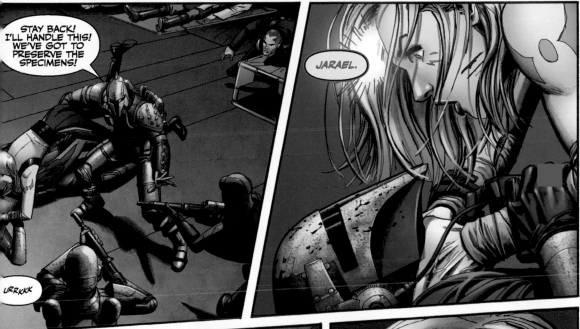

STAY BACK! I'LL HANDLE THIS! WE'VE GOT TO PRESERVE THE SPECIMENS!

JARAEL.

URRKKK

I'D LIKE TO WATCH YOU DEAL WITH HER LATER, DEMAGOL. NOW, HOW ABOUT THAT TOUR OF THE CAMP YOU PROMISED?

WHAT -- WHAT HAPPENED? YOU HAD HIM!

I...HEARD SOMETHING...

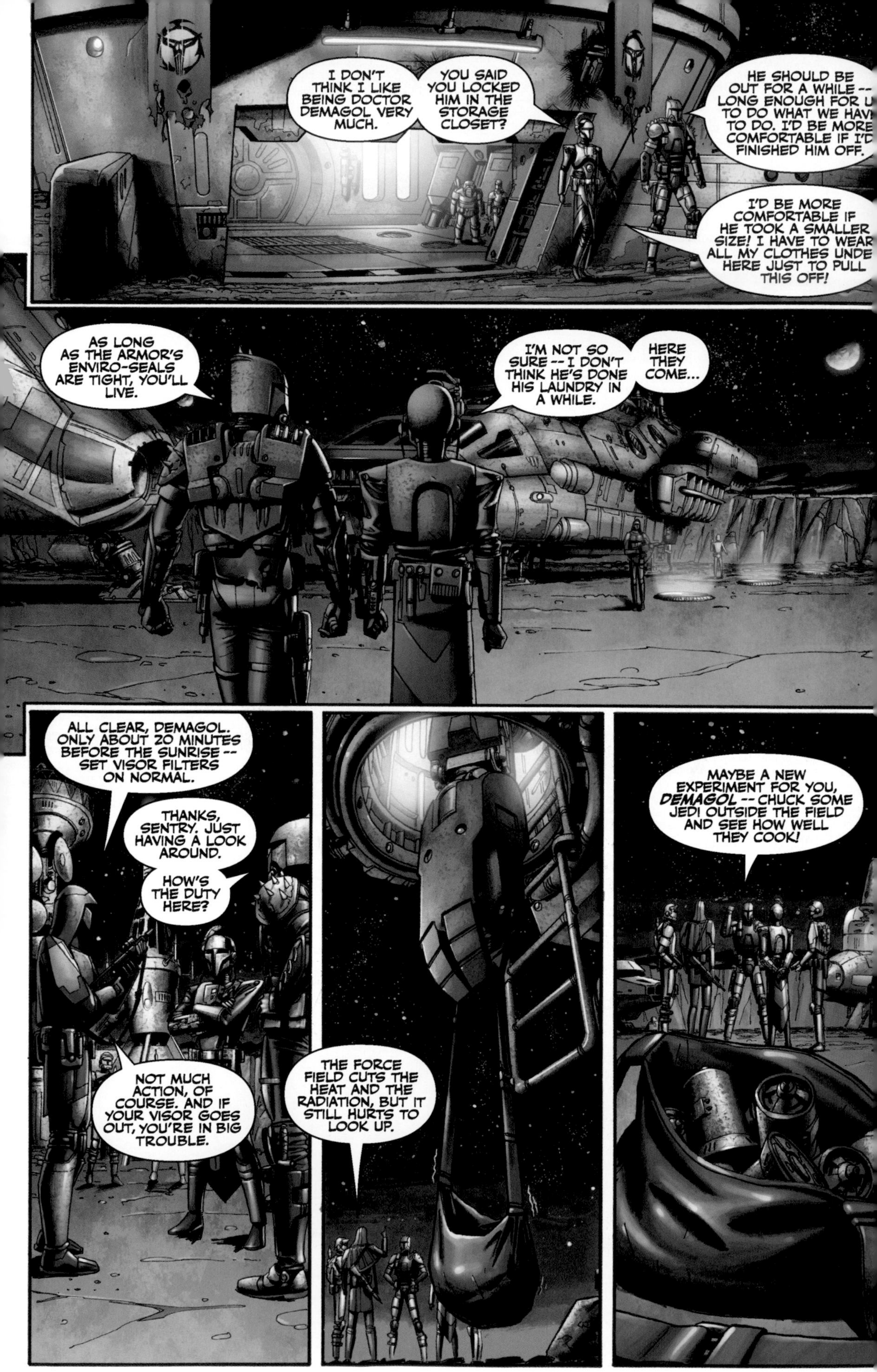
I DON'T THINK I LIKE BEING DOCTOR DEMAGOL VERY MUCH.
YOU SAID YOU LOCKED HIM IN THE STORAGE CLOSET?
HE SHOULD BE OUT FOR A WHILE -- LONG ENOUGH FOR U TO DO WHAT WE HAV TO DO. I'D BE MORE COMFORTABLE IF I'D FINISHED HIM OFF.
I'D BE MORE COMFORTABLE IF HE TOOK A SMALLER SIZE! I HAVE TO WEAR ALL MY CLOTHES UNDE HERE JUST TO PULL THIS OFF!
AS LONG AS THE ARMOR'S ENVIRO-SEALS ARE TIGHT, YOU'LL LIVE.
I'M NOT SO SURE -- I DON'T THINK HE'S DONE HIS LAUNDRY IN A WHILE.
HERE THEY COME...
ALL CLEAR, DEMAGOL. ONLY ABOUT 20 MINUTES BEFORE THE SUNRISE -- SET VISOR FILTERS ON NORMAL.
THANKS, SENTRY. JUST HAVING A LOOK AROUND.
HOW'S THE DUTY HERE?
NOT MUCH ACTION, OF COURSE. AND IF YOUR VISOR GOES OUT, YOU'RE IN BIG TROUBLE.
THE FORCE FIELD CUTS THE HEAT AND THE RADIATION, BUT IT STILL HURTS TO LOOK UP.
MAYBE A NEW EXPERIMENT FOR YOU, DEMAGOL -- CHUCK SOME JEDI OUTSIDE THE FIELD AND SEE HOW WELL THEY COOK!

I GUESS WE'LL SEE MORE JEDI NOW THAT THE INVASION IS ON.

I'VE JUST COME FROM THERE. WHO'D LIKE TO HEAR ABOUT IT?

TINK!

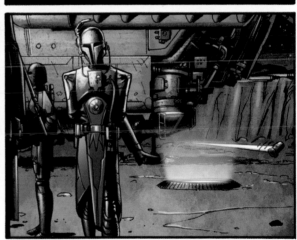

TINK!

TINK!

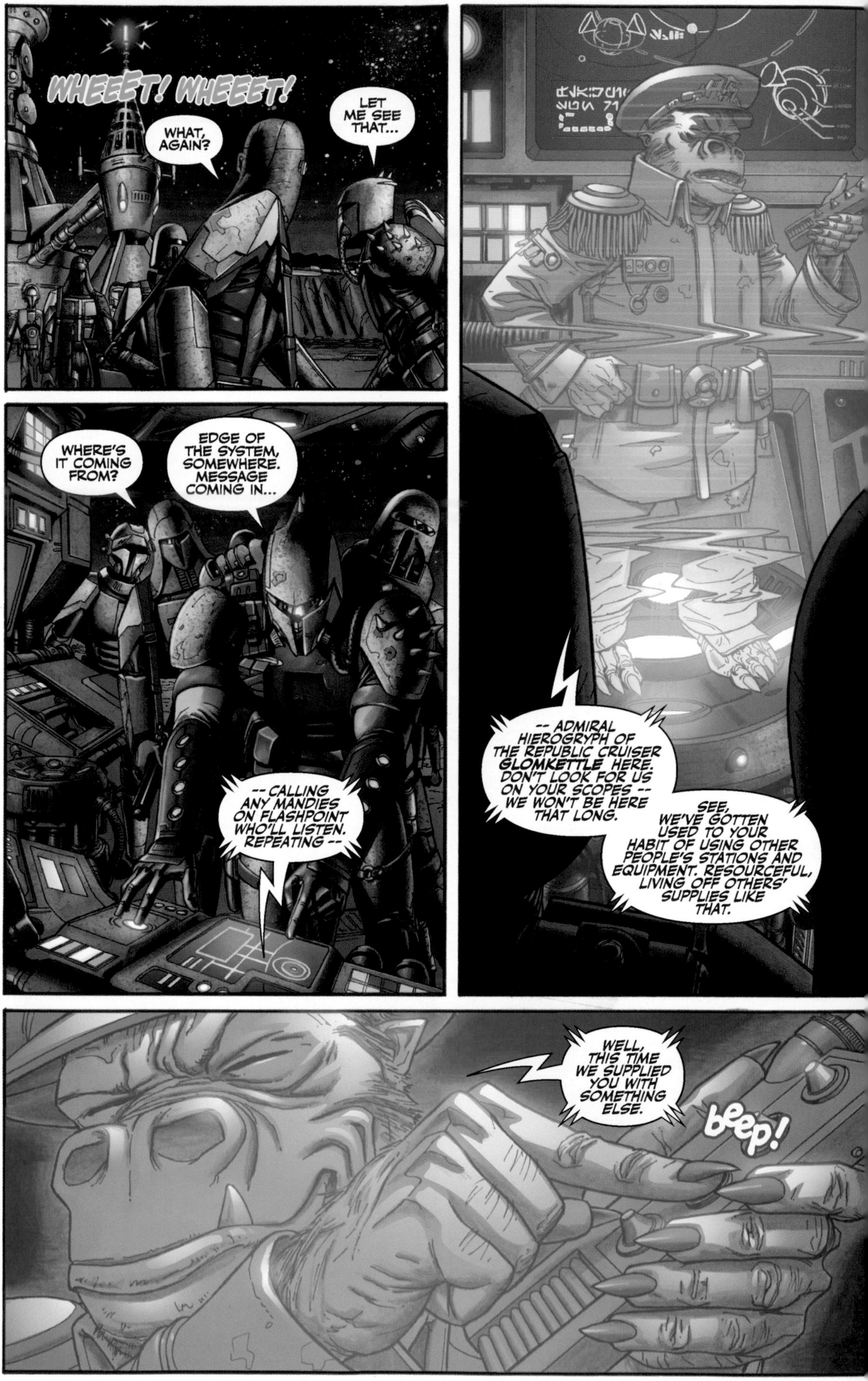
WHEEET! WHEEET!
WHAT, AGAIN?
LET ME SEE THAT...
WHERE'S IT COMING FROM?
EDGE OF THE SYSTEM, SOMEWHERE. MESSAGE COMING IN...
--CALLING ANY MANDIES ON FLASHPOINT WHO'LL LISTEN. REPEATING --
-- ADMIRAL HIEROGRYPH OF THE REPUBLIC CRUISER GLOMKETTLE HERE. DON'T LOOK FOR US ON YOUR SCOPES -- WE WON'T BE HERE THAT LONG.
SEE, WE'VE GOTTEN USED TO YOUR HABIT OF USING OTHER PEOPLE'S STATIONS AND EQUIPMENT. RESOURCEFUL, LIVING OFF OTHERS' SUPPLIES LIKE THAT.
WELL, THIS TIME WE SUPPLIED YOU WITH SOMETHING ELSE.
beep!

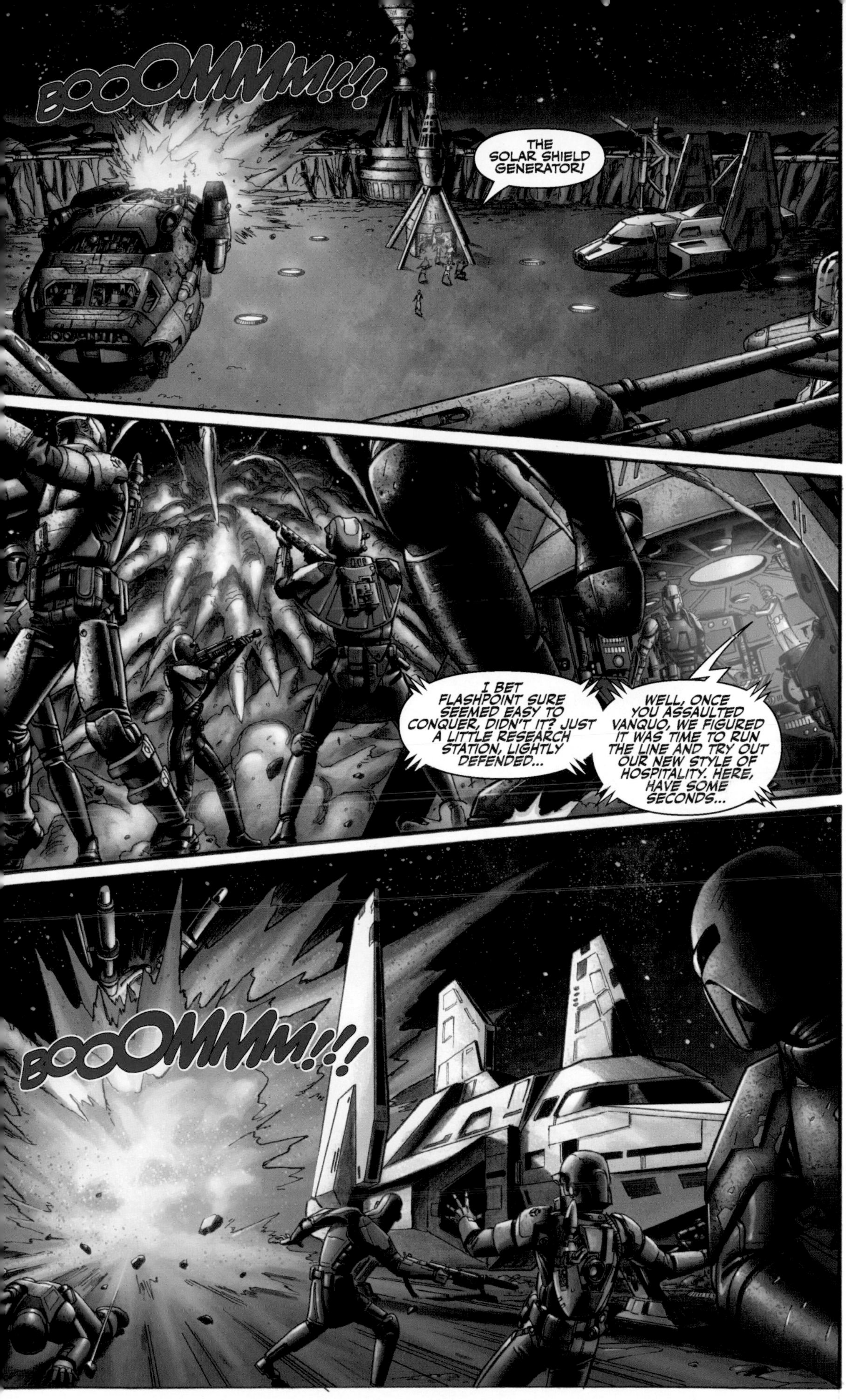
BOOOMMMM!!!
THE SOLAR SHIELD GENERATOR!
I BET FLASHPOINT SURE SEEMED EASY TO CONQUER, DIDN'T IT? JUST A LITTLE RESEARCH STATION, LIGHTLY DEFENDED...
WELL, ONCE YOU ASSAULTED VANQUO, WE FIGURED IT WAS TIME TO RUN THE LINE AND TRY OUT OUR NEW STYLE OF HOSPITALITY. HERE, HAVE SOME SECONDS...
BOOOMMMM!!!

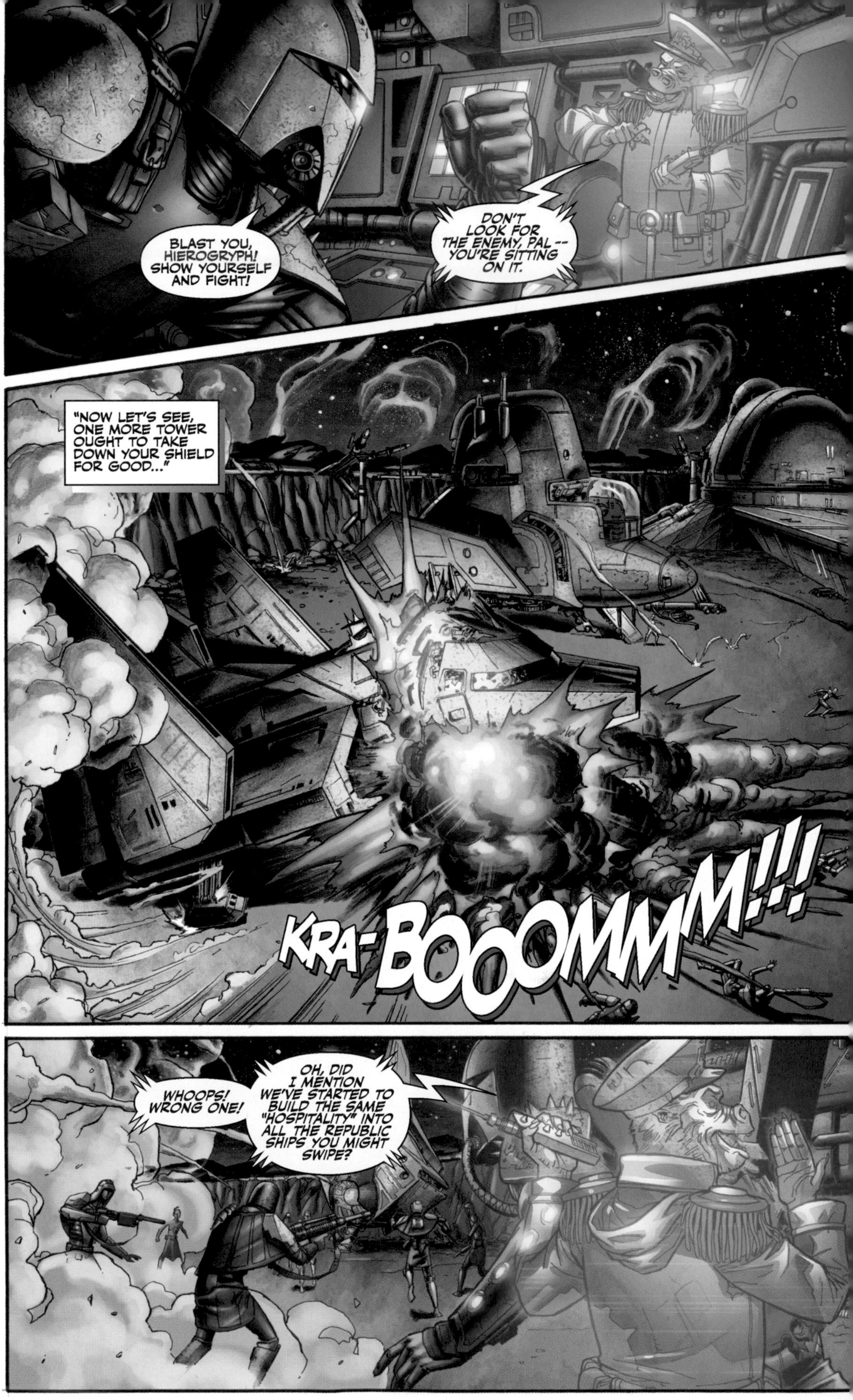
BLAST YOU, HIEROGRYPH! SHOW YOURSELF AND FIGHT!
DON'T LOOK FOR THE ENEMY, PAL -- YOU'RE SITTING ON IT.
"NOW LET'S SEE, ONE MORE TOWER OUGHT TO TAKE DOWN YOUR SHIELD FOR GOOD..."
KRA-BOOOMMM!!!
WHOOPS! WRONG ONE!
OH, DID I MENTION WE'VE STARTED TO BUILD THE SAME "HOSPITALITY" INTO ALL THE REPUBLIC SHIPS YOU MIGHT SWIPE?

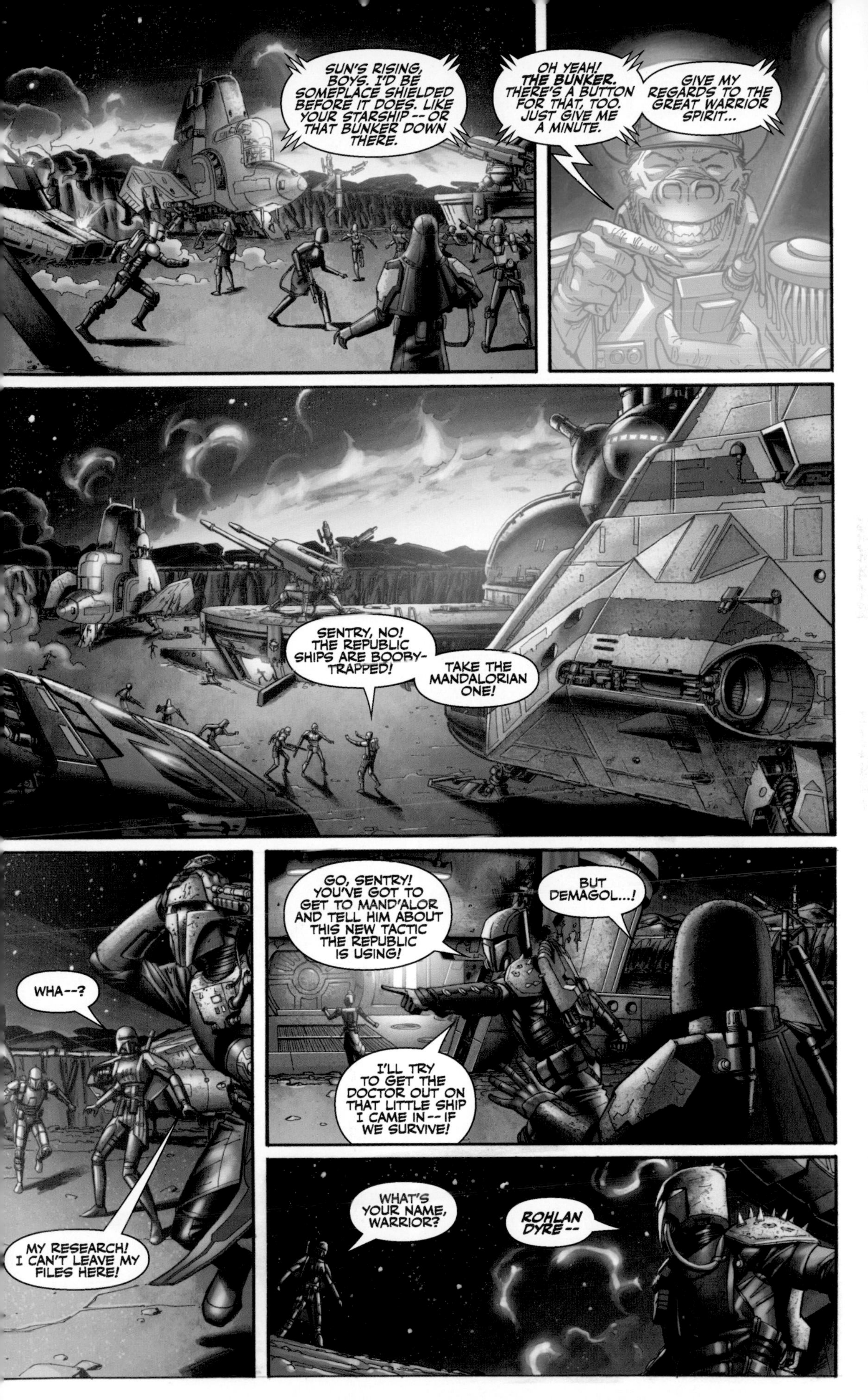
SUN'S RISING, BOYS. I'D BE SOMEPLACE SHIELDED BEFORE IT DOES. LIKE YOUR STARSHIP -- OR THAT BUNKER DOWN THERE.
OH YEAH! THE BUNKER. THERE'S A BUTTON FOR THAT, TOO. JUST GIVE ME A MINUTE.
GIVE MY REGARDS TO THE GREAT WARRIOR SPIRIT...
SENTRY, NO! THE REPUBLIC SHIPS ARE BOOBY-TRAPPED!
TAKE THE MANDALORIAN ONE!
WHA--?
MY RESEARCH! I CAN'T LEAVE MY FILES HERE!
GO, SENTRY! YOU'VE GOT TO GET TO MAND'ALOR AND TELL HIM ABOUT THIS NEW TACTIC THE REPUBLIC IS USING!
BUT DEMAGOL...!
I'LL TRY TO GET THE DOCTOR OUT ON THAT LITTLE SHIP I CAME IN -- IF WE SURVIVE!
WHAT'S YOUR NAME, WARRIOR?
ROHLAN DYRE --

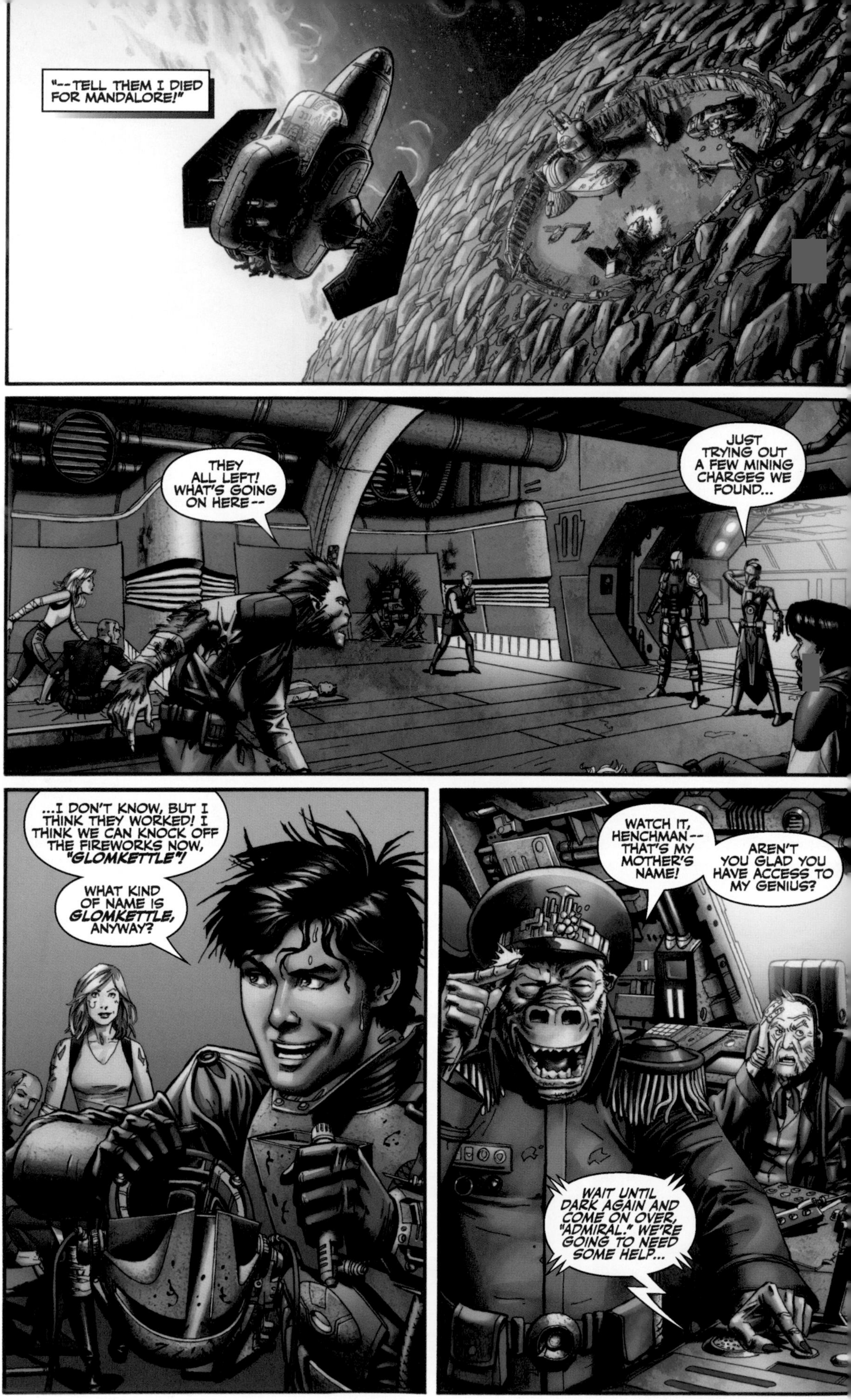
"--TELL THEM I DIED FOR MANDALORE!"
THEY ALL LEFT! WHAT'S GOING ON HERE--
JUST TRYING OUT A FEW MINING CHARGES WE FOUND...
...I DON'T KNOW, BUT I THINK THEY WORKED! I THINK WE CAN KNOCK OFF THE FIREWORKS NOW, "GLOMKETTLE"!
WHAT KIND OF NAME IS GLOMKETTLE, ANYWAY?
WATCH IT, HENCHMAN-- THAT'S MY MOTHER'S NAME!
AREN'T YOU GLAD YOU HAVE ACCESS TO MY GENIUS?
WAIT UNTIL DARK AGAIN AND COME ON OVER, "ADMIRAL." WE'RE GOING TO NEED SOME HELP...

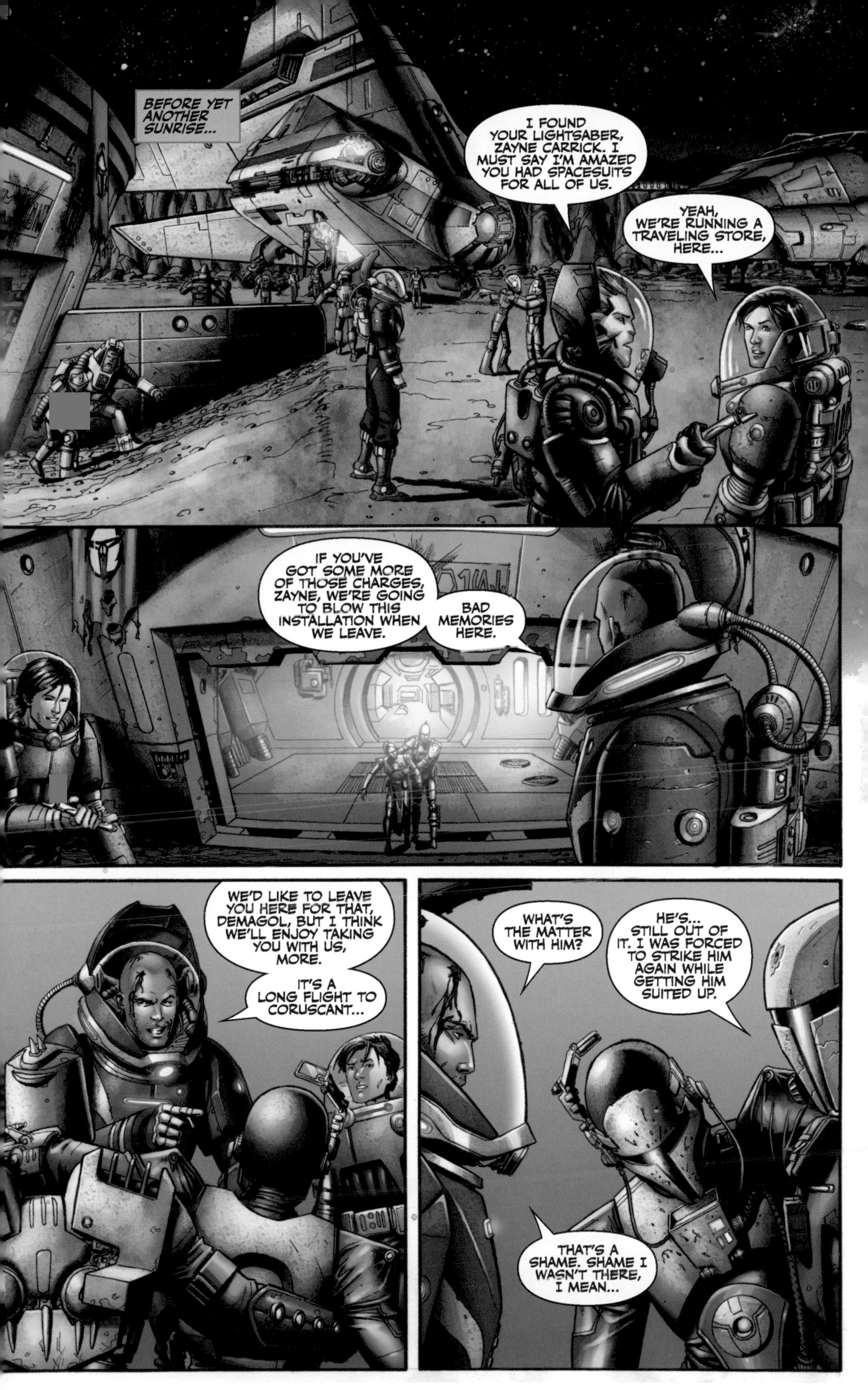
BEFORE YET ANOTHER SUNRISE...
I FOUND YOUR LIGHTSABER, ZAYNE CARRICK. I MUST SAY I'M AMAZED YOU HAD SPACESUITS FOR ALL OF US.
YEAH, WE'RE RUNNING A TRAVELING STORE, HERE...
IF YOU'VE GOT SOME MORE OF THOSE CHARGES, ZAYNE, WE'RE GOING TO BLOW THIS INSTALLATION WHEN WE LEAVE.
BAD MEMORIES HERE.
WE'D LIKE TO LEAVE YOU HERE FOR THAT, DEMAGOL, BUT I THINK WE'LL ENJOY TAKING YOU WITH US, MORE.
IT'S A LONG FLIGHT TO CORUSCANT...
WHAT'S THE MATTER WITH HIM?
HE'S... STILL OUT OF IT. I WAS FORCED TO STRIKE HIM AGAIN WHILE GETTING HIM SUITED UP.
THAT'S A SHAME. SHAME I WASN'T THERE, I MEAN...

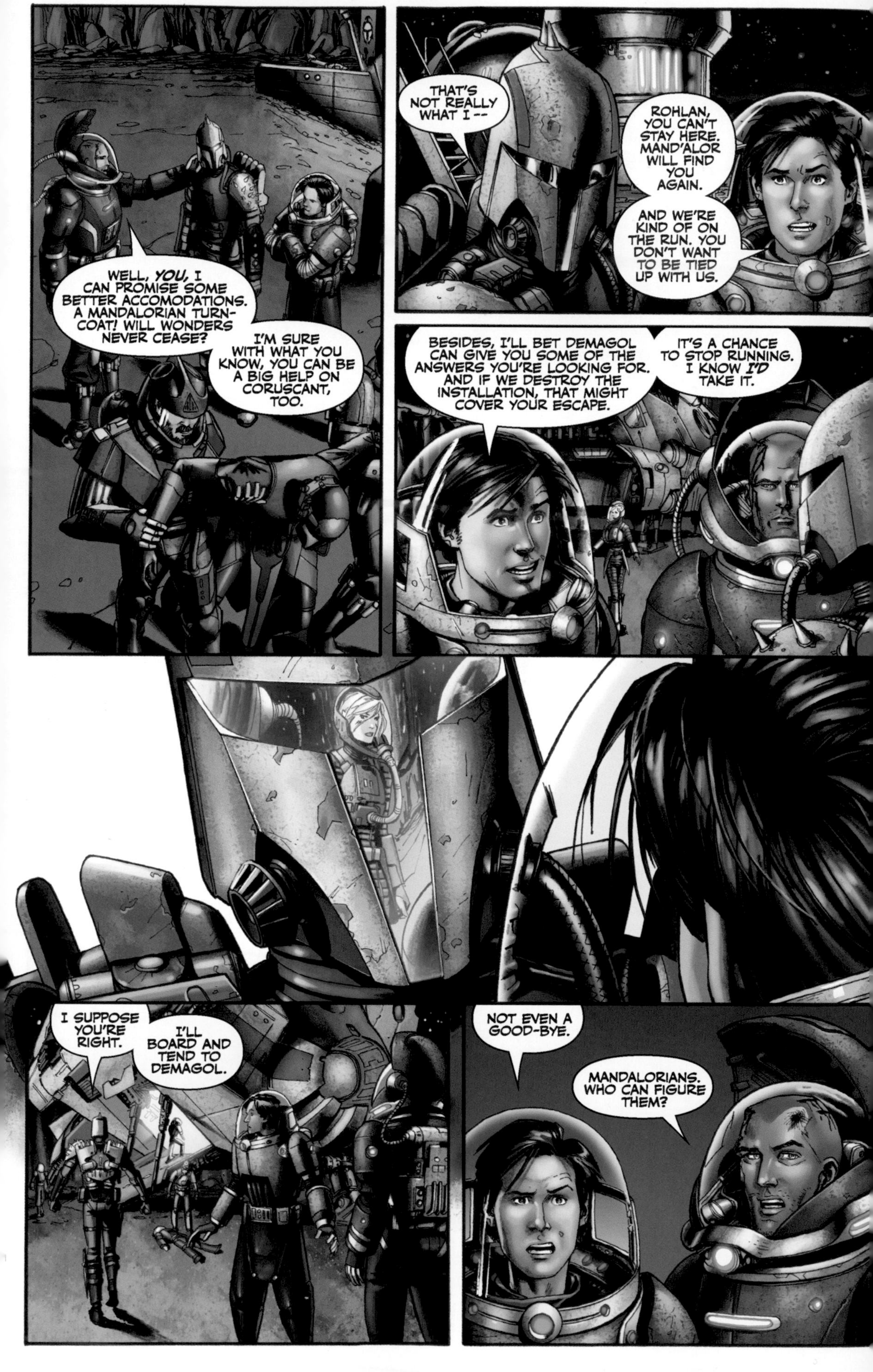
WELL, *YOU,* I CAN PROMISE SOME BETTER ACCOMODATIONS. A MANDALORIAN TURN-COAT! WILL WONDERS NEVER CEASE?
I'M SURE WITH WHAT YOU KNOW, YOU CAN BE A BIG HELP ON CORUSCANT, TOO.
THAT'S NOT REALLY WHAT I --
ROHLAN, YOU CAN'T STAY HERE. MAND'ALOR WILL FIND YOU AGAIN.
AND WE'RE KIND OF ON THE RUN. YOU DON'T WANT TO BE TIED UP WITH US.
BESIDES, I'LL BET DEMAGOL CAN GIVE YOU SOME OF THE ANSWERS YOU'RE LOOKING FOR. AND IF WE DESTROY THE INSTALLATION, THAT MIGHT COVER YOUR ESCAPE.
IT'S A CHANCE TO STOP RUNNING. I KNOW *I'D* TAKE IT.
I SUPPOSE YOU'RE RIGHT.
I'LL BOARD AND TEND TO DEMAGOL.
NOT EVEN A GOOD-BYE.
MANDALORIANS. WHO CAN FIGURE THEM?

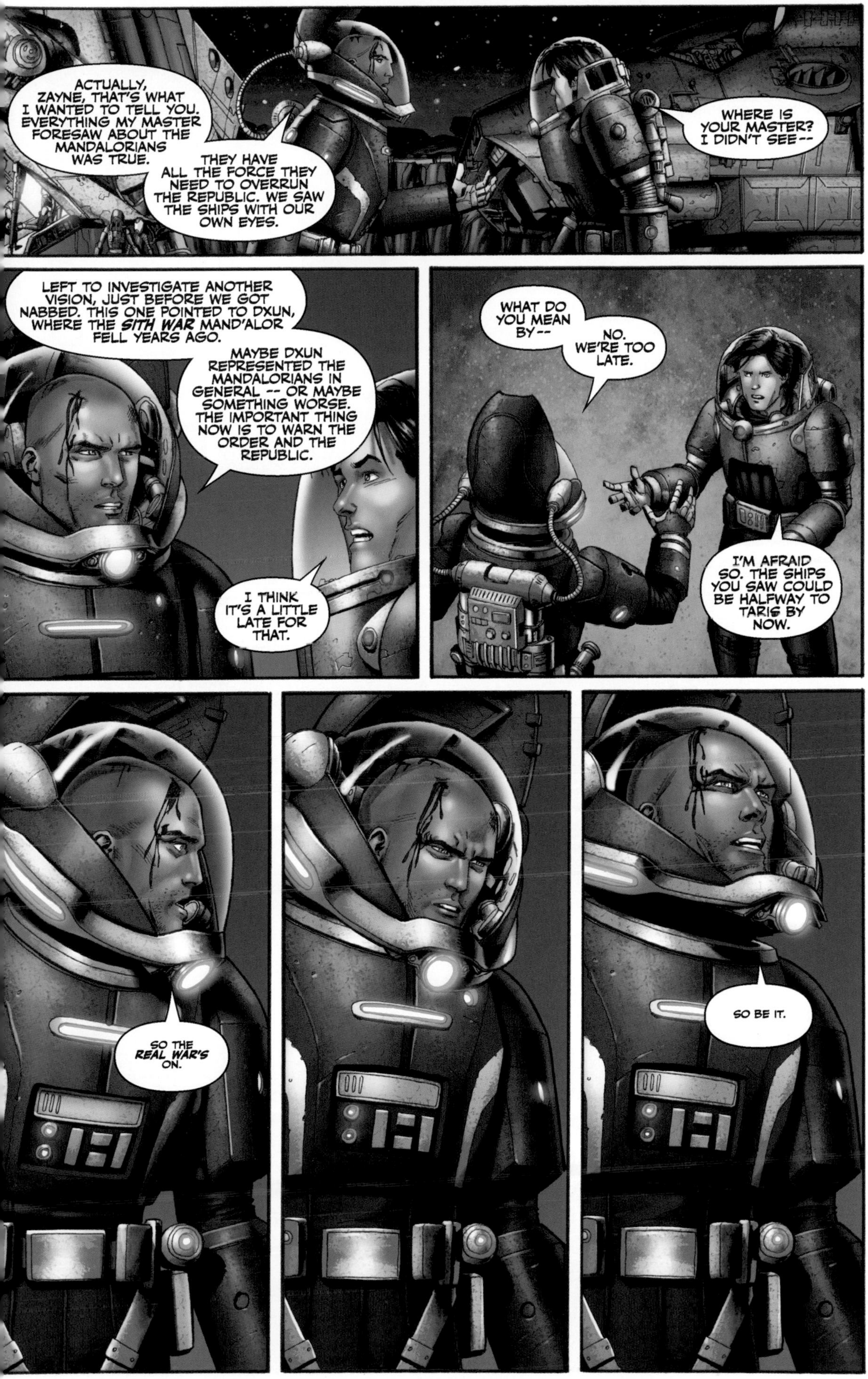
ACTUALLY, ZAYNE, THAT'S WHAT I WANTED TO TELL YOU. EVERYTHING MY MASTER FORESAW ABOUT THE MANDALORIANS WAS TRUE.
THEY HAVE ALL THE FORCE THEY NEED TO OVERRUN THE REPUBLIC. WE SAW THE SHIPS WITH OUR OWN EYES.
WHERE IS YOUR MASTER? I DIDN'T SEE--
LEFT TO INVESTIGATE ANOTHER VISION, JUST BEFORE WE GOT NABBED. THIS ONE POINTED TO DXUN, WHERE THE *SITH WAR* MAND'ALOR FELL YEARS AGO.
MAYBE DXUN REPRESENTED THE MANDALORIANS IN GENERAL -- OR MAYBE SOMETHING WORSE. THE IMPORTANT THING NOW IS TO WARN THE ORDER AND THE REPUBLIC.
I THINK IT'S A LITTLE LATE FOR THAT.
WHAT DO YOU MEAN BY--
NO. WE'RE TOO LATE.
I'M AFRAID SO. THE SHIPS YOU SAW COULD BE HALFWAY TO TARIS BY NOW.
SO THE *REAL WAR'S* ON.
SO BE IT.

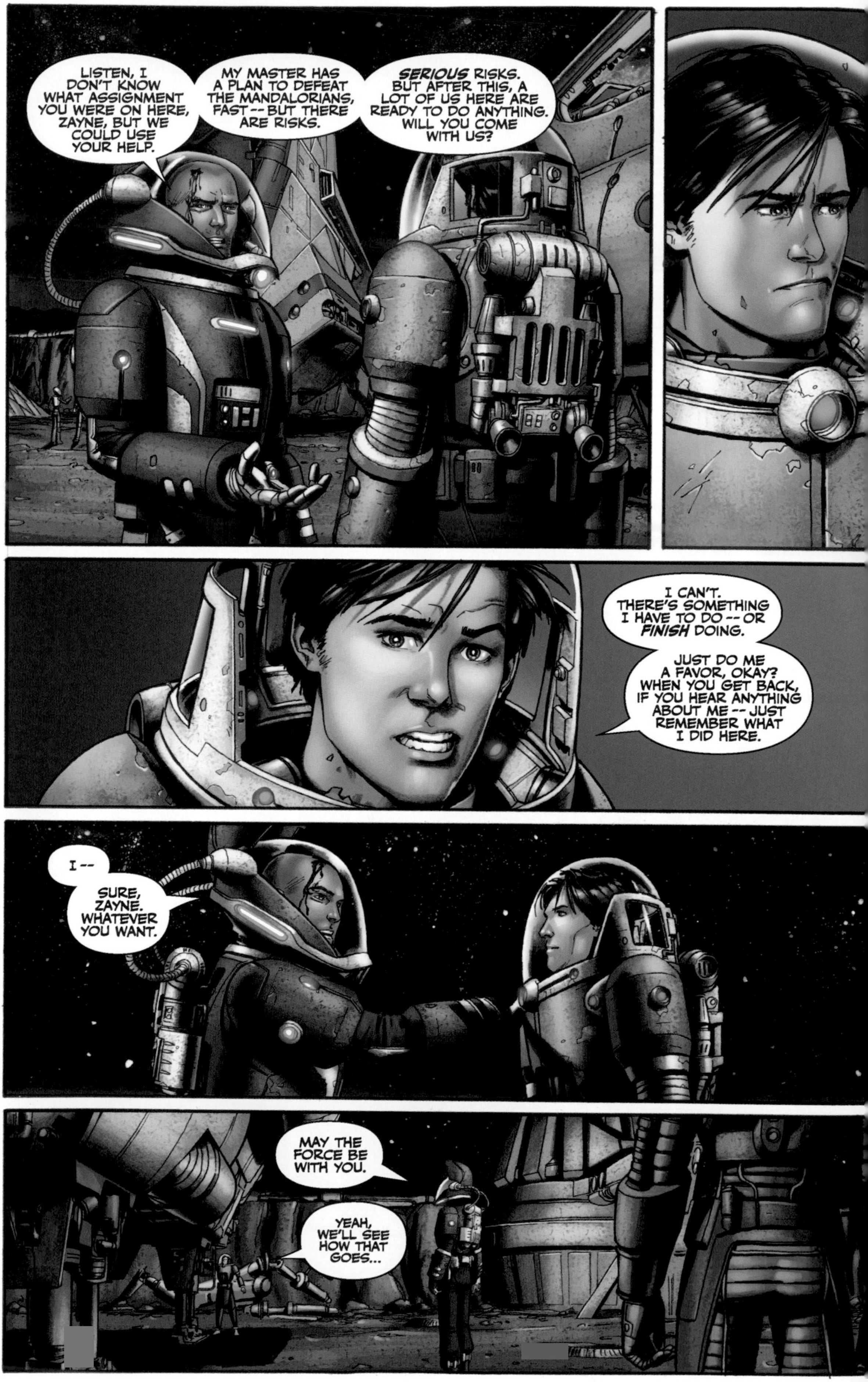
LISTEN, I DON'T KNOW WHAT ASSIGNMENT YOU WERE ON HERE, ZAYNE, BUT WE COULD USE YOUR HELP.
MY MASTER HAS A PLAN TO DEFEAT THE MANDALORIANS, FAST -- BUT THERE ARE RISKS.
SERIOUS RISKS. BUT AFTER THIS, A LOT OF US HERE ARE READY TO DO ANYTHING. WILL YOU COME WITH US?
I CAN'T. THERE'S SOMETHING I HAVE TO DO -- OR FINISH DOING.
JUST DO ME A FAVOR, OKAY? WHEN YOU GET BACK, IF YOU HEAR ANYTHING ABOUT ME -- JUST REMEMBER WHAT I DID HERE.
I --
SURE, ZAYNE. WHATEVER YOU WANT.
MAY THE FORCE BE WITH YOU.
YEAH, WE'LL SEE HOW THAT GOES...

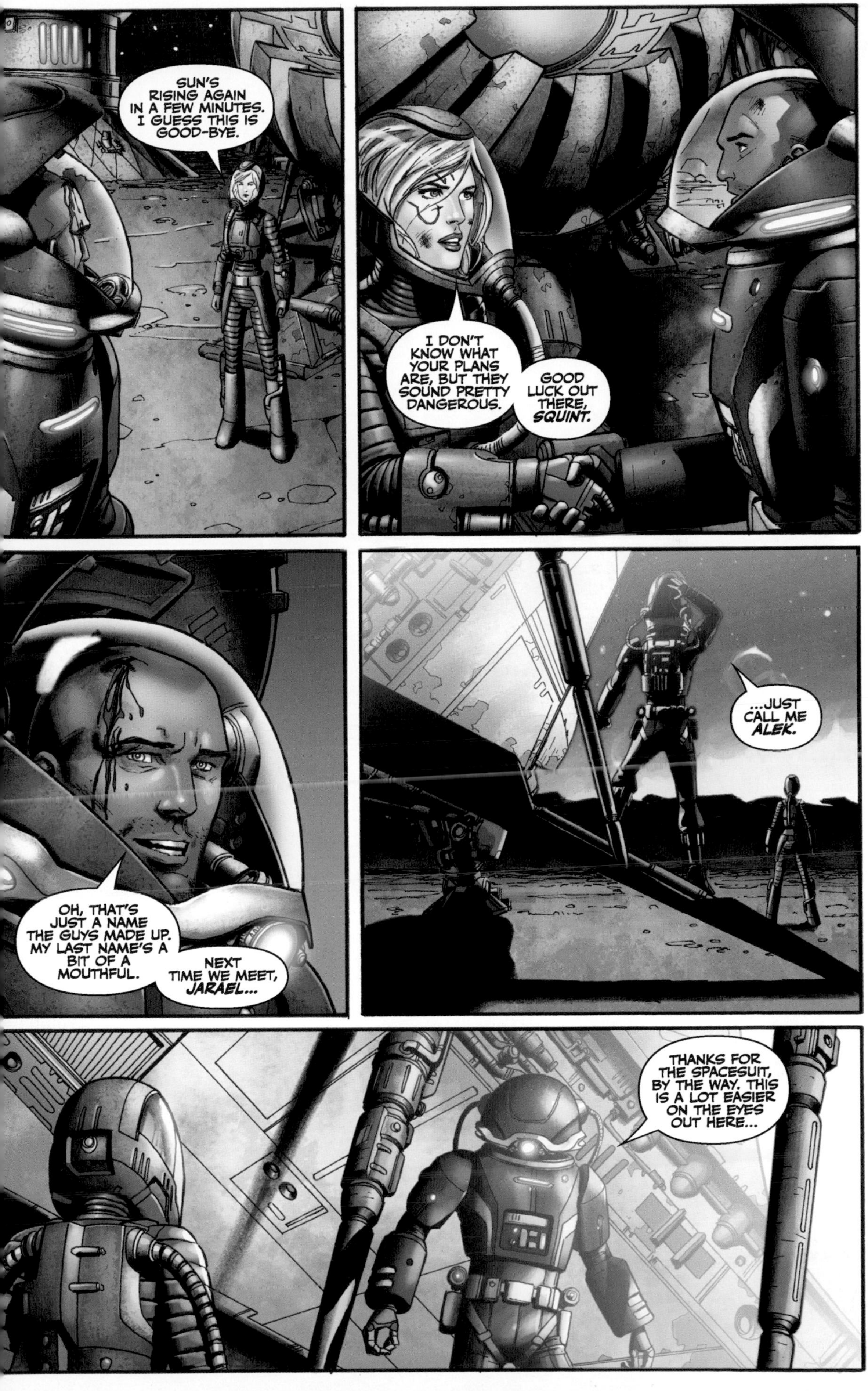
SUN'S RISING AGAIN IN A FEW MINUTES. I GUESS THIS IS GOOD-BYE.
I DON'T KNOW WHAT YOUR PLANS ARE, BUT THEY SOUND PRETTY DANGEROUS.
GOOD LUCK OUT THERE, *SQUINT.*
OH, THAT'S JUST A NAME THE GUYS MADE UP. MY LAST NAME'S A BIT OF A MOUTHFUL.
NEXT TIME WE MEET, *JARAEL...*
...JUST CALL ME *ALEK.*
THANKS FOR THE SPACESUIT, BY THE WAY. THIS IS A LOT EASIER ON THE EYES OUT HERE...

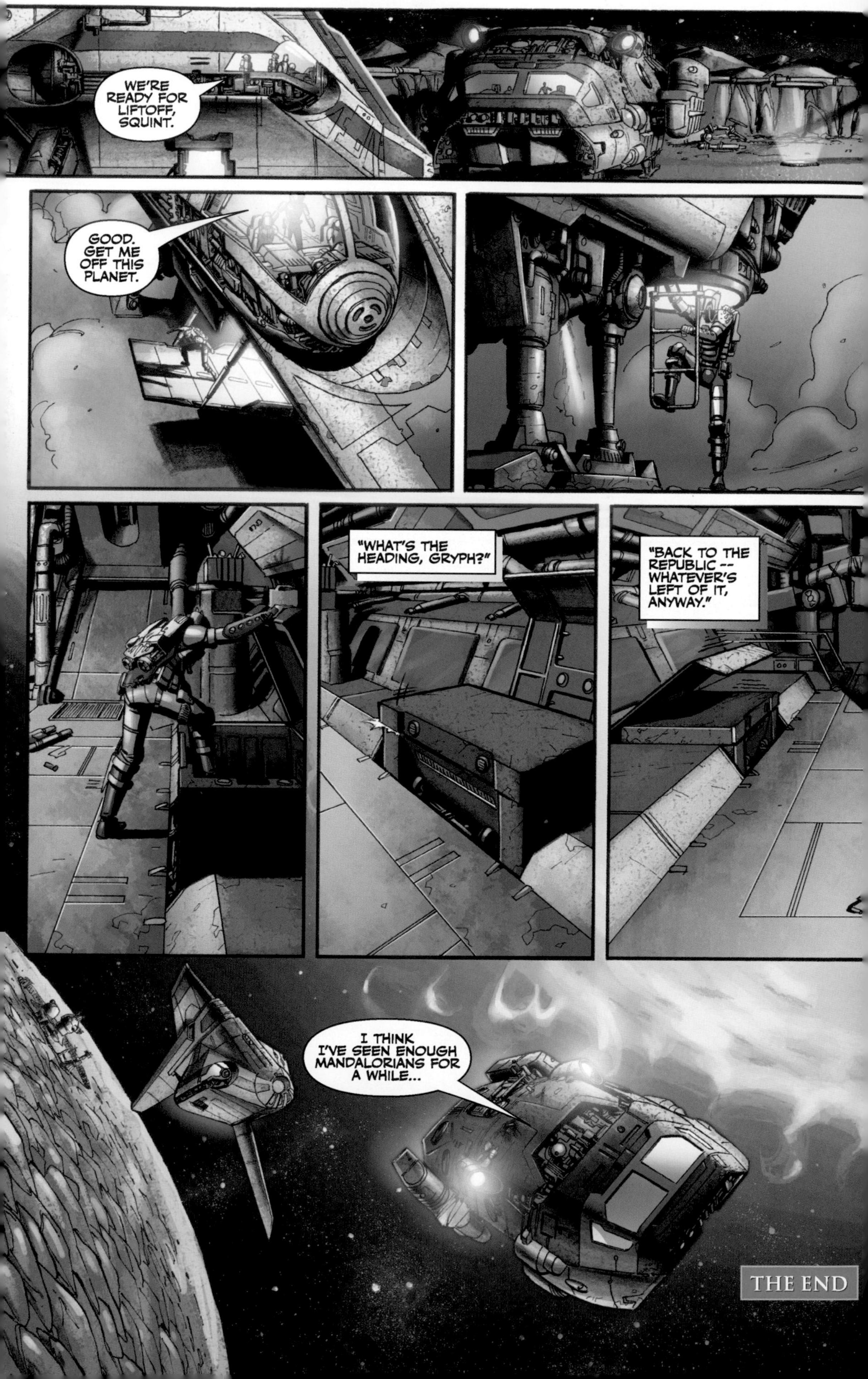
WE'RE READY FOR LIFTOFF, SQUINT.
GOOD. GET ME OFF THIS PLANET.
"WHAT'S THE HEADING, GRYPH?"
"BACK TO THE REPUBLIC -- WHATEVER'S LEFT OF IT, ANYWAY."
I THINK I'VE SEEN ENOUGH MANDALORIANS FOR A WHILE...
THE END

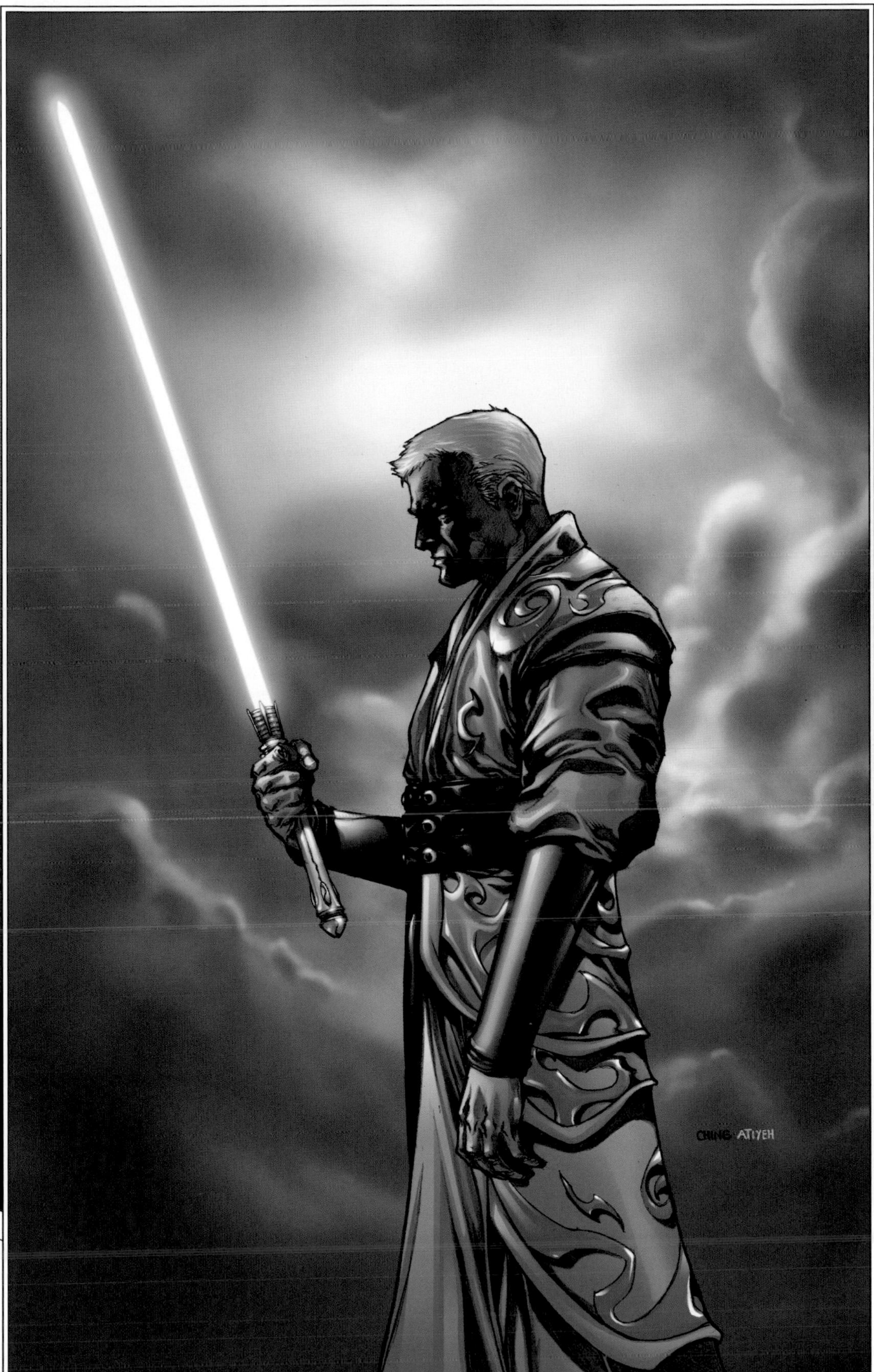
CHING ATIYEH

ILLUSTRATION BY BRIAN CHING AND MICHAEL ATIYEH

HOMECOMING

art by Brian Ching

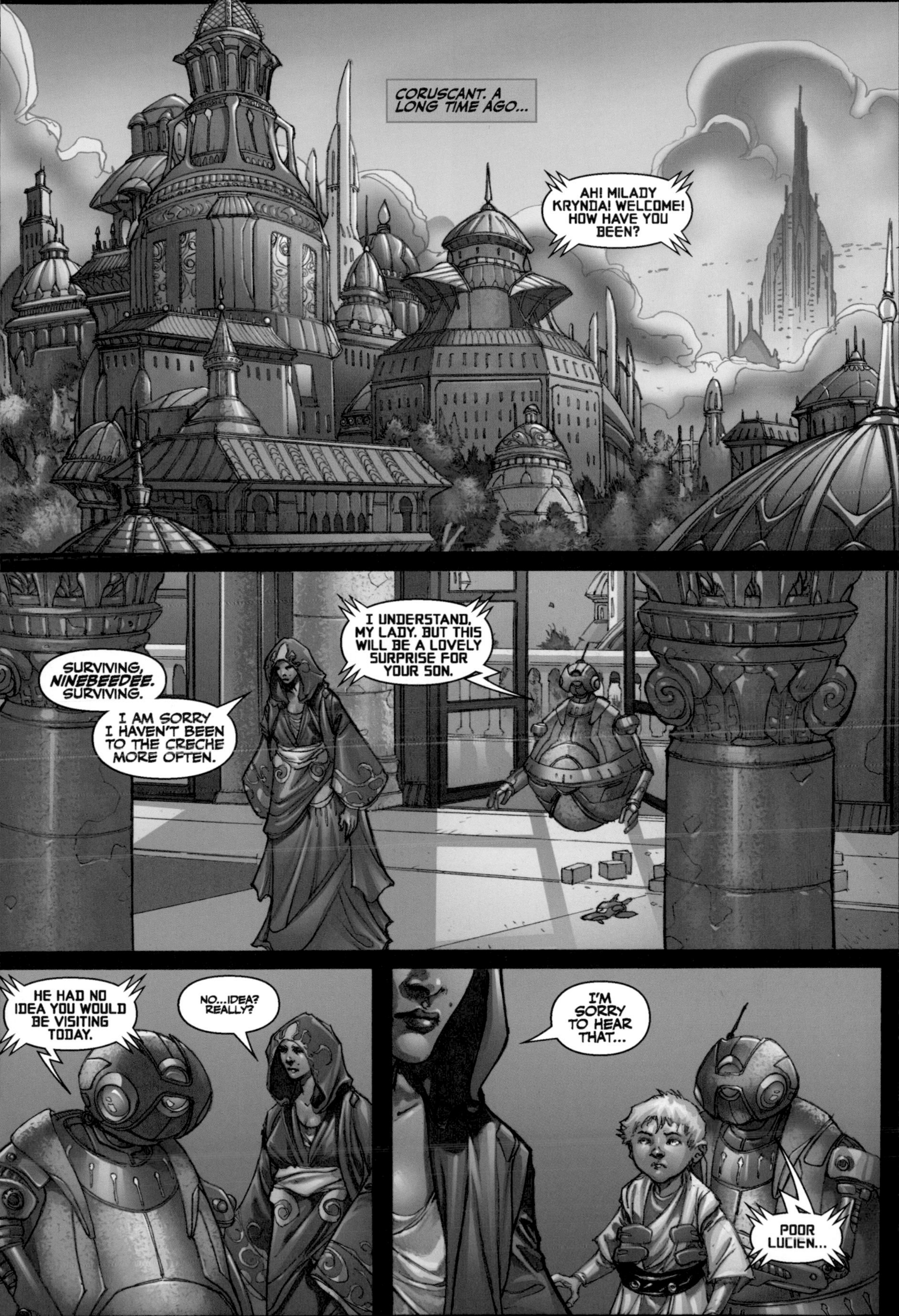
CORUSCANT. A LONG TIME AGO...
AH! MILADY KRYNDA! WELCOME! HOW HAVE YOU BEEN?
SURVIVING, NINEBEEDEE. SURVIVING.
I AM SORRY I HAVEN'T BEEN TO THE CRECHE MORE OFTEN.
I UNDERSTAND, MY LADY. BUT THIS WILL BE A LOVELY SURPRISE FOR YOUR SON.
HE HAD NO IDEA YOU WOULD BE VISITING TODAY.
NO...IDEA? REALLY?
I'M SORRY TO HEAR THAT...
POOR LUCIEN...

CORUSCANT. TODAY.

WHERE ARE YOU?

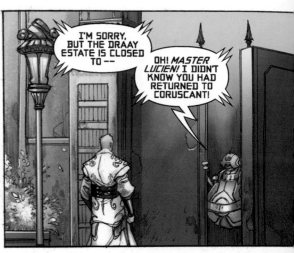

I'M SORRY, BUT THE DRAAY ESTATE IS CLOSED TO --

OH! *MASTER LUCIEN!* I DIDN'T KNOW YOU HAD RETURNED TO CORUSCANT!

IT WAS A SUDDEN DECISION. I NEED TO SEE MY MOTHER.

I'M SORRY, BUT HER LADYSHIP IS NOT SEEING GUESTS AT THIS TIME.

I'M NOT A GUEST, NINEBEEDEE! THIS IS MY HOUSE!

AND I WILL ALERT THE HOUSEHOLD TO YOUR ARRIVAL. PLEASE STAND BY.

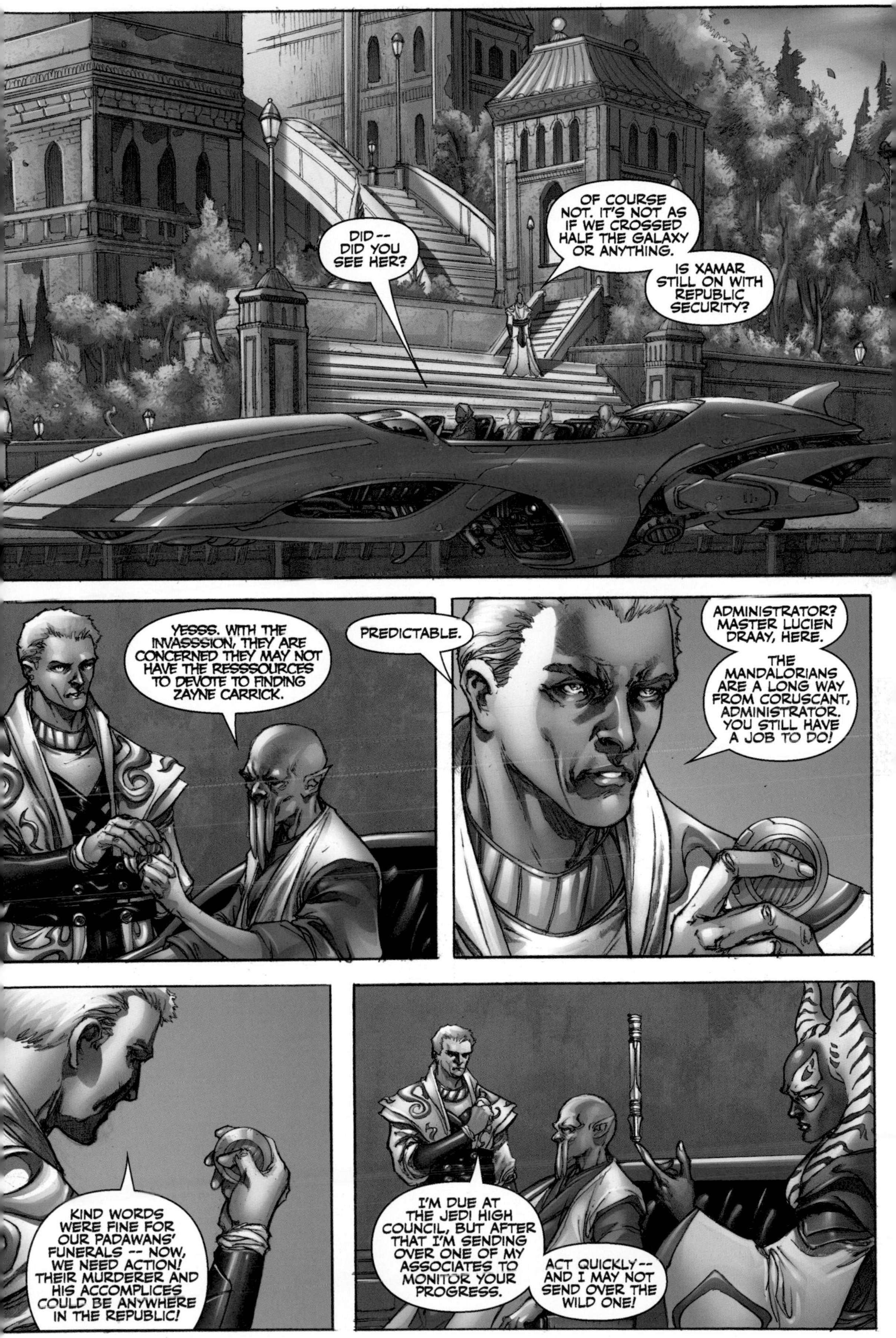
DID-- DID YOU SEE HER?
OF COURSE NOT. IT'S NOT AS IF WE CROSSED HALF THE GALAXY OR ANYTHING.
IS XAMAR STILL ON WITH REPUBLIC SECURITY?
YESSS. WITH THE INVASSSION, THEY ARE CONCERNED THEY MAY NOT HAVE THE RESSSOURCES TO DEVOTE TO FINDING ZAYNE CARRICK.
PREDICTABLE.
ADMINISTRATOR? MASTER LUCIEN DRAAY, HERE.
THE MANDALORIANS ARE A LONG WAY FROM CORUSCANT, ADMINISTRATOR. YOU STILL HAVE A JOB TO DO!
KIND WORDS WERE FINE FOR OUR PADAWANS' FUNERALS -- NOW, WE NEED ACTION! THEIR MURDERER AND HIS ACCOMPLICES COULD BE ANYWHERE IN THE REPUBLIC!
I'M DUE AT THE JEDI HIGH COUNCIL, BUT AFTER THAT I'M SENDING OVER ONE OF MY ASSOCIATES TO MONITOR YOUR PROGRESS.
ACT QUICKLY-- AND I MAY NOT SEND OVER THE WILD ONE!

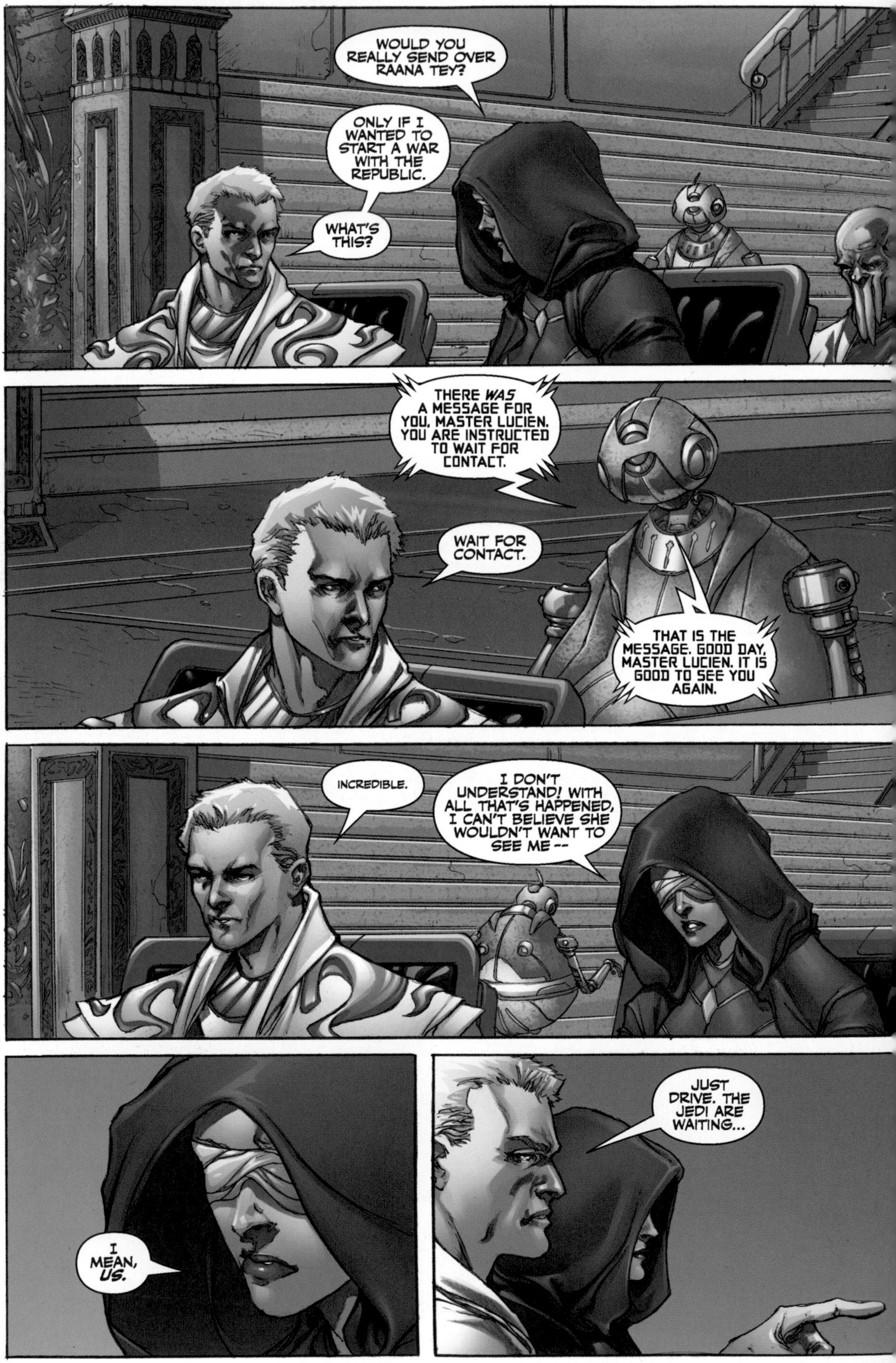
WOULD YOU REALLY SEND OVER RAANA TEY?
ONLY IF I WANTED TO START A WAR WITH THE REPUBLIC.
WHAT'S THIS?
THERE *WAS* A MESSAGE FOR YOU, MASTER LUCIEN. YOU ARE INSTRUCTED TO WAIT FOR CONTACT.
WAIT FOR CONTACT.
THAT IS THE MESSAGE. GOOD DAY, MASTER LUCIEN. IT IS GOOD TO SEE YOU AGAIN.
INCREDIBLE.
I DON'T UNDERSTAND! WITH ALL THAT'S HAPPENED, I CAN'T BELIEVE SHE WOULDN'T WANT TO SEE ME --
I MEAN, *US.*
JUST DRIVE. THE JEDI ARE WAITING...

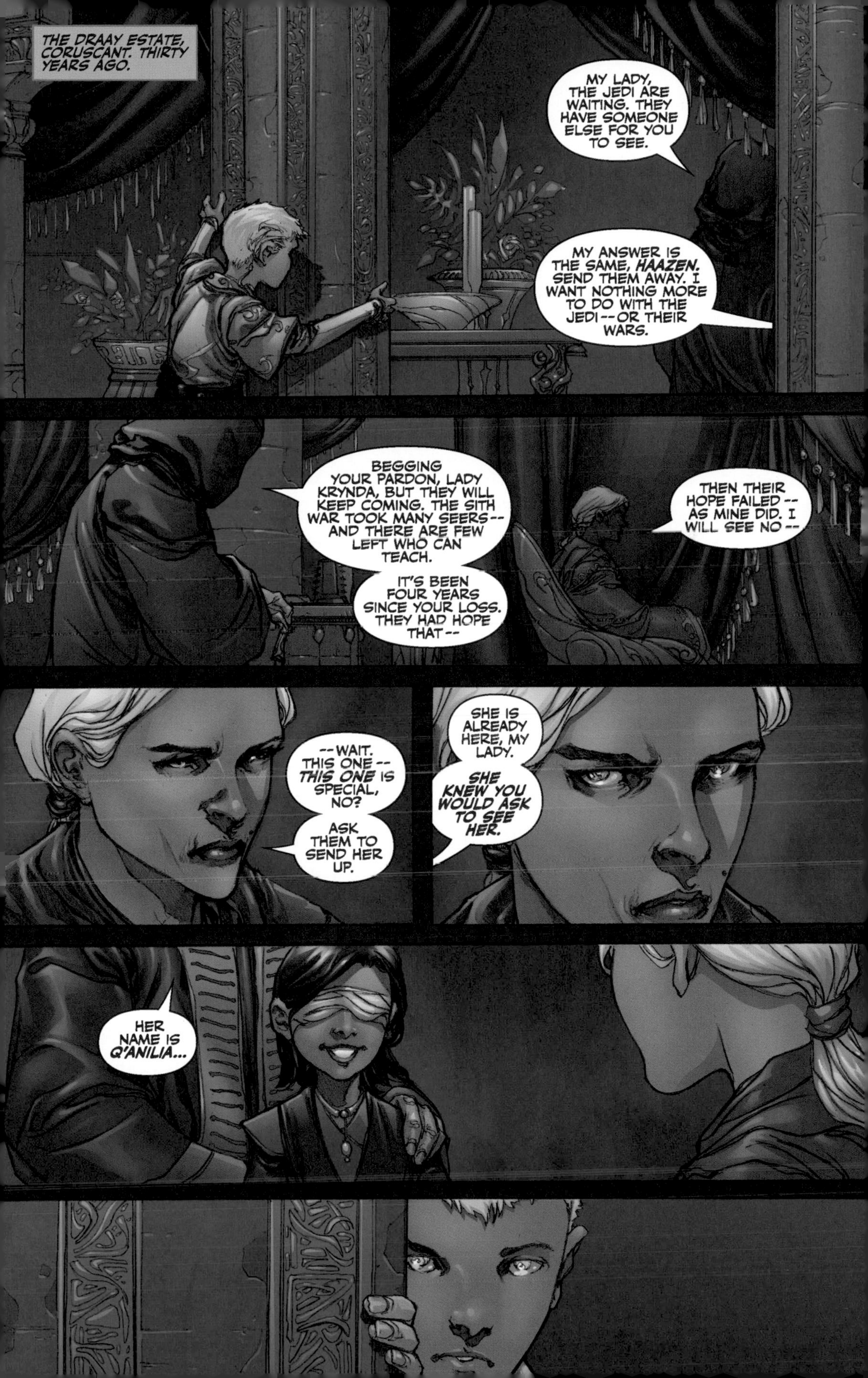

THE DRAAY ESTATE, CORUSCANT. THIRTY YEARS AGO.
MY LADY, THE JEDI ARE WAITING. THEY HAVE SOMEONE ELSE FOR YOU TO SEE.
MY ANSWER IS THE SAME, HAAZEN. SEND THEM AWAY. I WANT NOTHING MORE TO DO WITH THE JEDI--OR THEIR WARS.
BEGGING YOUR PARDON, LADY KRYNDA, BUT THEY WILL KEEP COMING. THE SITH WAR TOOK MANY SEERS--AND THERE ARE FEW LEFT WHO CAN TEACH.
IT'S BEEN FOUR YEARS SINCE YOUR LOSS. THEY HAD HOPE THAT--
THEN THEIR HOPE FAILED--AS MINE DID. I WILL SEE NO--
--WAIT. THIS ONE--THIS ONE IS SPECIAL, NO?
ASK THEM TO SEND HER UP.
SHE IS ALREADY HERE, MY LADY.
SHE KNEW YOU WOULD ASK TO SEE HER.
HER NAME IS Q'ANILIA...

THE JEDI HIGH COUNCIL, CORUSCANT. TODAY.

...AND WHILE YOUR REPORT ON WHAT YOU SAW AT *ONDERON* AND *DXUN* IS, OF COURSE, DISTURBING--

-- NONETHELESS, YOU HAD NO BUSINESS INVESTIGATING ON YOUR OWN!

WE'RE STILL REBUILDING OUR RANKS FROM THE LAST WAR. WE CAN'T AFFORD THIS KIND OF ADVENTURISM, EVEN IF WE *WERE* SUPPORTING IT!

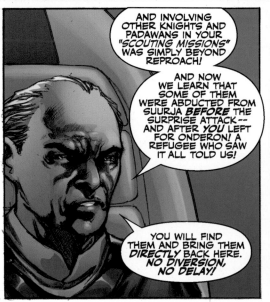

AND INVOLVING OTHER KNIGHTS AND PADAWANS IN YOUR "SCOUTING MISSIONS" WAS SIMPLY BEYOND REPROACH!

AND NOW WE LEARN THAT SOME OF THEM WERE ABDUCTED FROM *SUURJA* BEFORE THE SURPRISE ATTACK -- AND AFTER *YOU* LEFT FOR ONDERON! A REFUGEE WHO SAW IT ALL TOLD US!

YOU WILL FIND THEM AND BRING THEM *DIRECTLY* BACK HERE. *NO DIVERSION, NO DELAY!*

THERE WAS NO PLACE FOR THE ORDER IN THE WRANGLING OVER THE OUTER RIM, AND THERE IS CERTAINLY NO PLACE FOR IT IN A WIDER MANDALORIAN WAR!

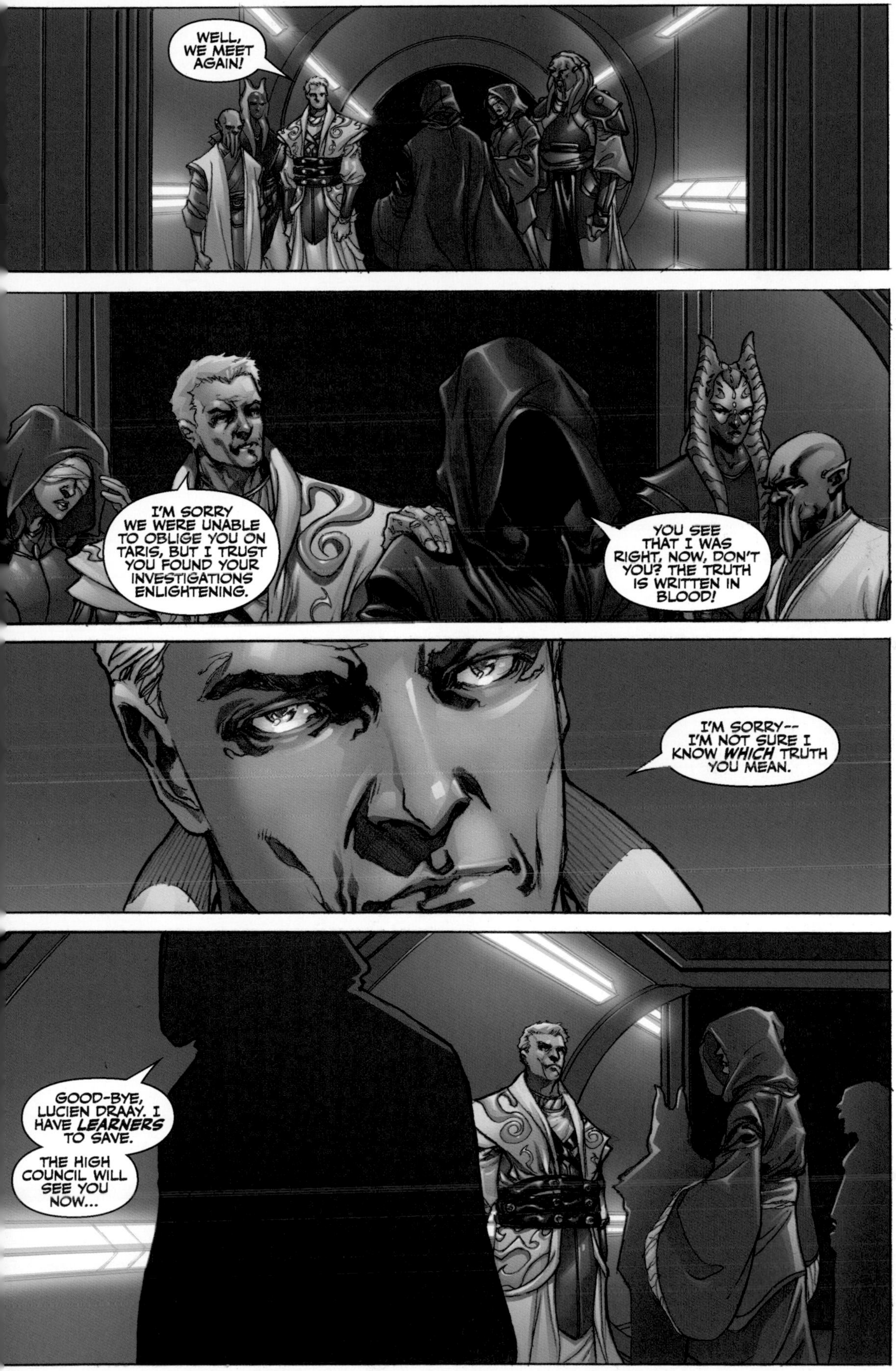
WELL, WE MEET AGAIN!
I'M SORRY WE WERE UNABLE TO OBLIGE YOU ON TARIS, BUT I TRUST YOU FOUND YOUR INVESTIGATIONS ENLIGHTENING.
YOU SEE THAT I WAS RIGHT, NOW, DON'T YOU? THE TRUTH IS WRITTEN IN BLOOD!
I'M SORRY-- I'M NOT SURE I KNOW *WHICH* TRUTH YOU MEAN.
GOOD-BYE, LUCIEN DRAAY. I HAVE *LEARNERS* TO SAVE.
THE HIGH COUNCIL WILL SEE YOU NOW...

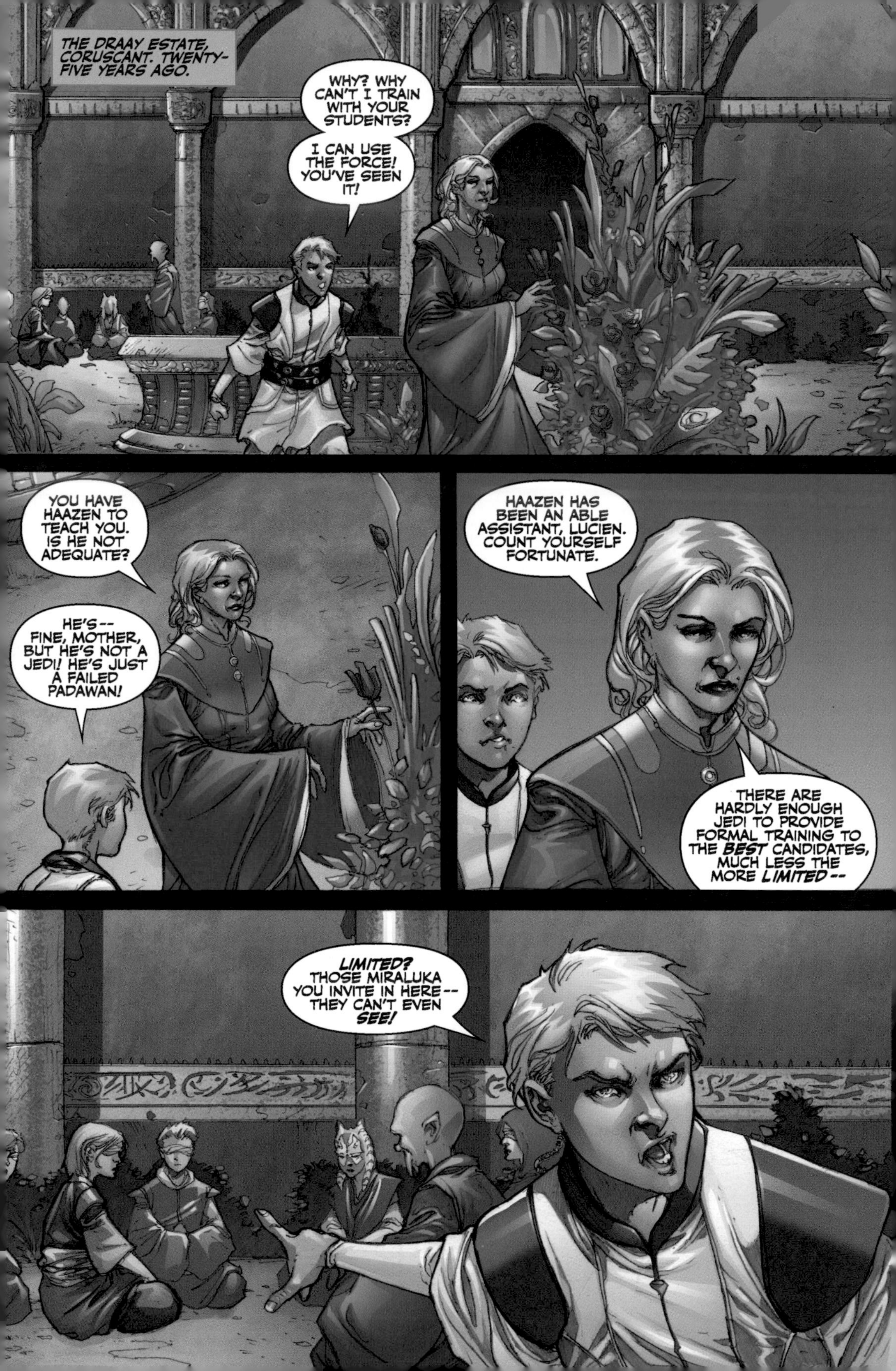
THE DRAAY ESTATE, CORUSCANT. TWENTY-FIVE YEARS AGO.
WHY? WHY CAN'T I TRAIN WITH YOUR STUDENTS?
I CAN USE THE FORCE! YOU'VE SEEN IT!
YOU HAVE HAAZEN TO TEACH YOU. IS HE NOT ADEQUATE?
HE'S-- FINE, MOTHER, BUT HE'S NOT A JEDI! HE'S JUST A FAILED PADAWAN!
HAAZEN HAS BEEN AN ABLE ASSISTANT, LUCIEN. COUNT YOURSELF FORTUNATE.
THERE ARE HARDLY ENOUGH JEDI TO PROVIDE FORMAL TRAINING TO THE *BEST* CANDIDATES, MUCH LESS THE MORE *LIMITED*--
LIMITED? THOSE MIRALUKA YOU INVITE IN HERE-- THEY CAN'T EVEN *SEE!*

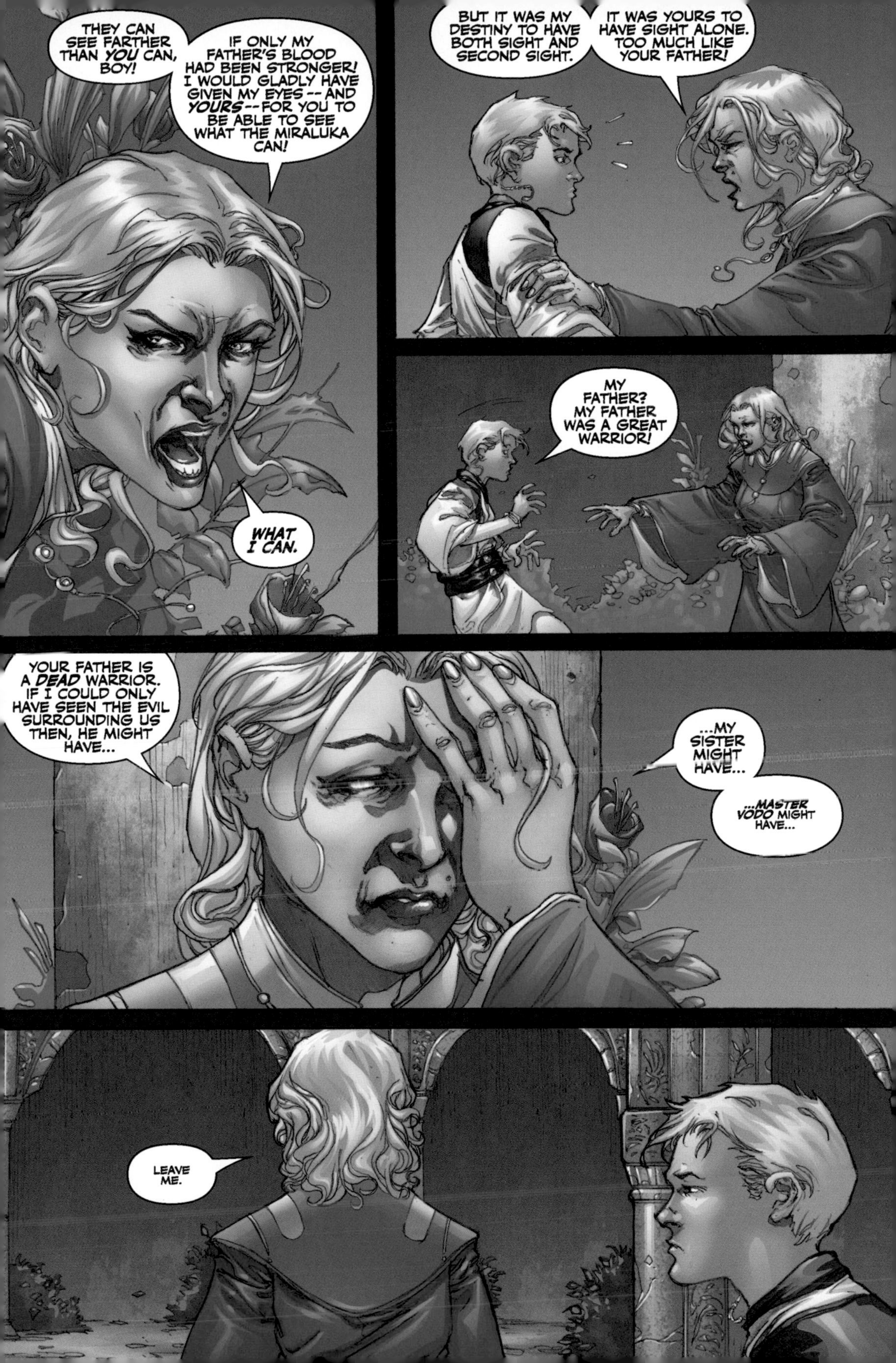
THEY CAN SEE FARTHER THAN *YOU* CAN, BOY!
IF ONLY MY FATHER'S BLOOD HAD BEEN STRONGER! I WOULD GLADLY HAVE GIVEN MY EYES -- AND *YOURS* -- FOR YOU TO BE ABLE TO SEE WHAT THE MIRALUKA CAN!
WHAT I CAN.
BUT IT WAS MY DESTINY TO HAVE BOTH SIGHT AND SECOND SIGHT.
IT WAS YOURS TO HAVE SIGHT ALONE. TOO MUCH LIKE YOUR FATHER!
MY FATHER? MY FATHER WAS A GREAT WARRIOR!
YOUR FATHER IS A *DEAD* WARRIOR. IF I COULD ONLY HAVE SEEN THE EVIL SURROUNDING US THEN, HE MIGHT HAVE...
...MY SISTER MIGHT HAVE...
...*MASTER VODO* MIGHT HAVE...
LEAVE ME.

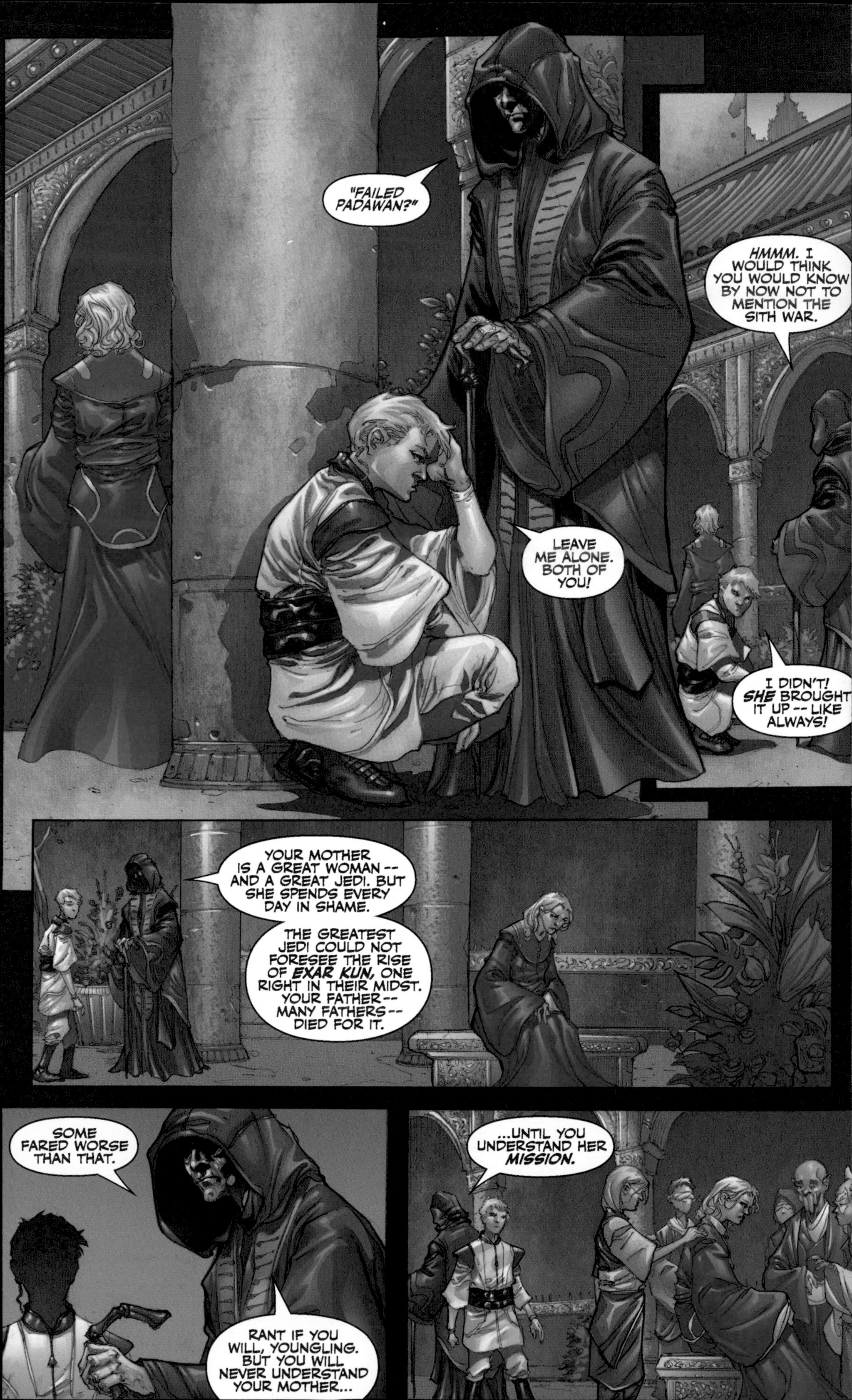
"FAILED PADAWAN?"
HMMM. I WOULD THINK YOU WOULD KNOW BY NOW NOT TO MENTION THE SITH WAR.
LEAVE ME ALONE. BOTH OF YOU!
I DIDN'T! SHE BROUGHT IT UP -- LIKE ALWAYS!
YOUR MOTHER IS A GREAT WOMAN -- AND A GREAT JEDI. BUT SHE SPENDS EVERY DAY IN SHAME.
THE GREATEST JEDI COULD NOT FORESEE THE RISE OF EXAR KUN, ONE RIGHT IN THEIR MIDST. YOUR FATHER -- MANY FATHERS -- DIED FOR IT.
SOME FARED WORSE THAN THAT.
RANT IF YOU WILL, YOUNGLING. BUT YOU WILL NEVER UNDERSTAND YOUR MOTHER...
...UNTIL YOU UNDERSTAND HER MISSION.

THE JEDI HIGH COUNCIL, CORUSCANT. TODAY.

-- AND IT APPEARS TO THIS COUNCIL THAT YOU HAVE *FAILED* IN THE MOST BASIC MISSION A JEDI INSTRUCTOR CAN HAVE.

AS MASTER VANDAR HAS SAID MANY TIMES: "WE'RE NOT JUST THEIR TEACHERS-- WE'RE THEIR PROTECTORS."

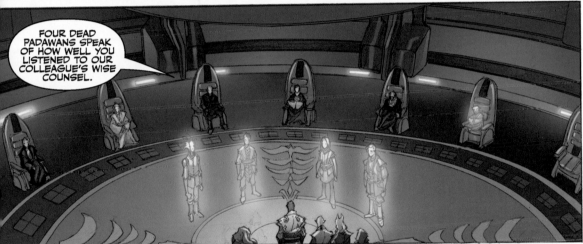

FOUR DEAD PADAWANS SPEAK OF HOW WELL YOU LISTENED TO OUR COLLEAGUE'S WISE COUNSEL.

IT IS *I* WHO SHOULD HAVE LISTENED, MASTER VROOK. NONE OF THESE JEDI WERE EAGER TO HAVE STUDENTS ASSIGNED TO THEM.

PERHAPS THAT RELUCTANCE WAS, IN FACT, WISDOM.

MASTERS OF THE COUNCIL...

...I DID IT. I'M GUILTY.

I KILLED THE PADAWANS OF TARIS.

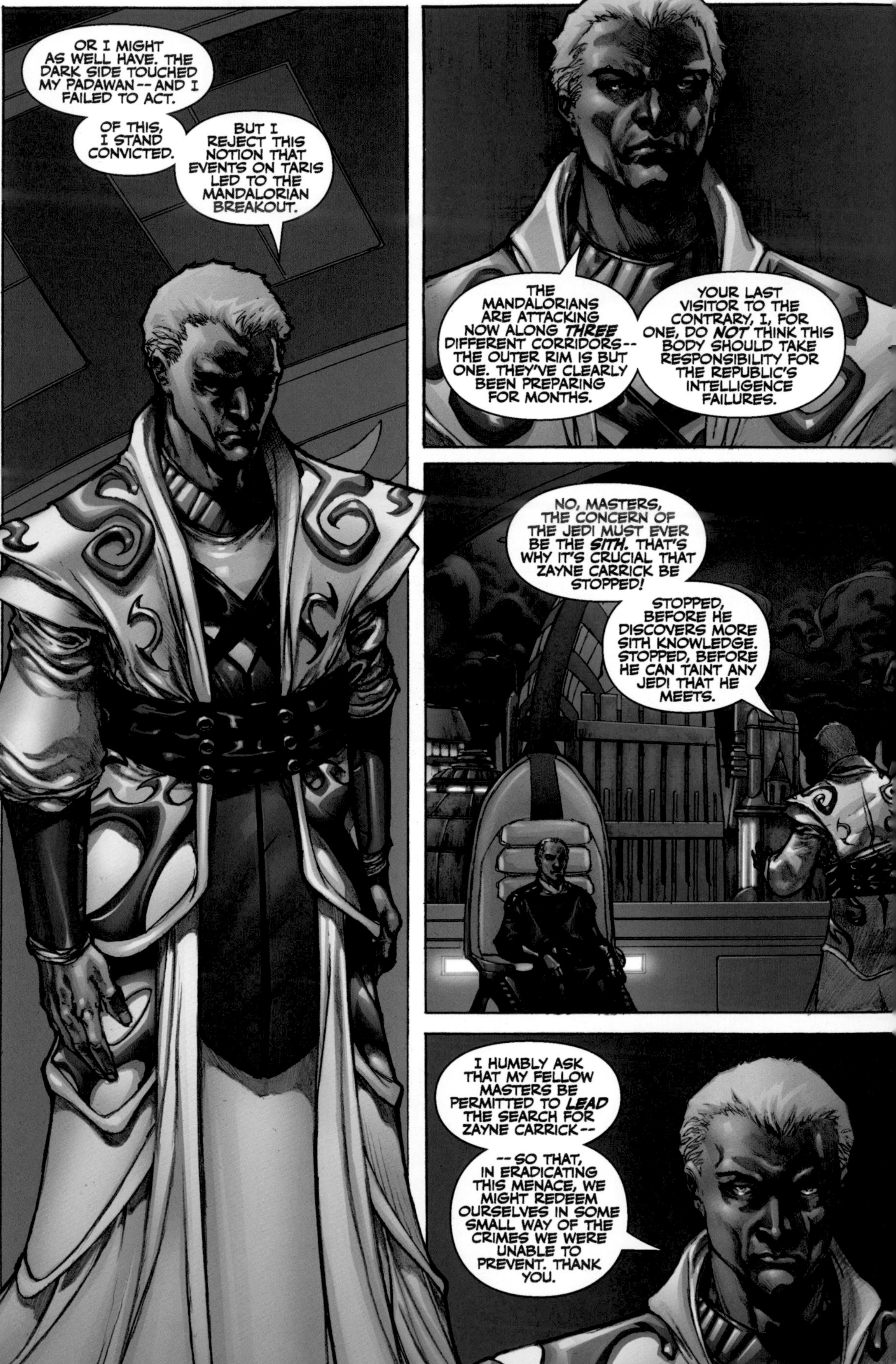
OR I MIGHT AS WELL HAVE. THE DARK SIDE TOUCHED MY PADAWAN-- AND I FAILED TO ACT.
OF THIS, I STAND CONVICTED.
BUT I REJECT THIS NOTION THAT EVENTS ON TARIS LED TO THE MANDALORIAN BREAKOUT.
THE MANDALORIANS ARE ATTACKING NOW ALONG *THREE* DIFFERENT CORRIDORS-- THE OUTER RIM IS BUT ONE. THEY'VE CLEARLY BEEN PREPARING FOR MONTHS.
YOUR LAST VISITOR TO THE CONTRARY, I, FOR ONE, DO *NOT* THINK THIS BODY SHOULD TAKE RESPONSIBILITY FOR THE REPUBLIC'S INTELLIGENCE FAILURES.
NO, MASTERS, THE CONCERN OF THE JEDI MUST EVER BE THE *SITH*. THAT'S WHY IT'S CRUCIAL THAT ZAYNE CARRICK BE STOPPED!
STOPPED, BEFORE HE DISCOVERS MORE SITH KNOWLEDGE. STOPPED, BEFORE HE CAN TAINT ANY JEDI THAT HE MEETS.
I HUMBLY ASK THAT MY FELLOW MASTERS BE PERMITTED TO *LEAD* THE SEARCH FOR ZAYNE CARRICK--
-- SO THAT, IN ERADICATING THIS MENACE, WE MIGHT REDEEM OURSELVES IN SOME SMALL WAY OF THE CRIMES WE WERE UNABLE TO PREVENT. THANK YOU.

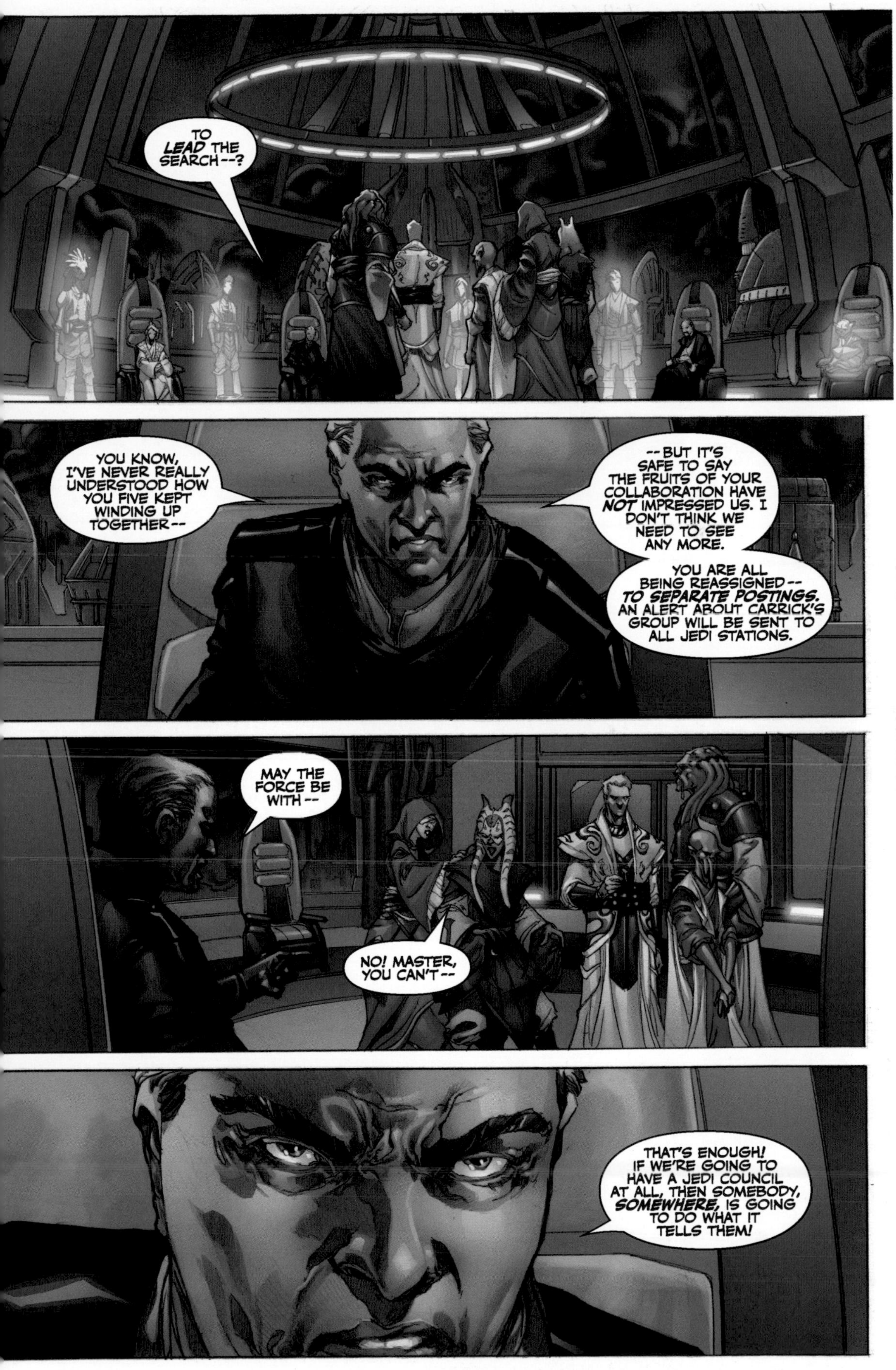
TO LEAD THE SEARCH--?
YOU KNOW, I'VE NEVER REALLY UNDERSTOOD HOW YOU FIVE KEPT WINDING UP TOGETHER--
--BUT IT'S SAFE TO SAY THE FRUITS OF YOUR COLLABORATION HAVE NOT IMPRESSED US. I DON'T THINK WE NEED TO SEE ANY MORE.
YOU ARE ALL BEING REASSIGNED-- TO SEPARATE POSTINGS. AN ALERT ABOUT CARRICK'S GROUP WILL BE SENT TO ALL JEDI STATIONS.
MAY THE FORCE BE WITH--
NO! MASTER, YOU CAN'T--
THAT'S ENOUGH! IF WE'RE GOING TO HAVE A JEDI COUNCIL AT ALL, THEN SOMEBODY, SOMEWHERE, IS GOING TO DO WHAT IT TELLS THEM!

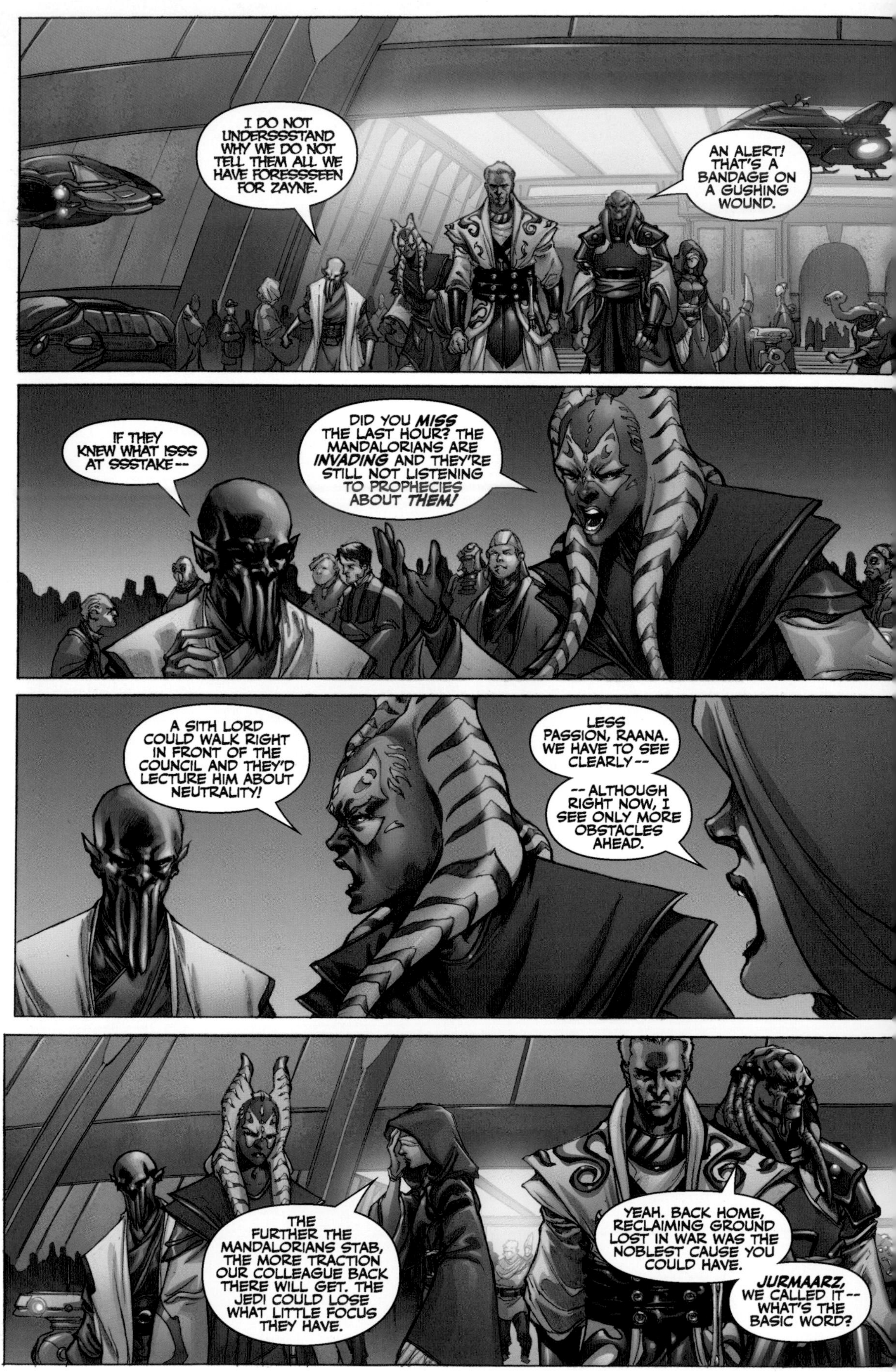
I DO NOT UNDERSSSTAND WHY WE DO NOT TELL THEM ALL WE HAVE FORESSSEEN FOR ZAYNE.
AN ALERT! THAT'S A BANDAGE ON A GUSHING WOUND.
IF THEY KNEW WHAT ISSS AT SSSTAKE--
DID YOU MISS THE LAST HOUR? THE MANDALORIANS ARE INVADING AND THEY'RE STILL NOT LISTENING TO PROPHECIES ABOUT THEM!
A SITH LORD COULD WALK RIGHT IN FRONT OF THE COUNCIL AND THEY'D LECTURE HIM ABOUT NEUTRALITY!
LESS PASSION, RAANA. WE HAVE TO SEE CLEARLY--
--ALTHOUGH RIGHT NOW, I SEE ONLY MORE OBSTACLES AHEAD.
THE FURTHER THE MANDALORIANS STAB, THE MORE TRACTION OUR COLLEAGUE BACK THERE WILL GET. THE JEDI COULD LOSE WHAT LITTLE FOCUS THEY HAVE.
YEAH. BACK HOME, RECLAIMING GROUND LOST IN WAR WAS THE NOBLEST CAUSE YOU COULD HAVE.
JURMAARZ, WE CALLED IT-- WHAT'S THE BASIC WORD?

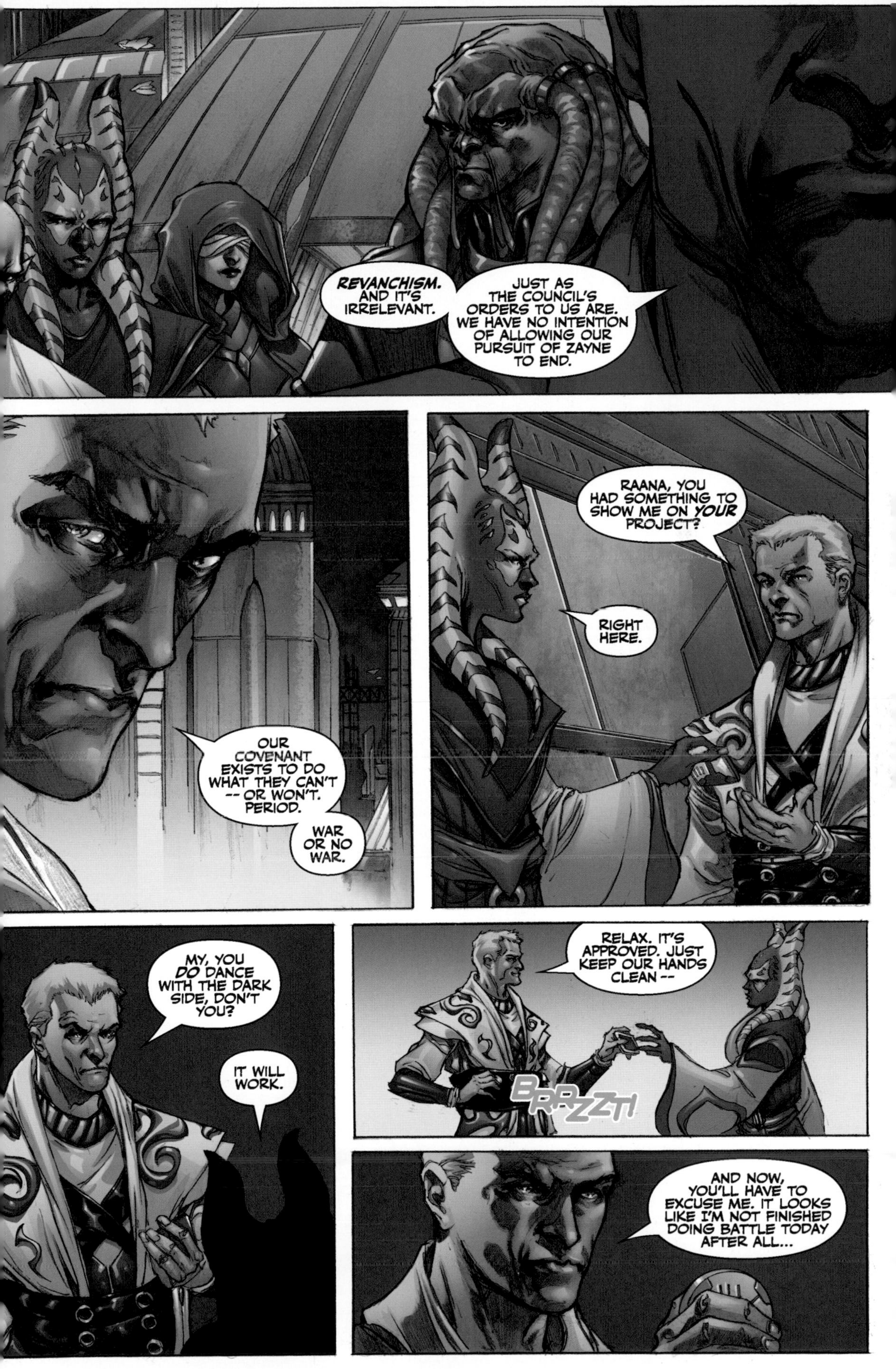
REVANCHISM. AND IT'S IRRELEVANT.
JUST AS THE COUNCIL'S ORDERS TO US ARE. WE HAVE NO INTENTION OF ALLOWING OUR PURSUIT OF ZAYNE TO END.
OUR COVENANT EXISTS TO DO WHAT THEY CAN'T -- OR WON'T. PERIOD.
WAR OR NO WAR.
RAANA, YOU HAD SOMETHING TO SHOW ME ON YOUR PROJECT?
RIGHT HERE.
MY, YOU DO DANCE WITH THE DARK SIDE, DON'T YOU?
IT WILL WORK.
RELAX. IT'S APPROVED. JUST KEEP OUR HANDS CLEAN --
BRRZZT!
AND NOW, YOU'LL HAVE TO EXCUSE ME. IT LOOKS LIKE I'M NOT FINISHED DOING BATTLE TODAY AFTER ALL...

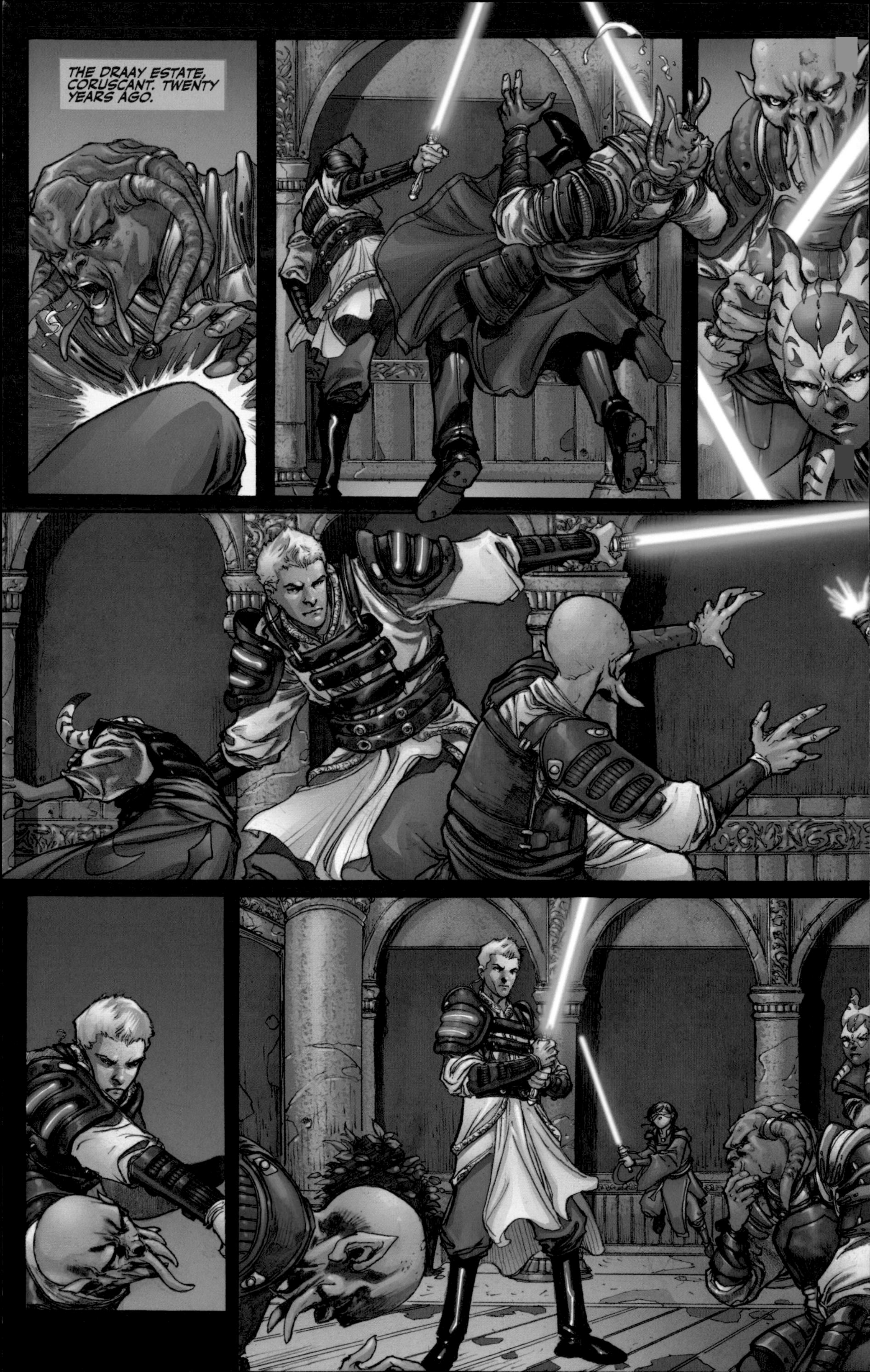
THE DRAAY ESTATE, CORUSCANT. TWENTY YEARS AGO.

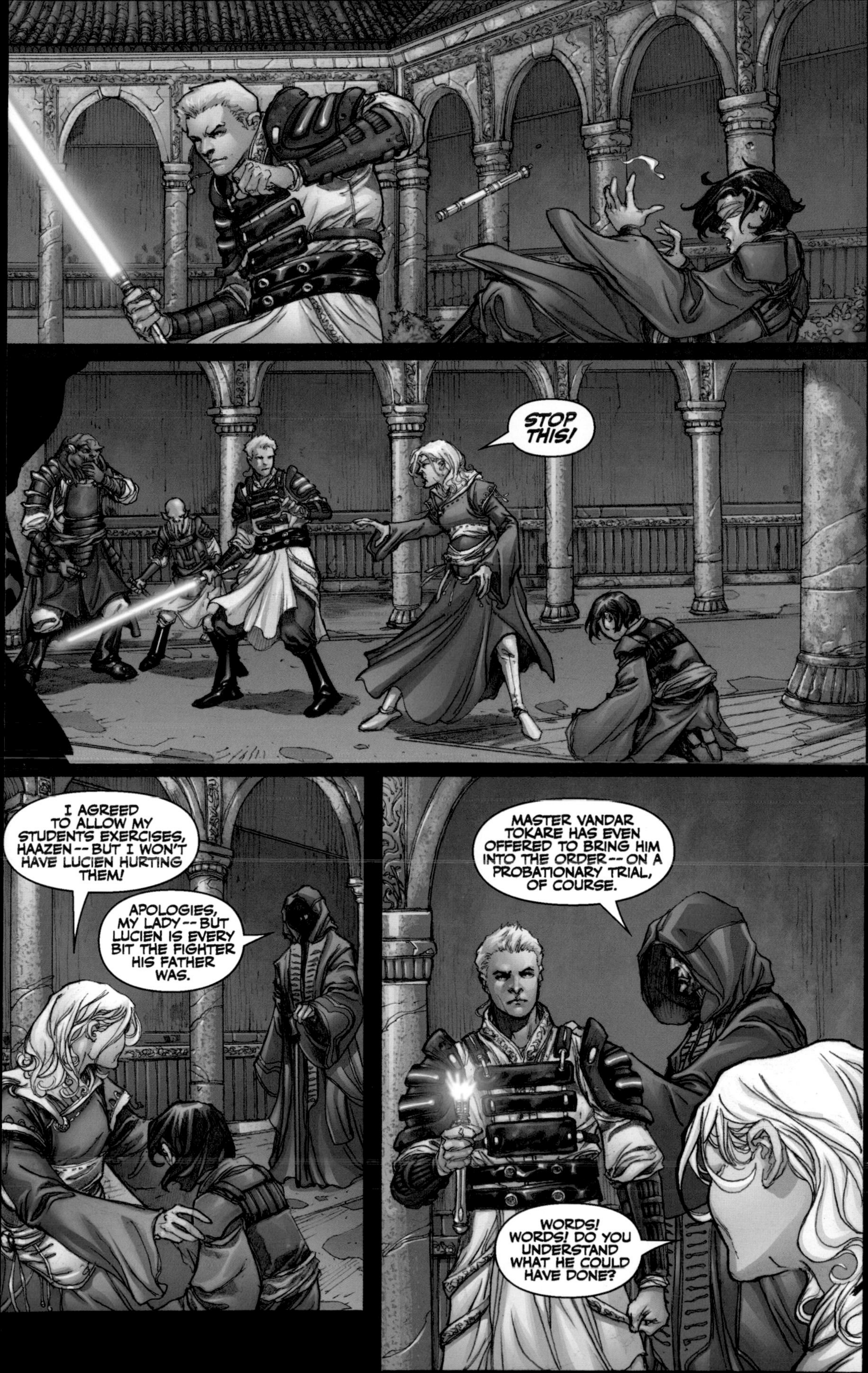
STOP THIS!
I AGREED TO ALLOW MY STUDENTS EXERCISES, HAAZEN-- BUT I WON'T HAVE LUCIEN HURTING THEM!
APOLOGIES, MY LADY-- BUT LUCIEN IS EVERY BIT THE FIGHTER HIS FATHER WAS.
MASTER VANDAR TOKARE HAS EVEN OFFERED TO BRING HIM INTO THE ORDER-- ON A PROBATIONARY TRIAL, OF COURSE.
WORDS! WORDS! DO YOU UNDERSTAND WHAT HE COULD HAVE DONE?

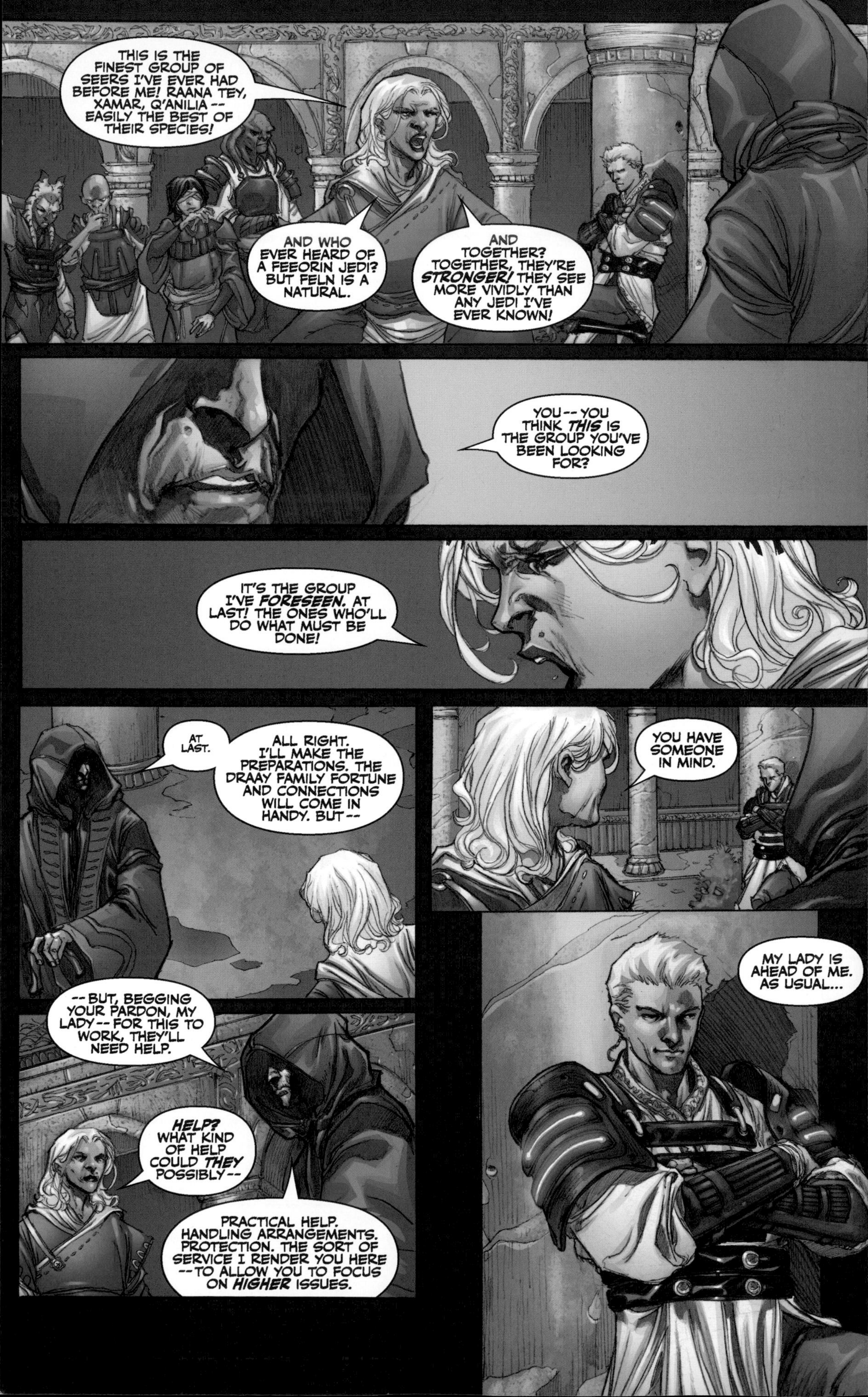
THIS IS THE FINEST GROUP OF SEERS I'VE EVER HAD BEFORE ME! RAANA TEY, XAMAR, Q'ANILIA -- EASILY THE BEST OF THEIR SPECIES!
AND WHO EVER HEARD OF A FEEORIN JEDI? BUT FELN IS A NATURAL.
AND TOGETHER? TOGETHER, THEY'RE STRONGER! THEY SEE MORE VIVIDLY THAN ANY JEDI I'VE EVER KNOWN!
YOU -- YOU THINK THIS IS THE GROUP YOU'VE BEEN LOOKING FOR?
IT'S THE GROUP I'VE FORESEEN. AT LAST! THE ONES WHO'LL DO WHAT MUST BE DONE!
AT LAST.
ALL RIGHT. I'LL MAKE THE PREPARATIONS. THE DRAAY FAMILY FORTUNE AND CONNECTIONS WILL COME IN HANDY. BUT --
YOU HAVE SOMEONE IN MIND.
-- BUT, BEGGING YOUR PARDON, MY LADY -- FOR THIS TO WORK, THEY'LL NEED HELP.
HELP? WHAT KIND OF HELP COULD THEY POSSIBLY --
PRACTICAL HELP. HANDLING ARRANGEMENTS. PROTECTION. THE SORT OF SERVICE I RENDER YOU HERE -- TO ALLOW YOU TO FOCUS ON HIGHER ISSUES.
MY LADY IS AHEAD OF ME. AS USUAL...

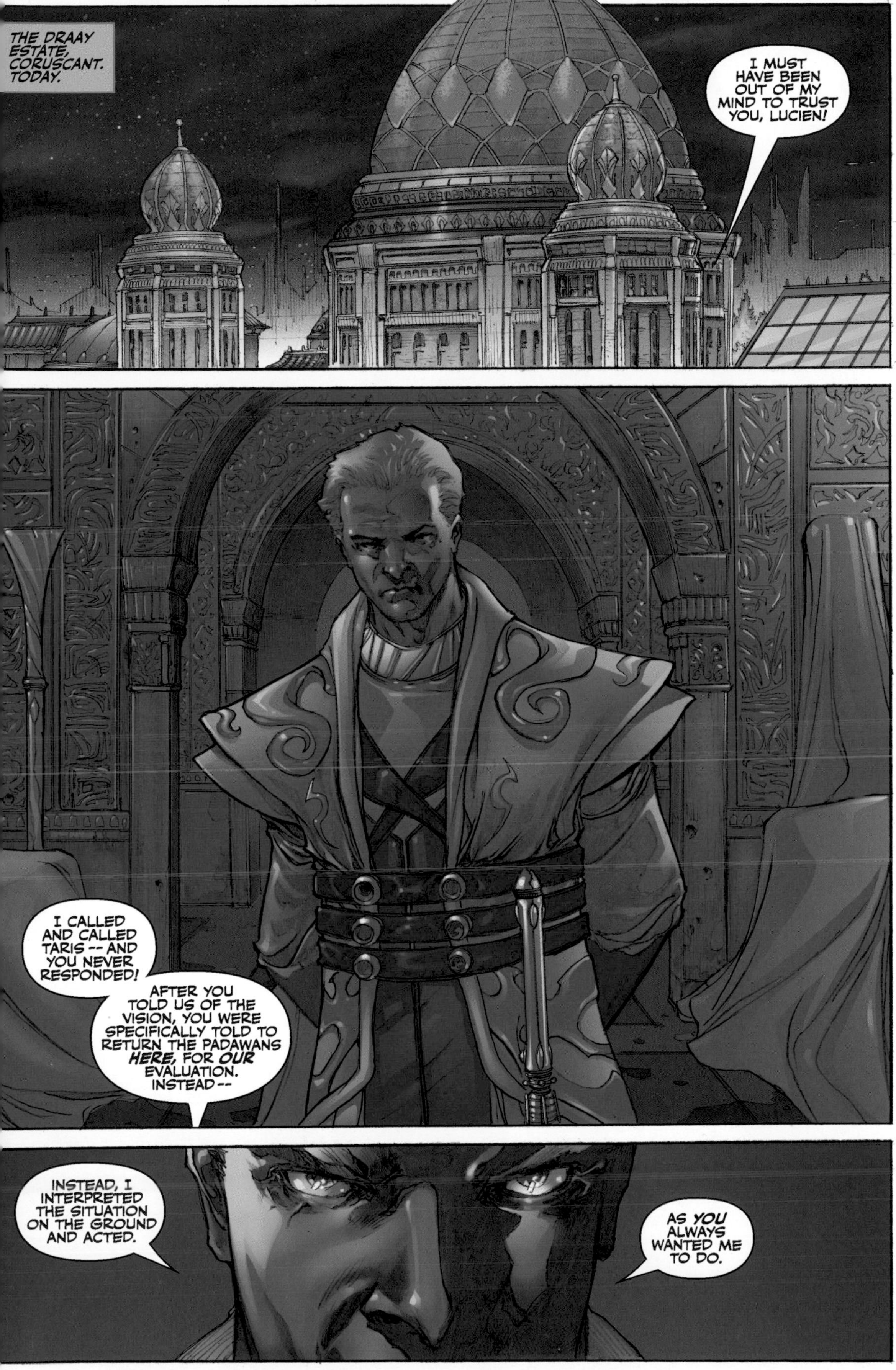
THE DRAAY ESTATE, CORUSCANT. TODAY.
I MUST HAVE BEEN OUT OF MY MIND TO TRUST YOU, LUCIEN!
I CALLED AND CALLED TARIS -- AND YOU NEVER RESPONDED!
AFTER YOU TOLD US OF THE VISION, YOU WERE SPECIFICALLY TOLD TO RETURN THE PADAWANS HERE, FOR OUR EVALUATION. INSTEAD --
INSTEAD, I INTERPRETED THE SITUATION ON THE GROUND AND ACTED.
AS YOU ALWAYS WANTED ME TO DO.

I NEVER WANTED YOU TO DO *THAT*.

NOW, THE COVENANT'S ONLY BARELY ESCAPED EXPOSURE, AND YOUR EFFECTIVENESS IS GREATLY REDUCED.

WHERE'S MY MOTHER, HAAZEN?

SHE'S HERE. CAN'T YOU FEEL HER PRESENCE?

NO. I MEAN, *YES.* I MEAN --

YOU'RE GETTING AS FEEBLE WITH THE PRESENT AS YOU ARE WITH THE FUTURE. YOUR HANDLING OF THE TARIS AFFAIR IS PROOF OF THAT!

AND I'VE BEEN EXAMINING SOME OF THE REPORTS IN VANDAR'S FILES. WHY DIDN'T YOU TELL US ABOUT ZAYNE CARRICK'S *"SPECIAL RELATIONSHIP"* WITH THE FORCE?

THERE WAS NO REASON TO. IT'S OF NO USE TO ANYONE.

YOU MEAN, THE JEDI DIDN'T KNOW WHAT TO DO WITH IT. MAYBE IT WAS HIS TEACHERS WHO WERE OF NO USE TO HIM! I WAS A SO-CALLED *"FAILED PADAWAN,"* MYSELF.

NO NEED TO GET NOSTALGIC, HAAZEN. YOU STILL ARE.

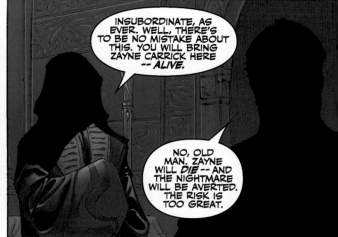

INSUBORDINATE, AS EVER. WELL, THERE'S TO BE NO MISTAKE ABOUT THIS. YOU WILL BRING ZAYNE CARRICK HERE -- *ALIVE.*

NO, OLD MAN. ZAYNE WILL *DIE* -- AND THE NIGHTMARE WILL BE AVERTED. THE RISK IS TOO GREAT.

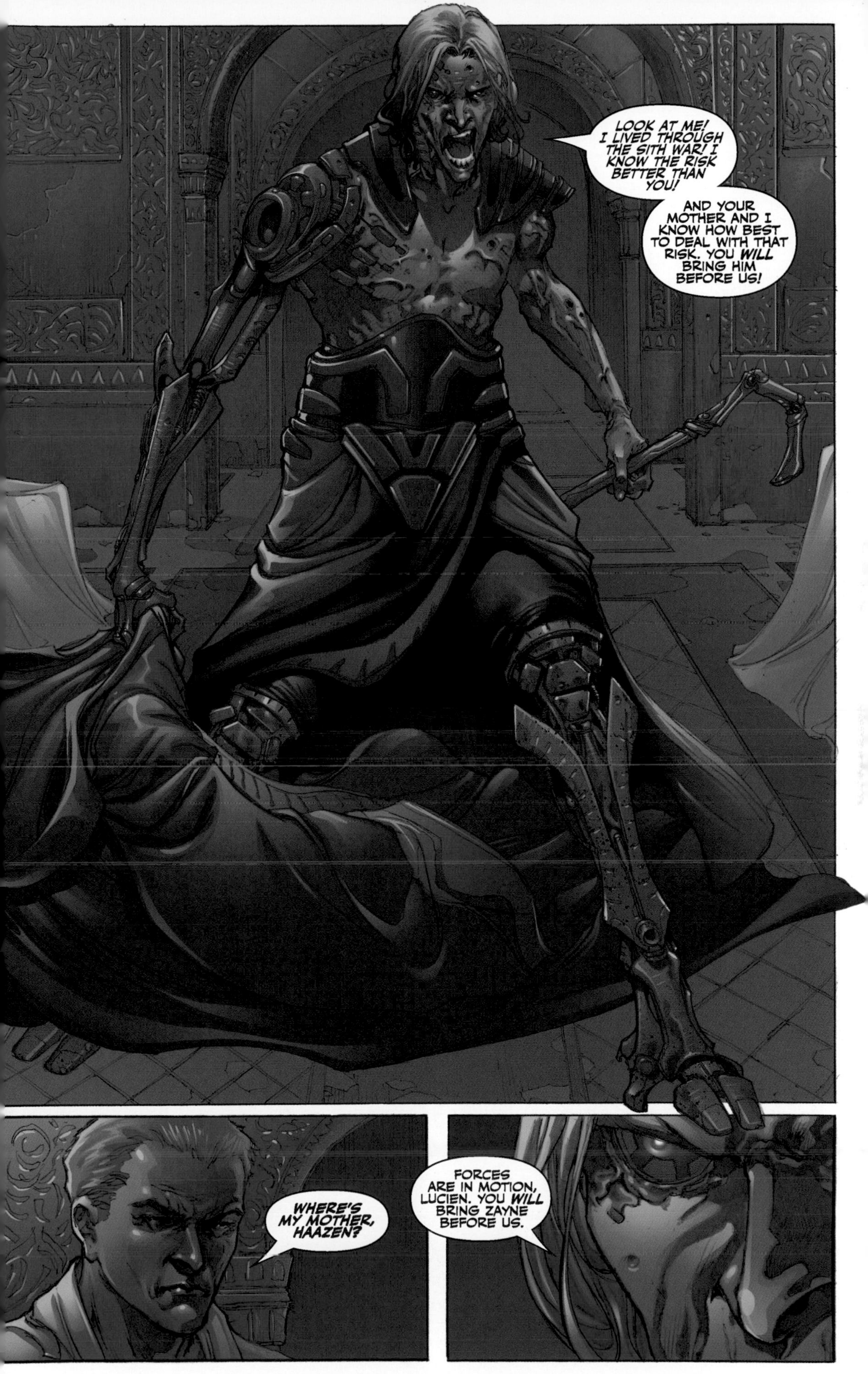
LOOK AT ME! I LIVED THROUGH THE SITH WAR! I KNOW THE RISK BETTER THAN YOU!
AND YOUR MOTHER AND I KNOW HOW BEST TO DEAL WITH THAT RISK. YOU *WILL* BRING HIM BEFORE US!
WHERE'S MY MOTHER, HAAZEN?
FORCES ARE IN MOTION, LUCIEN. YOU *WILL* BRING ZAYNE BEFORE US.

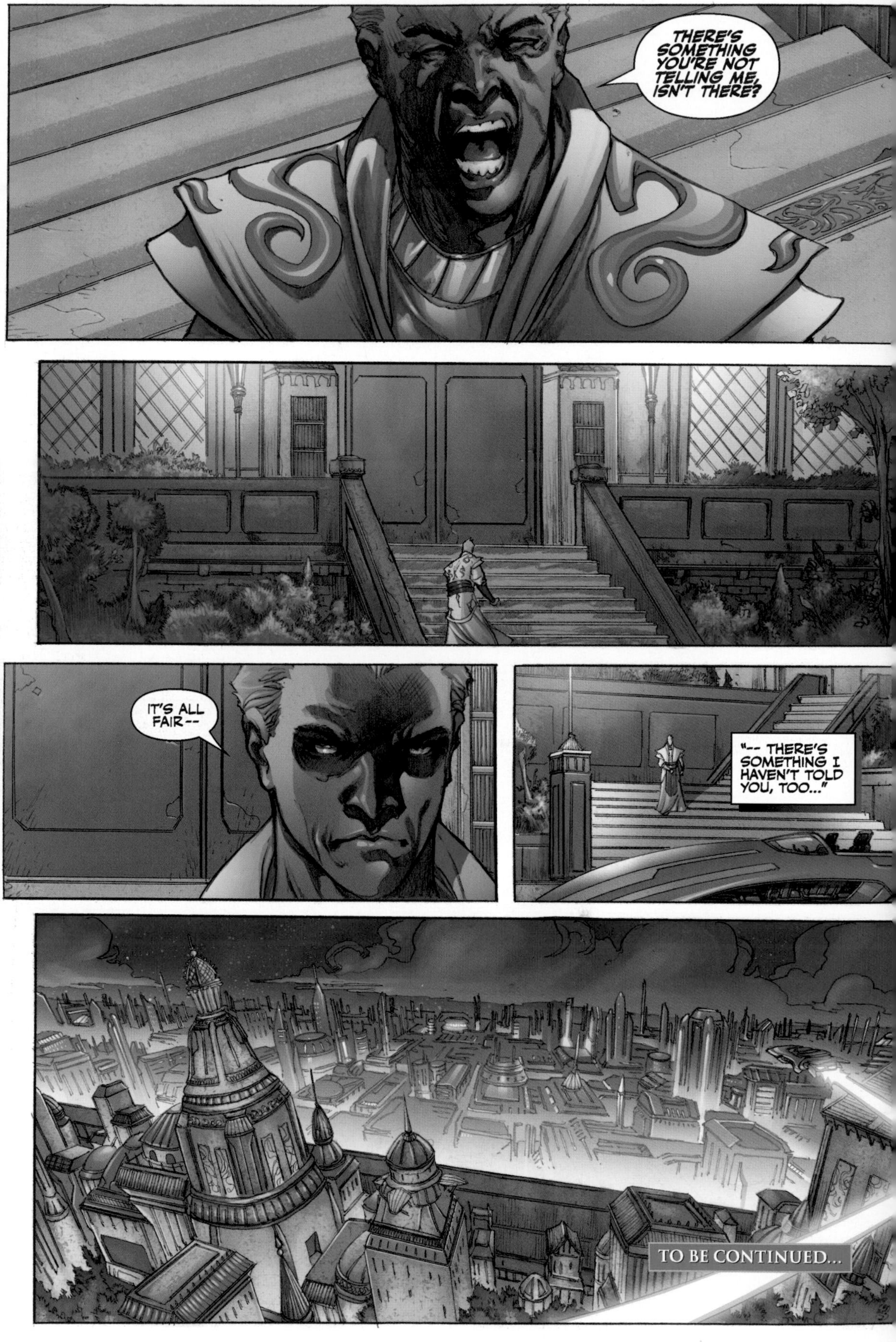
THERE'S SOMETHING YOU'RE NOT TELLING ME, ISN'T THERE?
IT'S ALL FAIR--
"-- THERE'S SOMETHING I HAVEN'T TOLD YOU, TOO..."
TO BE CONTINUED...

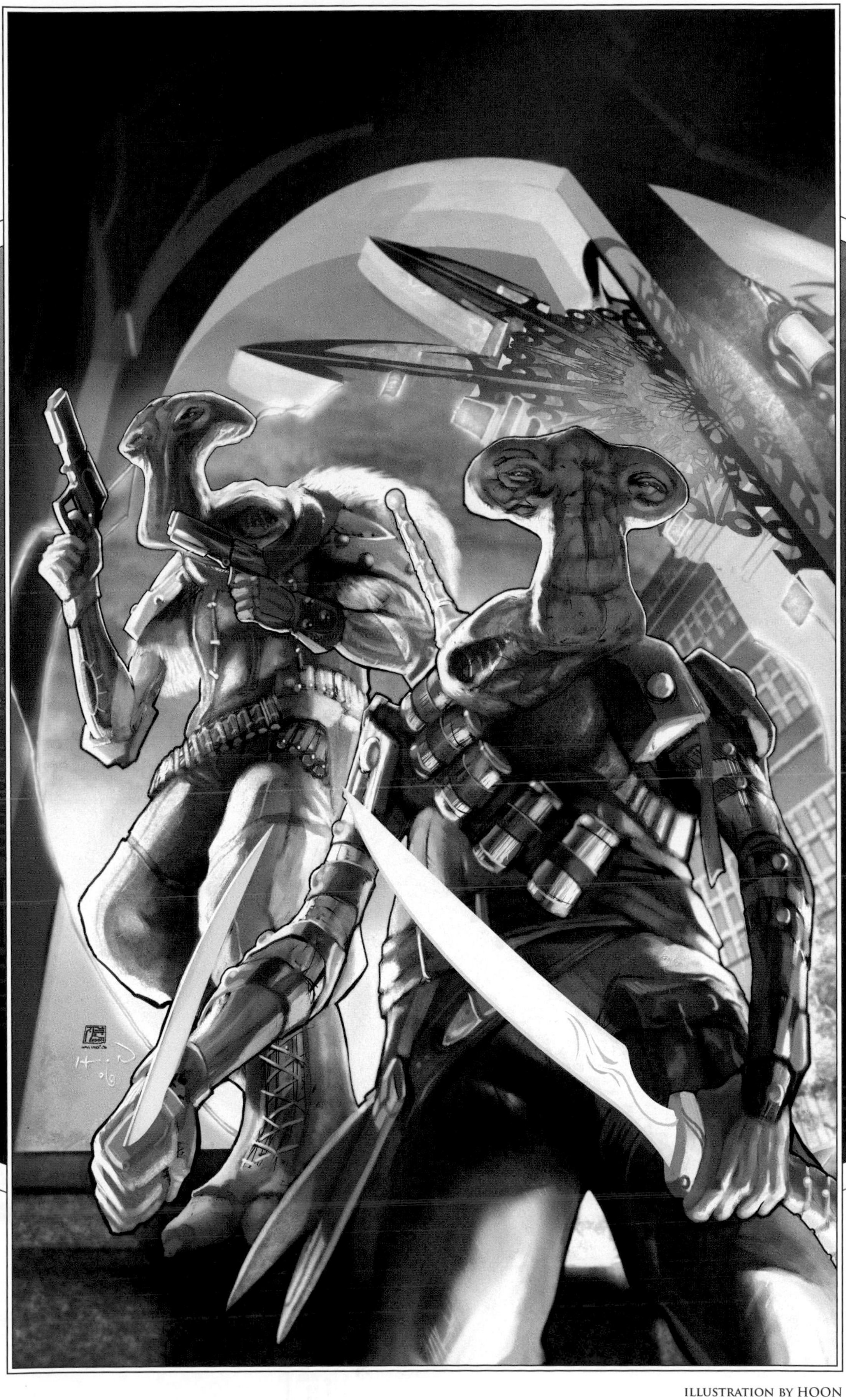

ILLUSTRATION BY HOON

REUNION

art by Brian Ching and Harvey Tolibao

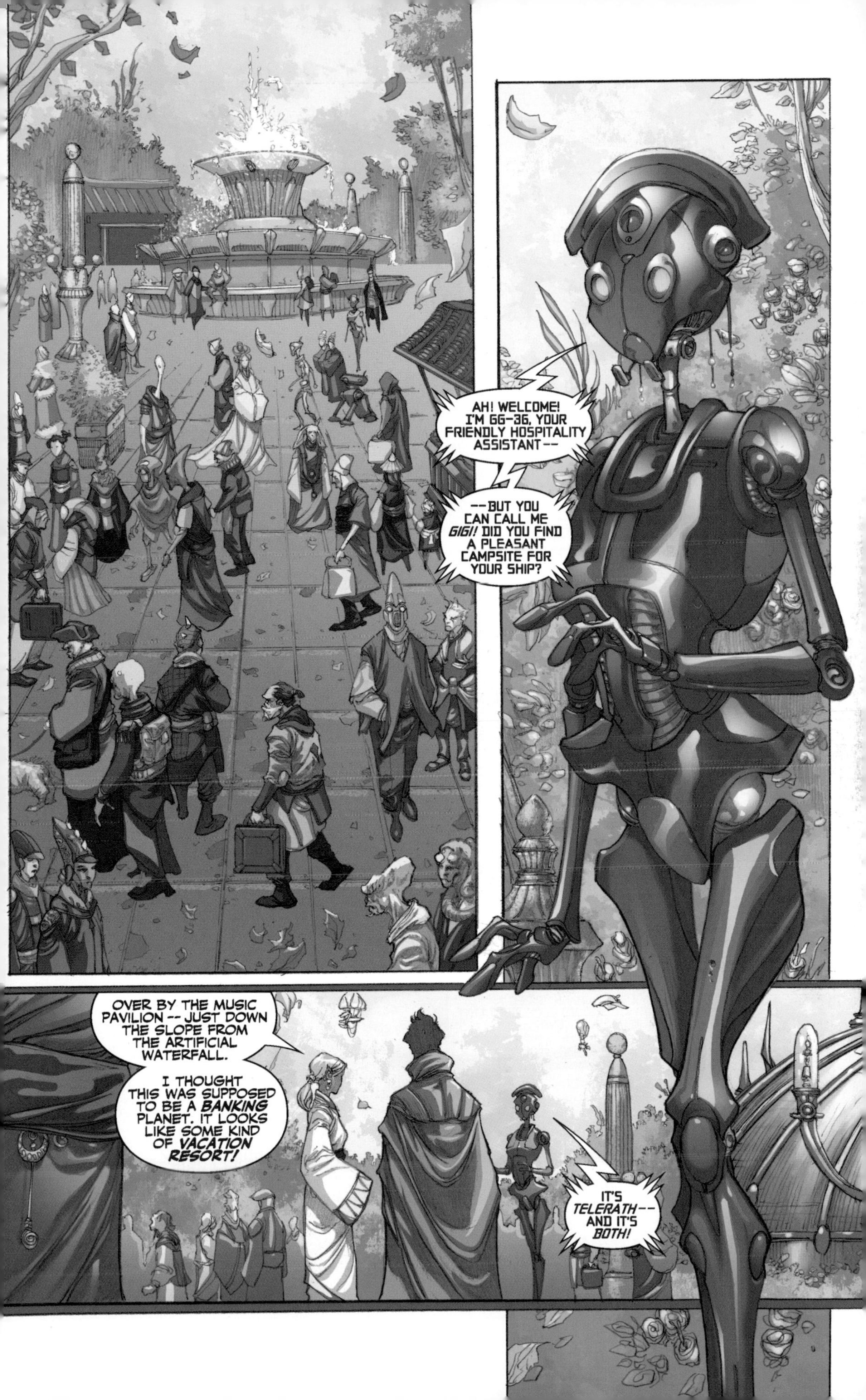
AH! WELCOME! I'M GG-36, YOUR FRIENDLY HOSPITALITY ASSISTANT--
--BUT YOU CAN CALL ME *GIGI!* DID YOU FIND A PLEASANT CAMPSITE FOR YOUR SHIP?
OVER BY THE MUSIC PAVILION -- JUST DOWN THE SLOPE FROM THE ARTIFICIAL WATERFALL.
I THOUGHT THIS WAS SUPPOSED TO BE A *BANKING* PLANET. IT LOOKS LIKE SOME KIND OF ***VACATION RESORT!***
IT'S *TELERATH*-- AND IT'S *BOTH!*

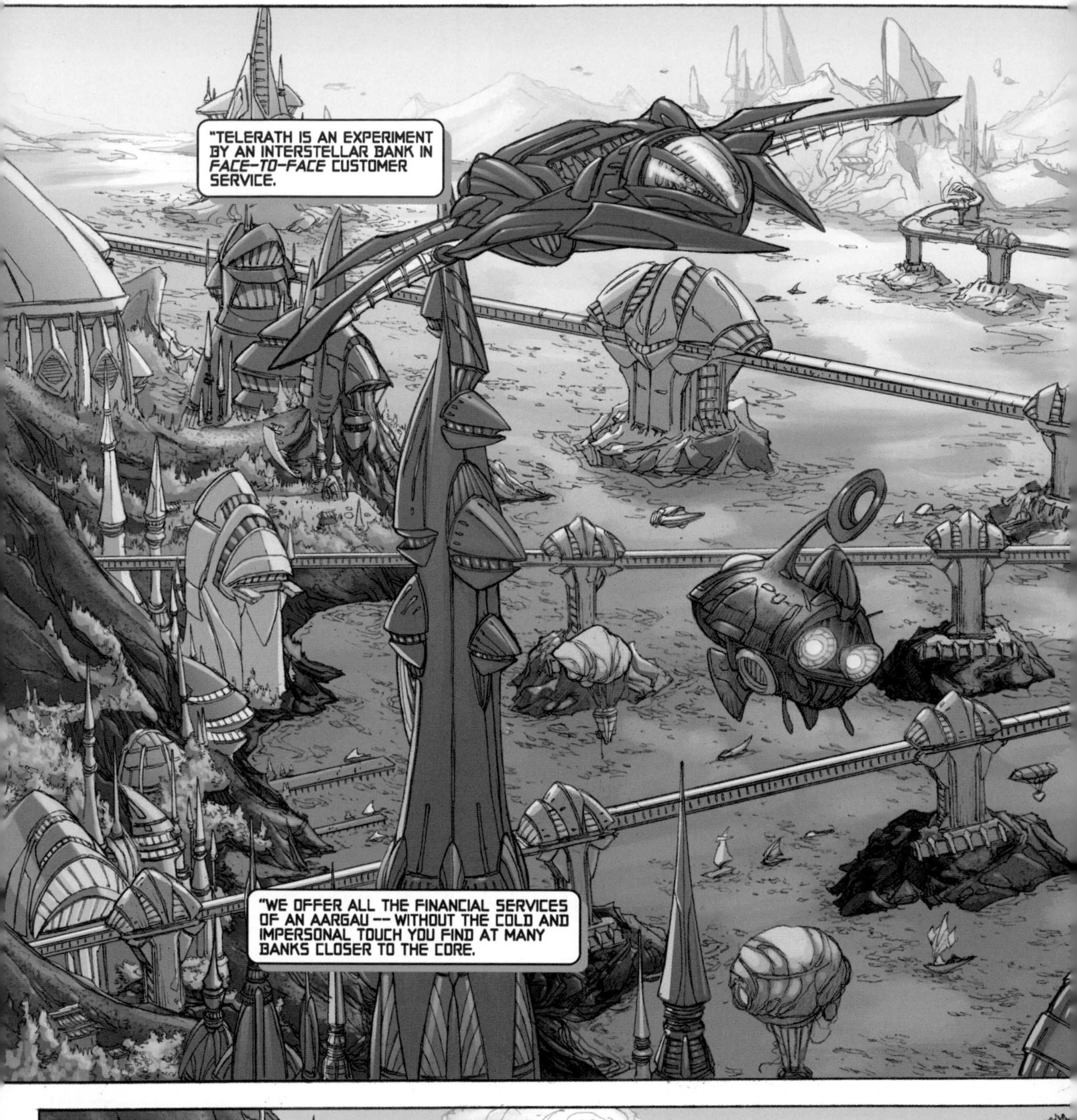
"TELERATH IS AN EXPERIMENT BY AN INTERSTELLAR BANK IN *FACE-TO-FACE* CUSTOMER SERVICE.
"WE OFFER ALL THE FINANCIAL SERVICES OF AN AARGAU -- WITHOUT THE COLD AND IMPERSONAL TOUCH YOU FIND AT MANY BANKS CLOSER TO THE CORE.

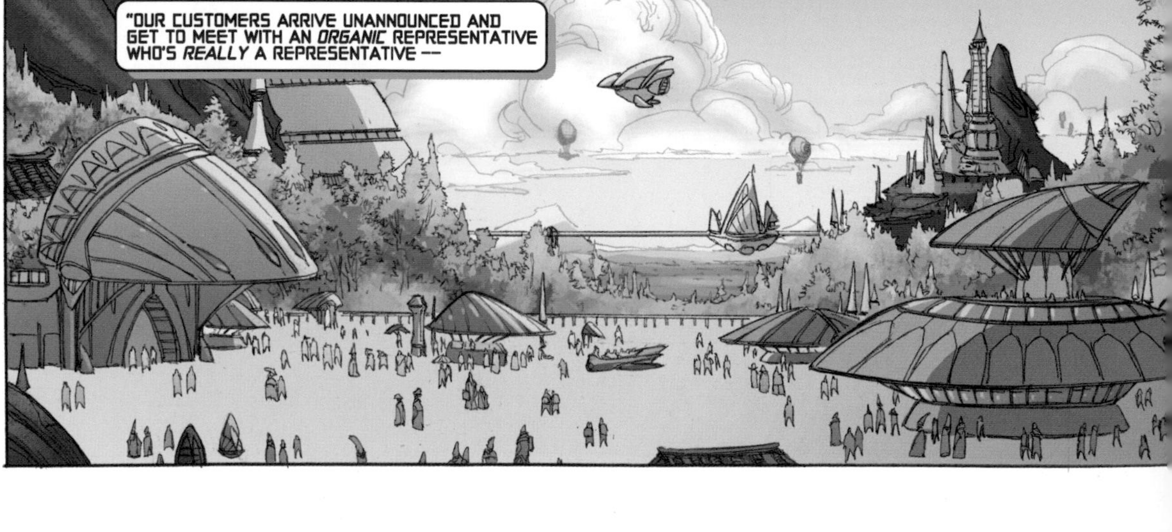
"OUR CUSTOMERS ARRIVE UNANNOUNCED AND GET TO MEET WITH AN *ORGANIC* REPRESENTATIVE WHO'S *REALLY* A REPRESENTATIVE --

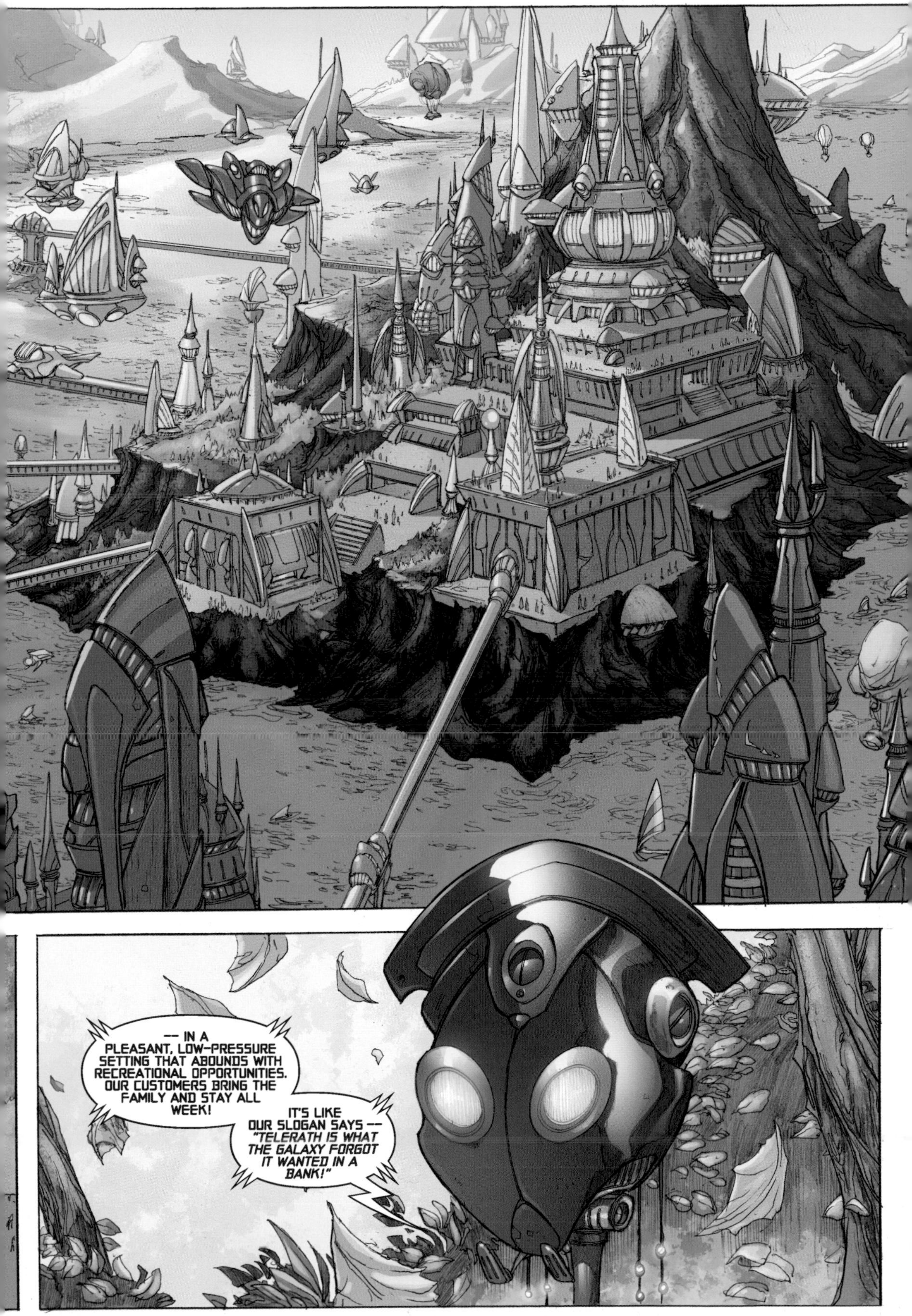
-- IN A PLEASANT, LOW-PRESSURE SETTING THAT ABOUNDS WITH RECREATIONAL OPPORTUNITIES. OUR CUSTOMERS BRING THE FAMILY AND STAY ALL WEEK!
IT'S LIKE OUR SLOGAN SAYS -- *"TELERATH IS WHAT THE GALAXY FORGOT IT WANTED IN A BANK!"*

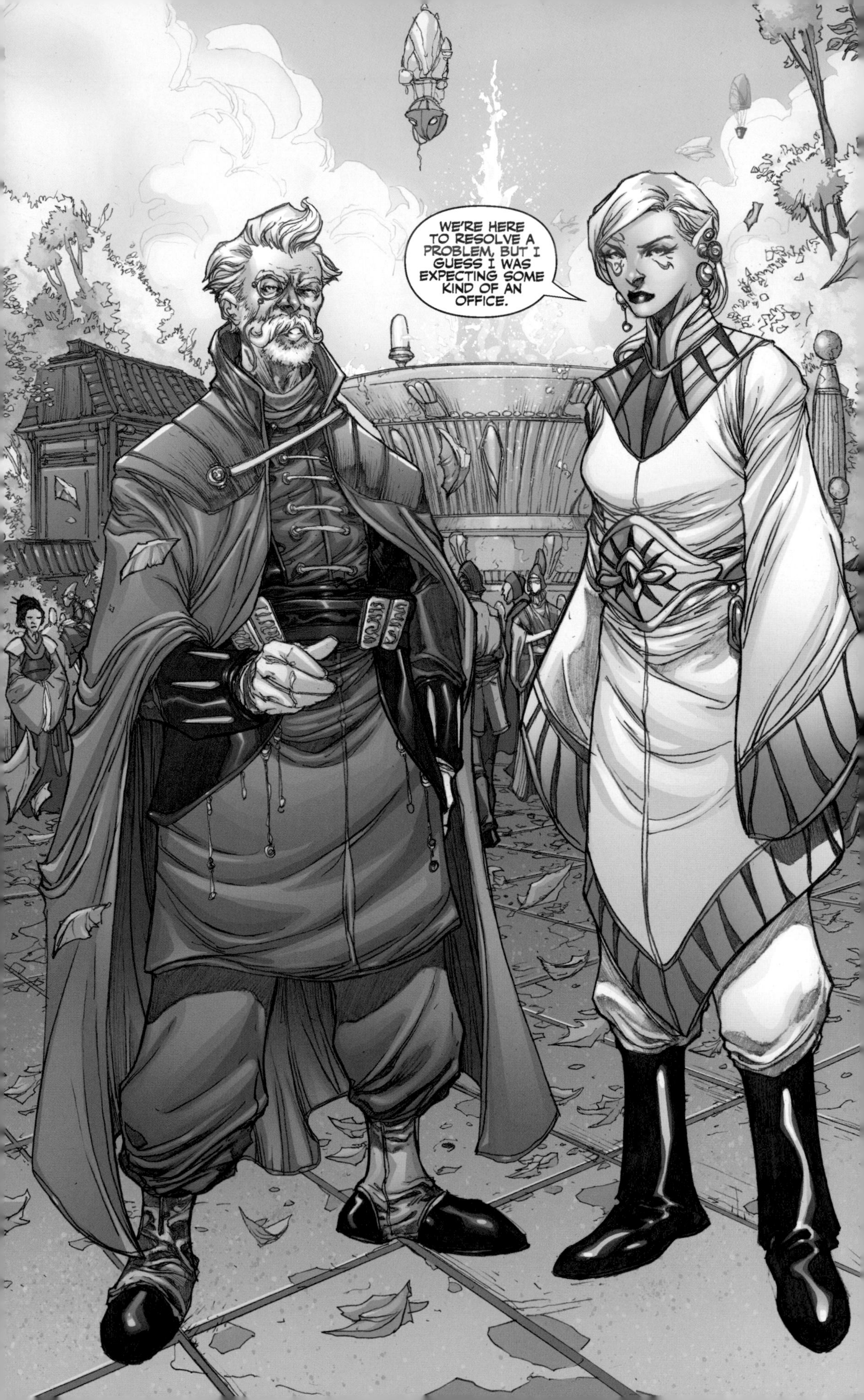
WE'RE HERE TO RESOLVE A PROBLEM, BUT I GUESS I WAS EXPECTING SOME KIND OF AN OFFICE.

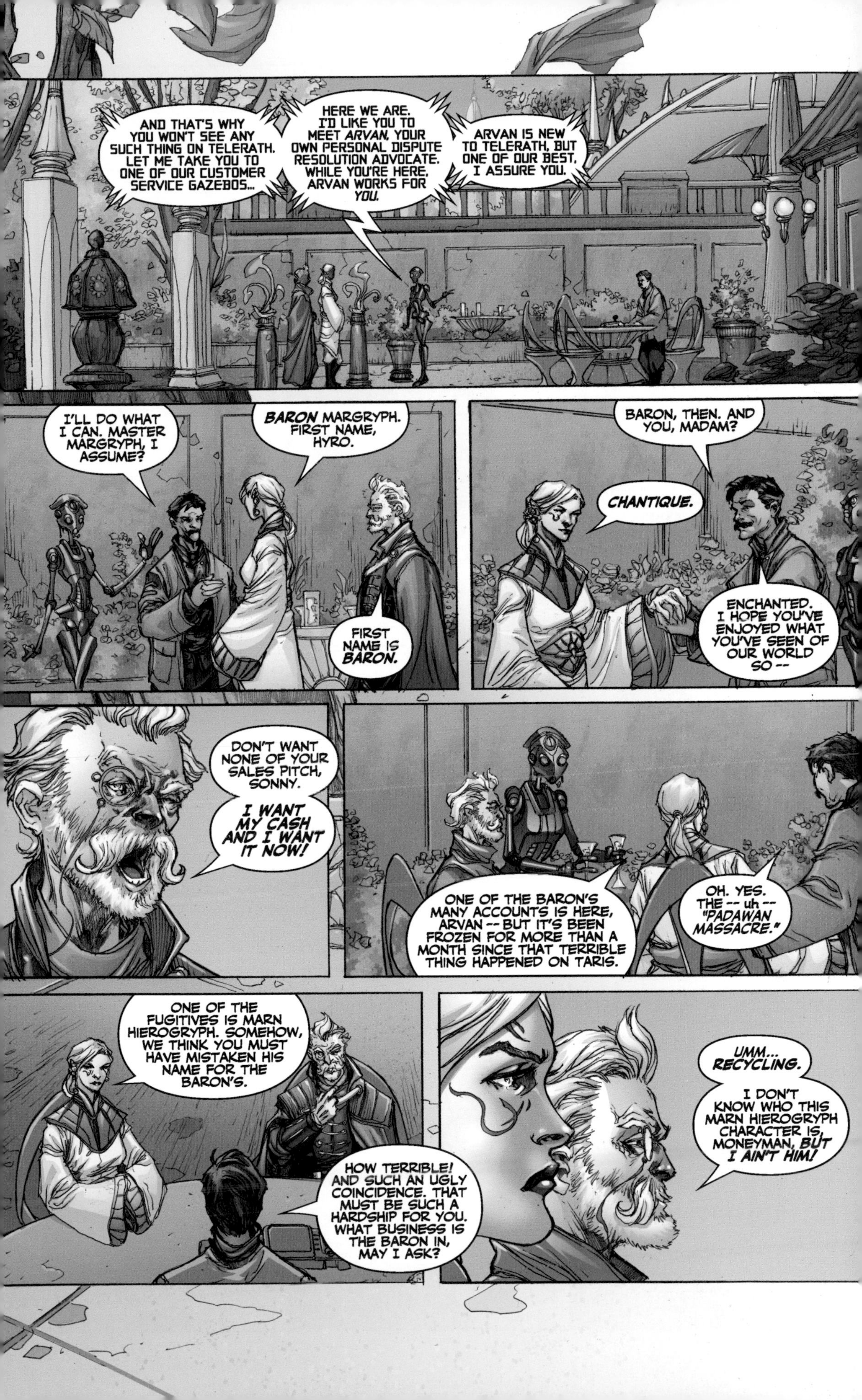
AND THAT'S WHY YOU WON'T SEE ANY SUCH THING ON TELERATH. LET ME TAKE YOU TO ONE OF OUR CUSTOMER SERVICE GAZEBOS...
HERE WE ARE. I'D LIKE YOU TO MEET ARVAN, YOUR OWN PERSONAL DISPUTE RESOLUTION ADVOCATE. WHILE YOU'RE HERE, ARVAN WORKS FOR YOU.
ARVAN IS NEW TO TELERATH, BUT ONE OF OUR BEST, I ASSURE YOU.
I'LL DO WHAT I CAN. MASTER MARGRYPH, I ASSUME?
BARON MARGRYPH. FIRST NAME, HYRO.
FIRST NAME IS BARON.
BARON, THEN. AND YOU, MADAM?
CHANTIQUE.
ENCHANTED. I HOPE YOU'VE ENJOYED WHAT YOU'VE SEEN OF OUR WORLD SO --
DON'T WANT NONE OF YOUR SALES PITCH, SONNY.
I WANT MY CASH AND I WANT IT NOW!
ONE OF THE BARON'S MANY ACCOUNTS IS HERE, ARVAN -- BUT IT'S BEEN FROZEN FOR MORE THAN A MONTH SINCE THAT TERRIBLE THING HAPPENED ON TARIS.
OH. YES. THE -- uh -- "PADAWAN MASSACRE."
ONE OF THE FUGITIVES IS MARN HIEROGRYPH. SOMEHOW, WE THINK YOU MUST HAVE MISTAKEN HIS NAME FOR THE BARON'S.
HOW TERRIBLE! AND SUCH AN UGLY COINCIDENCE. THAT MUST BE SUCH A HARDSHIP FOR YOU. WHAT BUSINESS IS THE BARON IN, MAY I ASK?
UMM... RECYCLING.
I DON'T KNOW WHO THIS MARN HIEROGRYPH CHARACTER IS, MONEYMAN, BUT I AIN'T HIM!

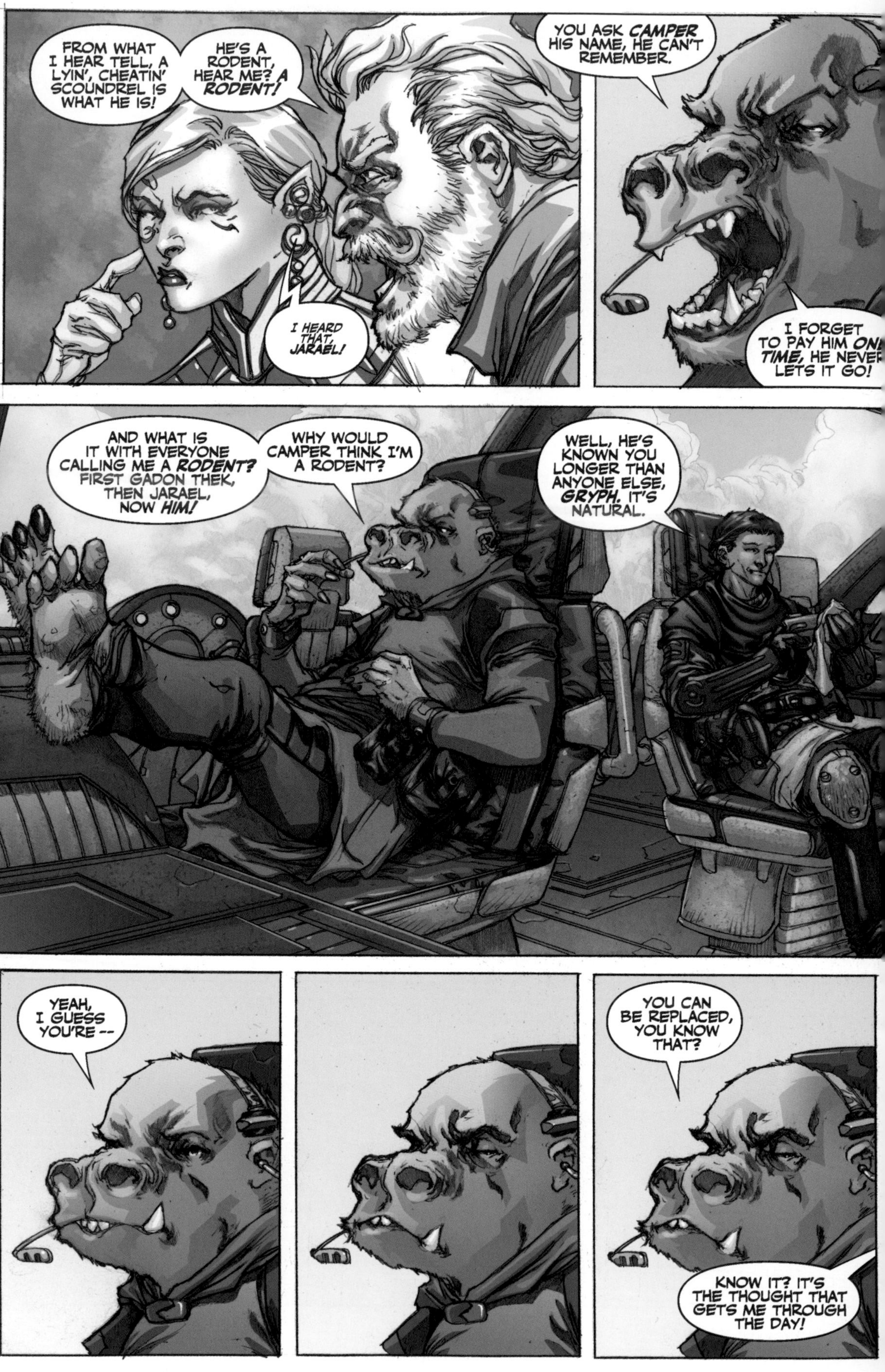
FROM WHAT I HEAR TELL, A LYIN', CHEATIN' SCOUNDREL IS WHAT HE IS!
HE'S A RODENT, HEAR ME? A *RODENT!*
I HEARD THAT, JARAEL!
YOU ASK *CAMPER* HIS NAME, HE CAN'T REMEMBER.
I FORGET TO PAY HIM ONE TIME, HE NEVER LETS IT GO!
AND WHAT IS IT WITH EVERYONE CALLING ME A *RODENT?* FIRST GADON THEK, THEN JARAEL, NOW *HIM!*
WHY WOULD CAMPER THINK I'M A RODENT?
WELL, HE'S KNOWN YOU LONGER THAN ANYONE ELSE, *GRYPH.* IT'S NATURAL.
YEAH, I GUESS YOU'RE --
YOU CAN BE REPLACED, YOU KNOW THAT?
KNOW IT? IT'S THE THOUGHT THAT GETS ME THROUGH THE DAY!

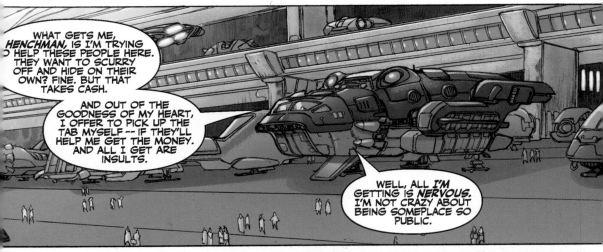

WHAT GETS ME, *HENCHMAN*, IS I'M TRYING TO HELP THESE PEOPLE HERE. THEY WANT TO SCURRY OFF AND HIDE ON THEIR OWN? FINE. BUT THAT TAKES CASH.

AND OUT OF THE GOODNESS OF MY HEART, I OFFER TO PICK UP THE TAB MYSELF -- IF THEY'LL HELP ME GET THE MONEY. AND ALL I GET ARE INSULTS.

WELL, ALL *I'M* GETTING IS *NERVOUS*. I'M NOT CRAZY ABOUT BEING SOMEPLACE SO PUBLIC.

MY ACCOUNT HERE WAS SAFE AND LEGAL THE WHOLE TIME I WAS ON THE WRONG SIDE OF THE LOCALS ON TARIS. IT TOOK *YOU* TO GET MY ACCOUNT FROZEN.

SORRY. I GUESS I WAS GOING TO LIVE WITHOUT POSSESSIONS, ONE WAY OR ANOTHER.

WELL, THIS IS SOME POSSESSION. A HUNDRED THOUSAND CREDS --

-- ENOUGH TO BANKROLL OUR NEXT BIG SCORE AND PUT *CAMPER* AND *JARAEL* IN THE JUNKYARD OF THEIR CHOICE, TO BOOT.

IT GOT THEM TO DO IT, I GUESS. YOU AND I SURE COULDN'T HAVE GONE IN THERE.

STILL, IT SEEMS DISHONEST, SOMEHOW.

WHAT KIND OF HENCHMAN TALK IS THAT? YOU DIDN'T MIND SO MUCH BACK ON VANQUO, WHEN WE WERE *STARVING*.

BESIDES, WE'RE NOT STEALING. THIS IS *MY* MONEY.

YEAH, BUT HOW'D YOU GET THE MONEY IN THE FIRST PLACE?

UH-HUH.

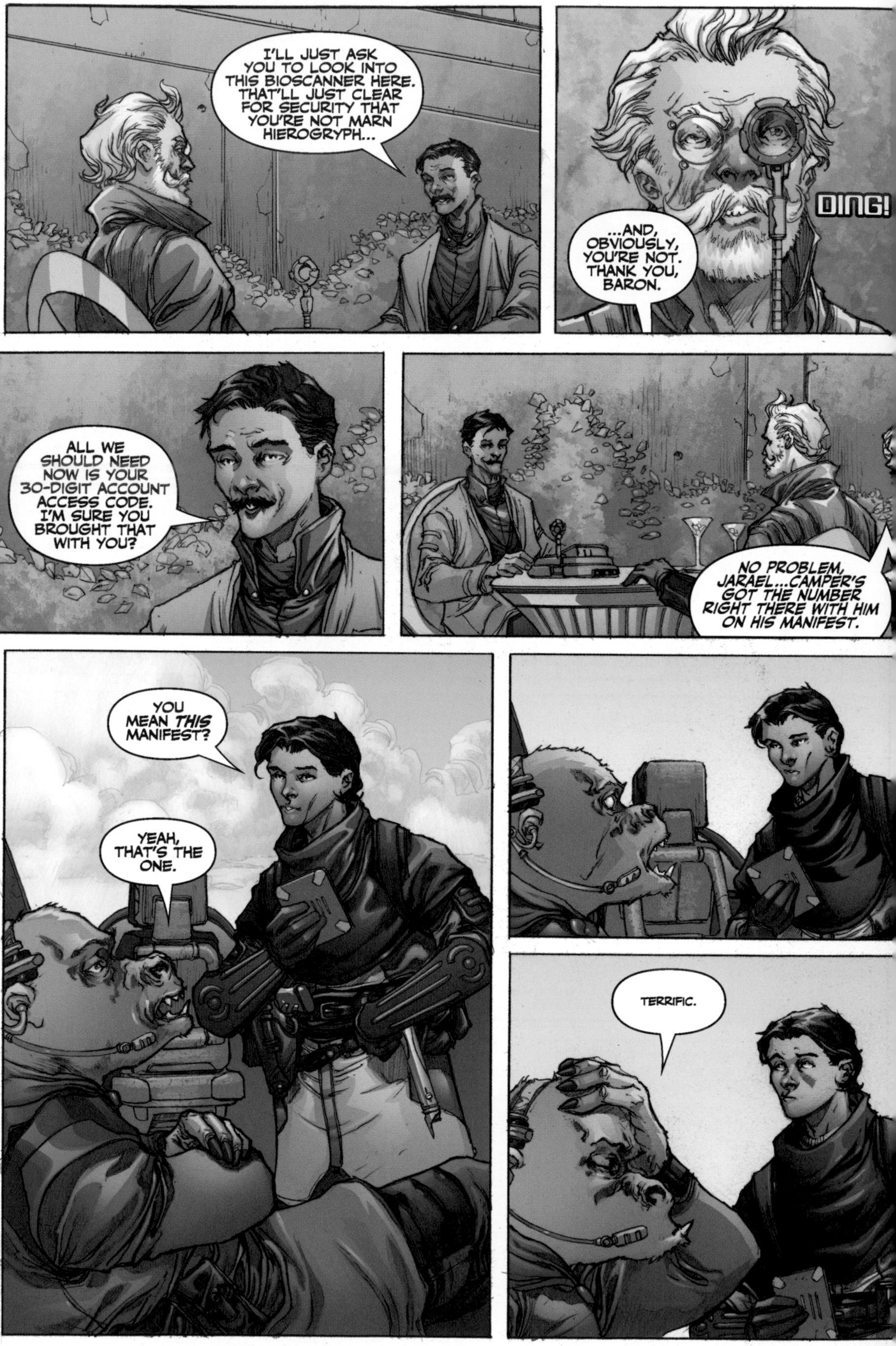
I'LL JUST ASK YOU TO LOOK INTO THIS BIOSCANNER HERE. THAT'LL JUST CLEAR FOR SECURITY THAT YOU'RE NOT MARN HIEROGRYPH...
DING!
...AND, OBVIOUSLY, YOU'RE NOT. THANK YOU, BARON.
ALL WE SHOULD NEED NOW IS YOUR 30-DIGIT ACCOUNT ACCESS CODE. I'M SURE YOU BROUGHT THAT WITH YOU?
NO PROBLEM, JARAEL...CAMPER'S GOT THE NUMBER RIGHT THERE WITH HIM ON HIS MANIFEST.
YOU MEAN *THIS* MANIFEST?
YEAH, THAT'S THE ONE.
TERRIFIC.

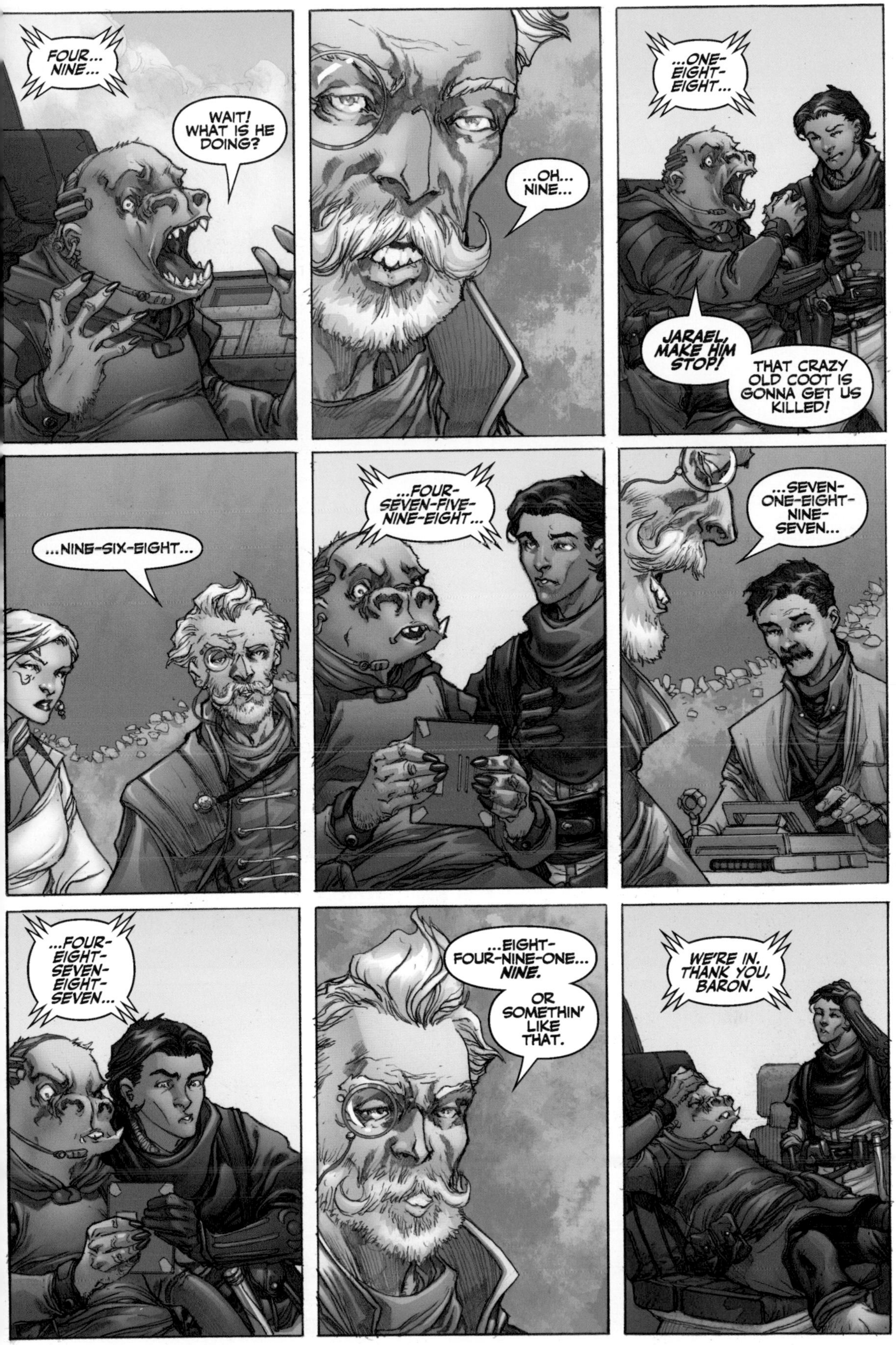
FOUR... NINE...
WAIT! WHAT IS HE DOING?
...OH... NINE...
...ONE- EIGHT- EIGHT...
JARAEL, MAKE HIM STOP!
THAT CRAZY OLD COOT IS GONNA GET US KILLED!
...NINE-SIX-EIGHT...
...FOUR- SEVEN-FIVE- NINE-EIGHT...
...SEVEN- ONE-EIGHT- NINE- SEVEN...
...FOUR- EIGHT- SEVEN- EIGHT- SEVEN...
...EIGHT- FOUR-NINE-ONE... NINE.
OR SOMETHIN' LIKE THAT.
WE'RE IN. THANK YOU, BARON.

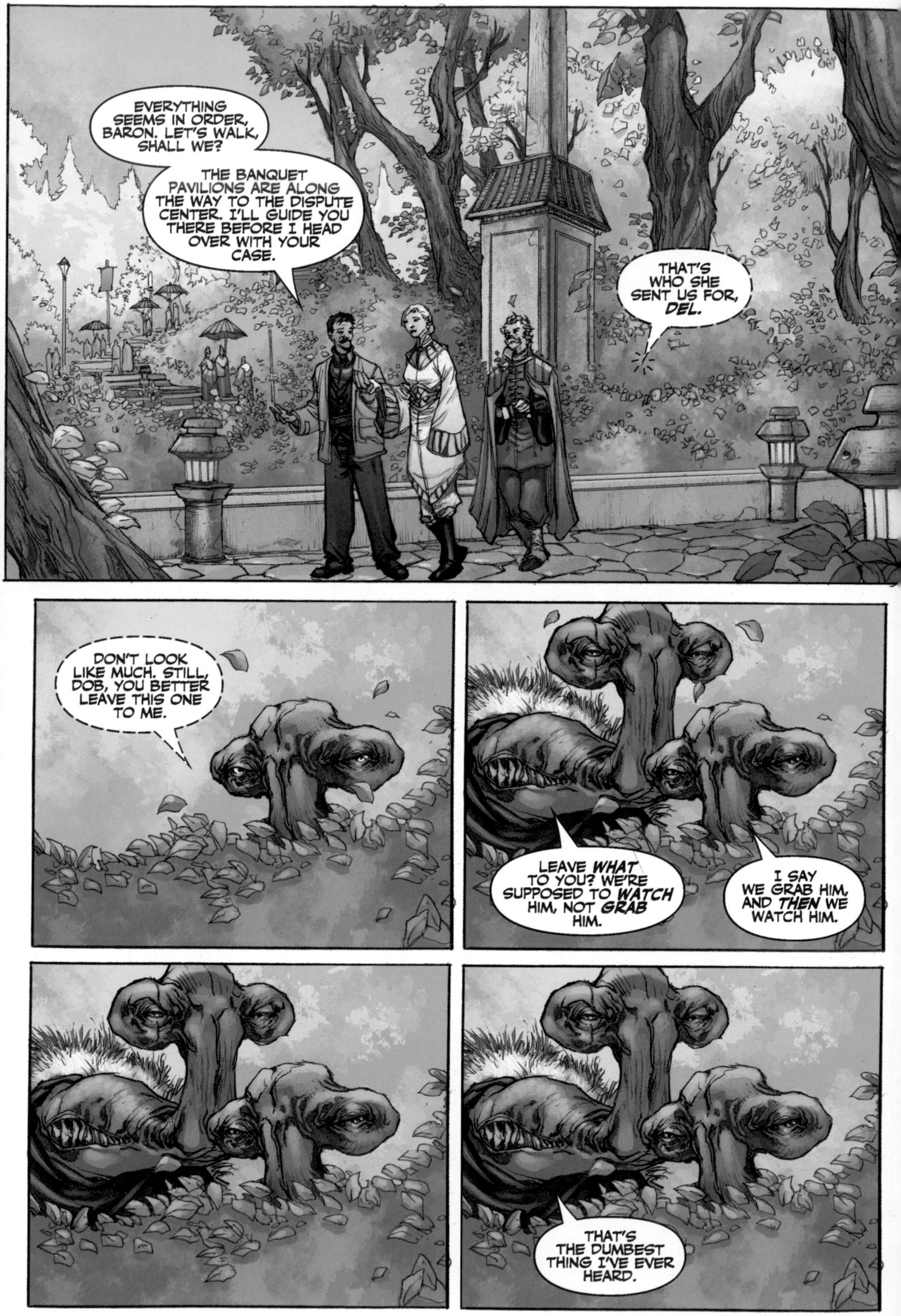
EVERYTHING SEEMS IN ORDER, BARON. LET'S WALK, SHALL WE?
THE BANQUET PAVILIONS ARE ALONG THE WAY TO THE DISPUTE CENTER. I'LL GUIDE YOU THERE BEFORE I HEAD OVER WITH YOUR CASE.
THAT'S WHO SHE SENT US FOR, DEL.
DON'T LOOK LIKE MUCH. STILL, DOB, YOU BETTER LEAVE THIS ONE TO ME.
LEAVE WHAT TO YOU? WE'RE SUPPOSED TO WATCH HIM, NOT GRAB HIM.
I SAY WE GRAB HIM, AND THEN WE WATCH HIM.
THAT'S THE DUMBEST THING I'VE EVER HEARD.

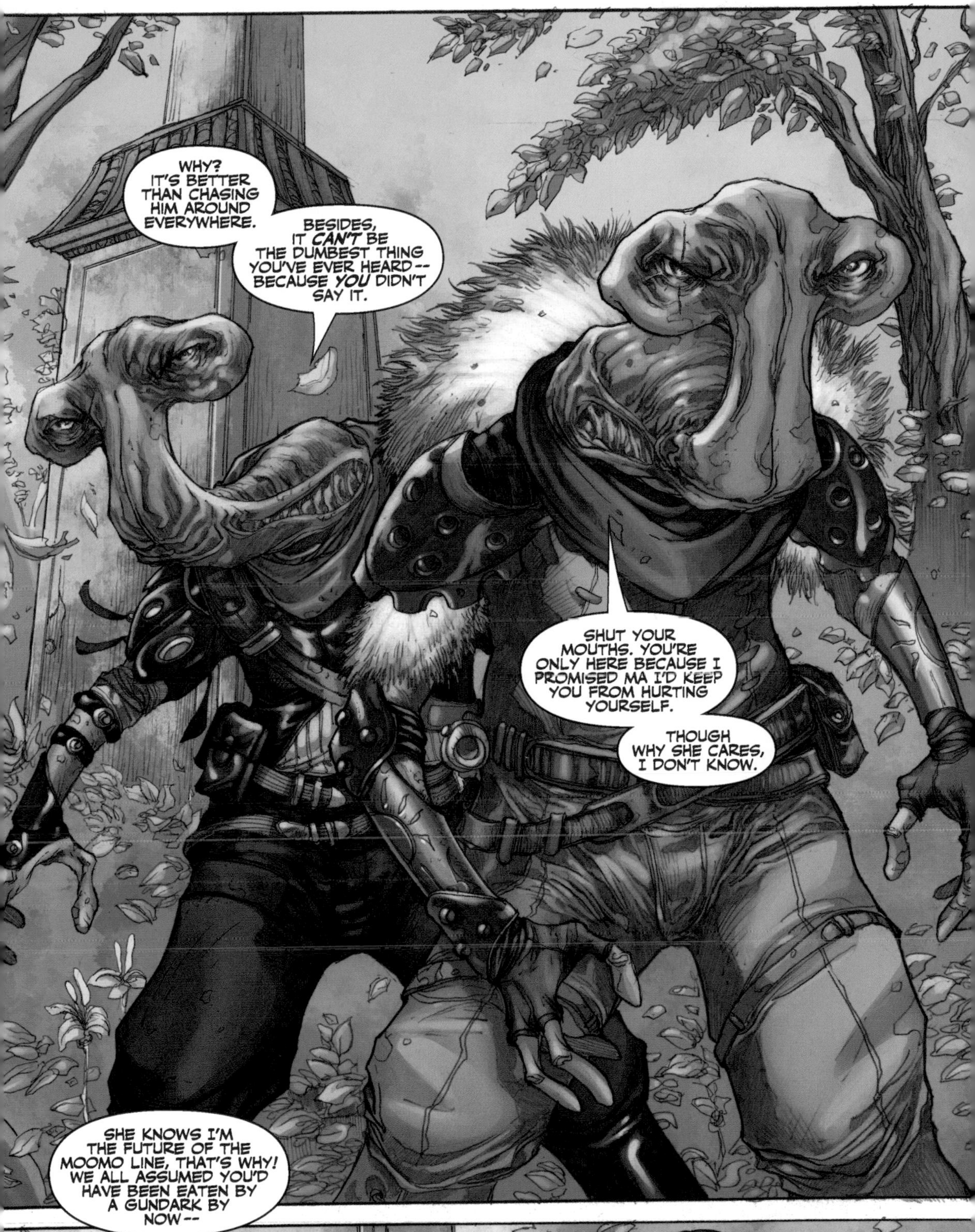
WHY? IT'S BETTER THAN CHASING HIM AROUND EVERYWHERE.
BESIDES, IT CAN'T BE THE DUMBEST THING YOU'VE EVER HEARD -- BECAUSE YOU DIDN'T SAY IT.
SHUT YOUR MOUTHS. YOU'RE ONLY HERE BECAUSE I PROMISED MA I'D KEEP YOU FROM HURTING YOURSELF.
THOUGH WHY SHE CARES, I DON'T KNOW.
SHE KNOWS I'M THE FUTURE OF THE MOOMO LINE, THAT'S WHY! WE ALL ASSUMED YOU'D HAVE BEEN EATEN BY A GUNDARK BY NOW --

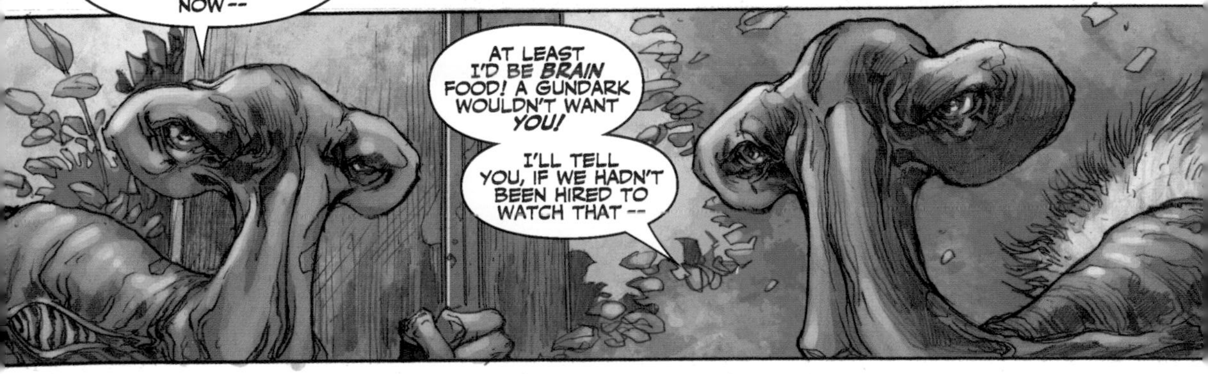
AT LEAST I'D BE BRAIN FOOD! A GUNDARK WOULDN'T WANT YOU!
I'LL TELL YOU, IF WE HADN'T BEEN HIRED TO WATCH THAT --

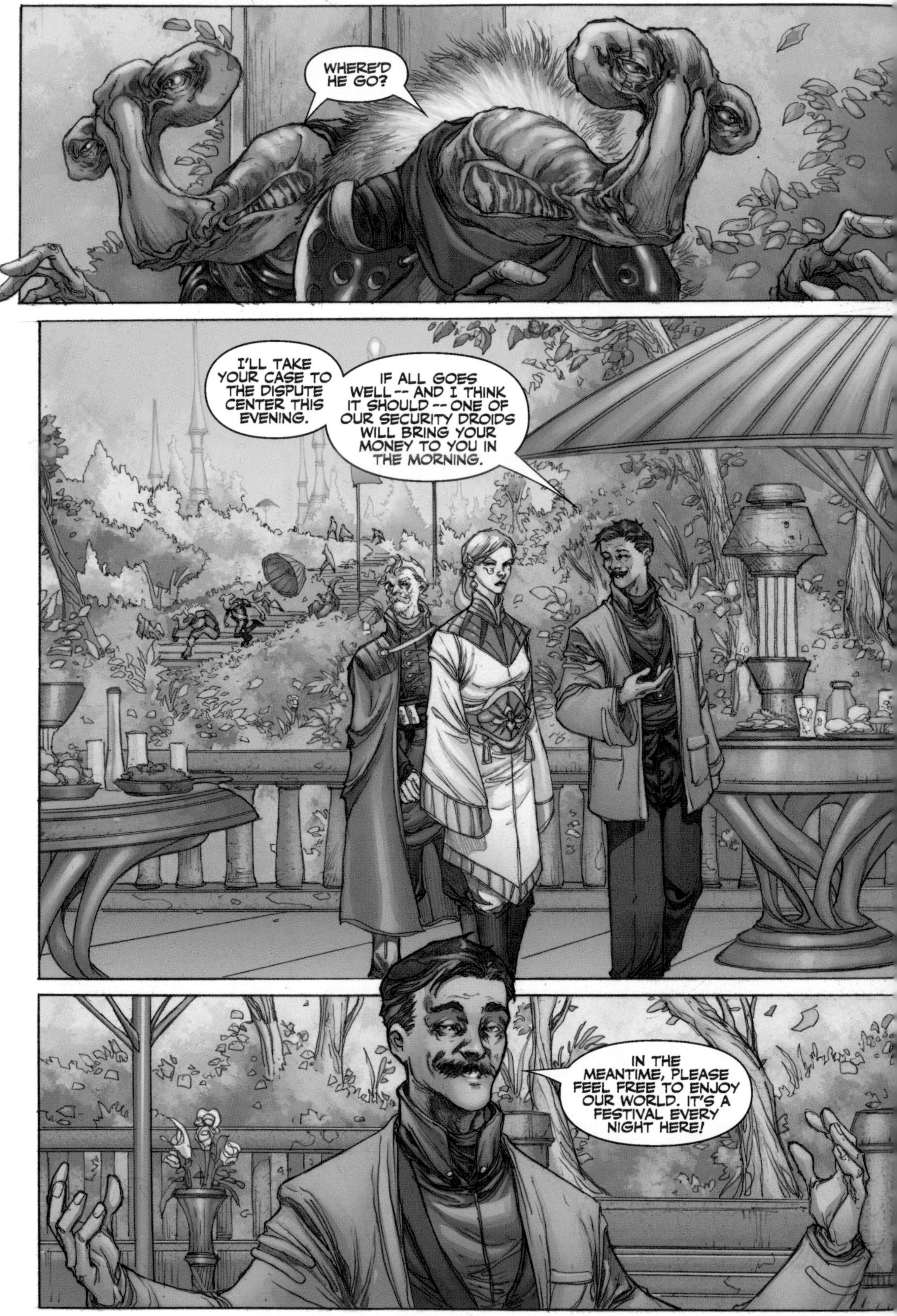
WHERE'D HE GO?
I'LL TAKE YOUR CASE TO THE DISPUTE CENTER THIS EVENING.
IF ALL GOES WELL -- AND I THINK IT SHOULD -- ONE OF OUR SECURITY DROIDS WILL BRING YOUR MONEY TO YOU IN THE MORNING.
IN THE MEANTIME, PLEASE FEEL FREE TO ENJOY OUR WORLD. IT'S A FESTIVAL EVERY NIGHT HERE!

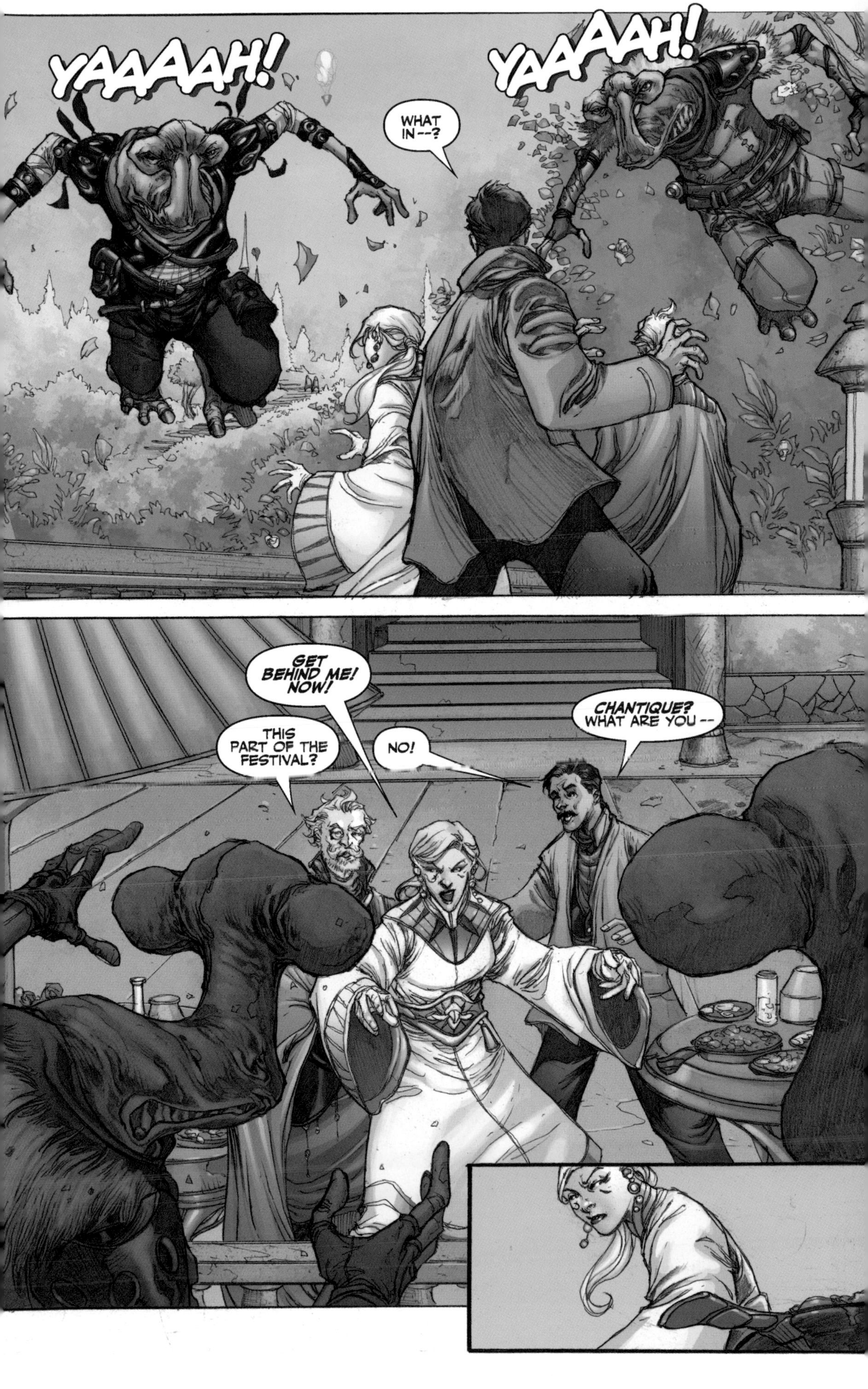
YAAAAH!
YAAAAH!
WHAT IN--?
GET BEHIND ME! NOW!
THIS PART OF THE FESTIVAL?
NO!
CHANTIQUE? WHAT ARE YOU --

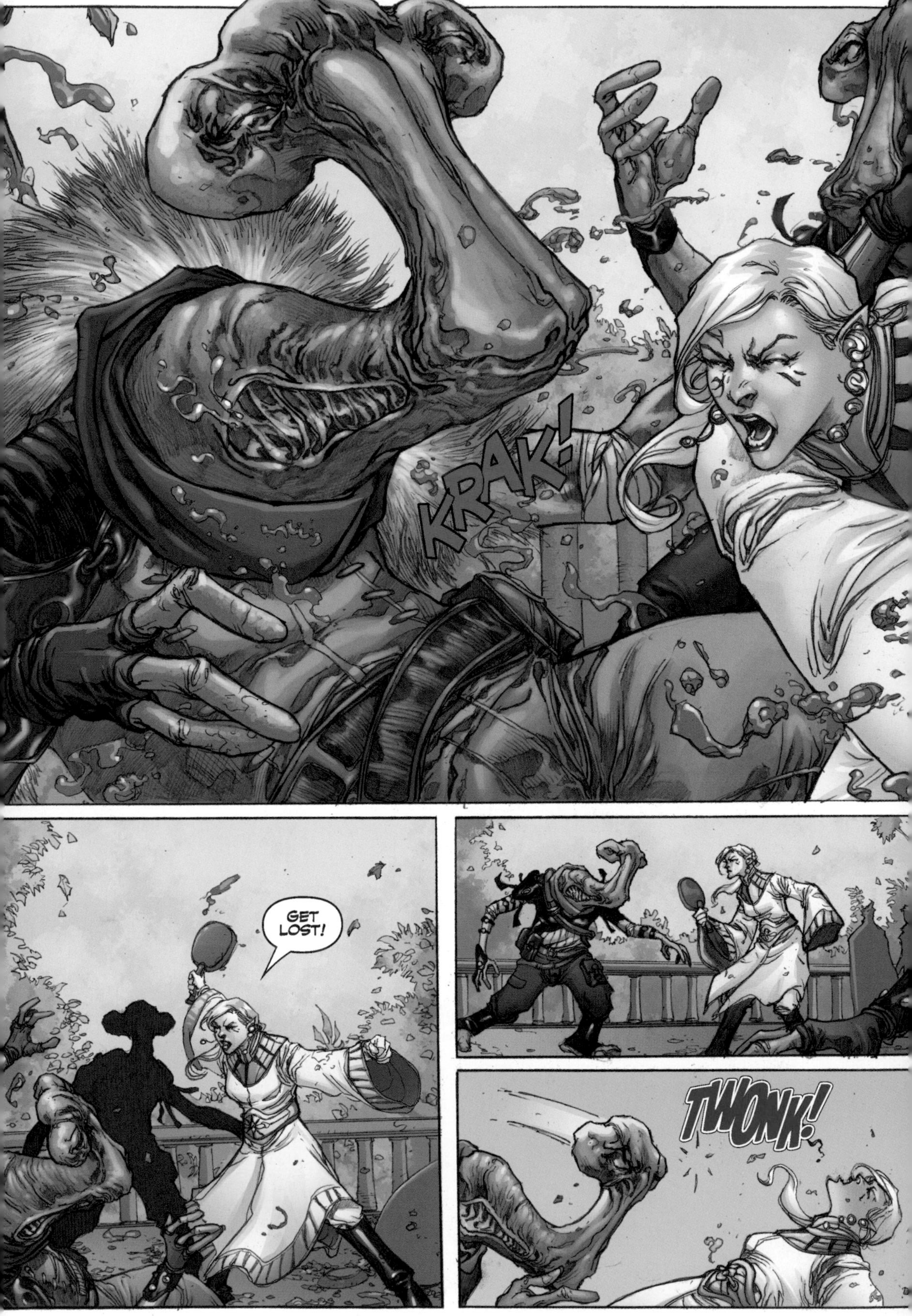
KRAK!
GET LOST!
TWONK!

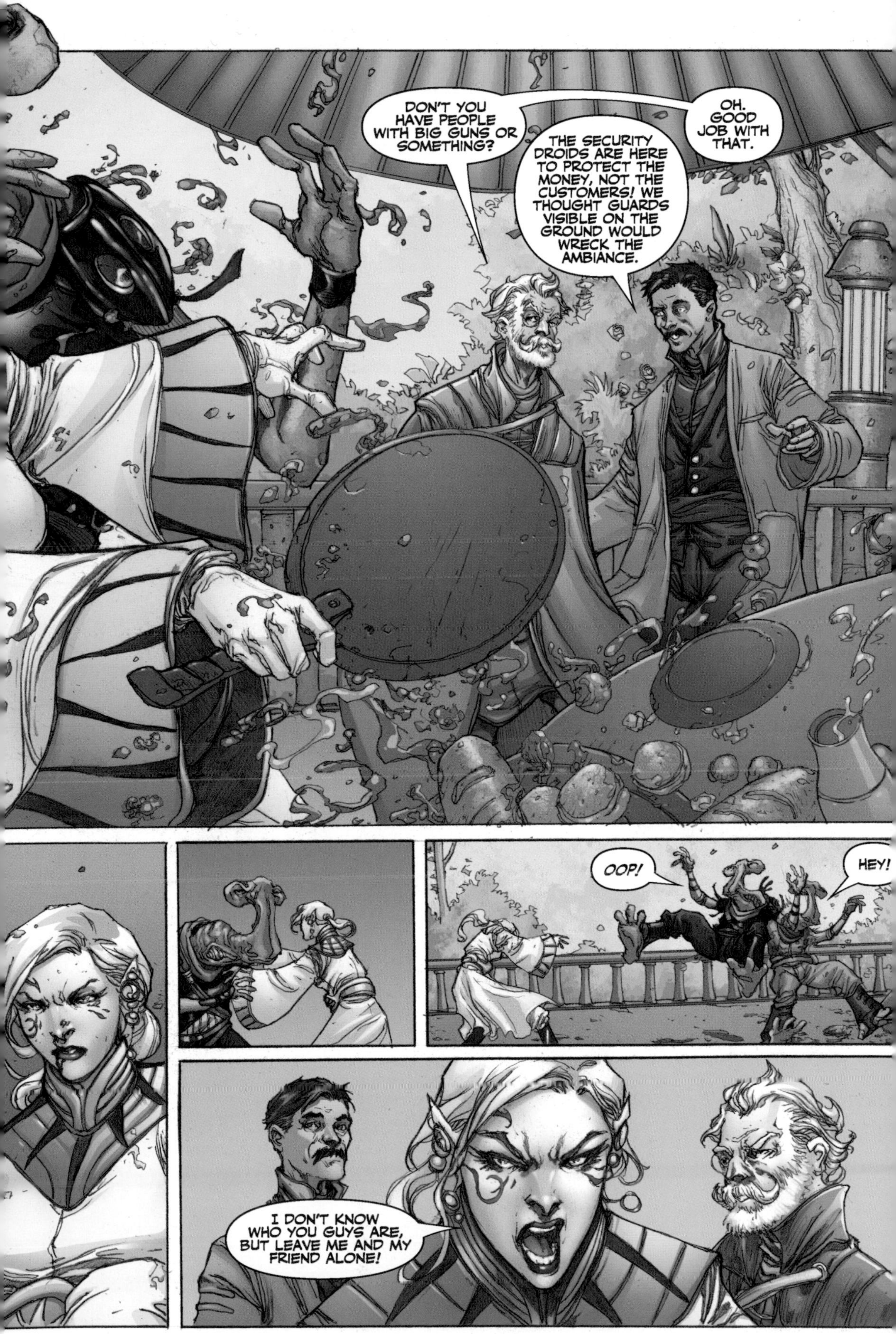
DON'T YOU HAVE PEOPLE WITH BIG GUNS OR SOMETHING?
THE SECURITY DROIDS ARE HERE TO PROTECT THE MONEY, NOT THE CUSTOMERS! WE THOUGHT GUARDS VISIBLE ON THE GROUND WOULD WRECK THE AMBIANCE.
OH. GOOD JOB WITH THAT.
OOP!
HEY!
I DON'T KNOW WHO YOU GUYS ARE, BUT LEAVE ME AND MY FRIEND ALONE!

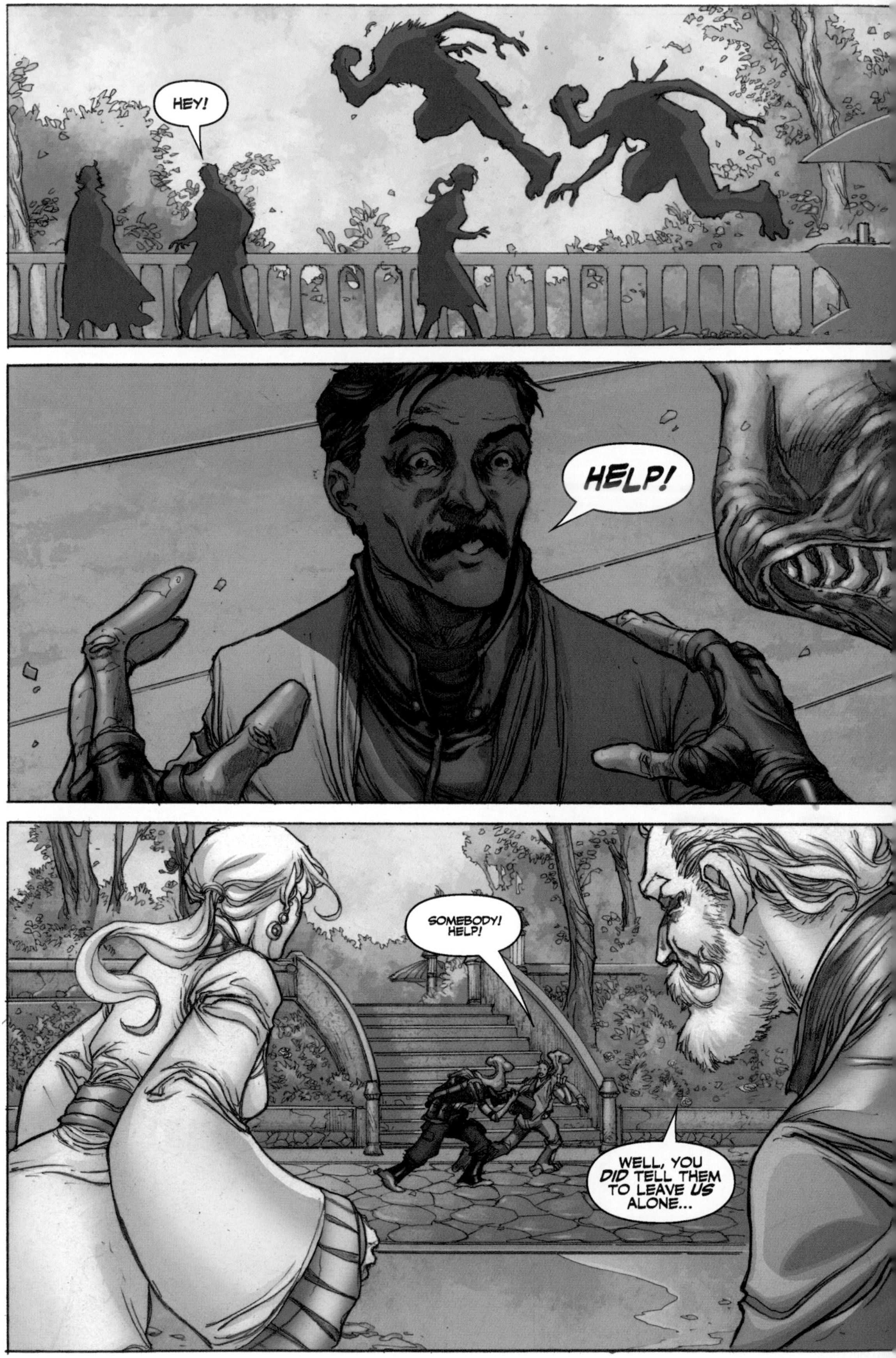
HEY!
HELP!
SOMEBODY! HELP!
WELL, YOU *DID* TELL THEM TO LEAVE *US* ALONE...

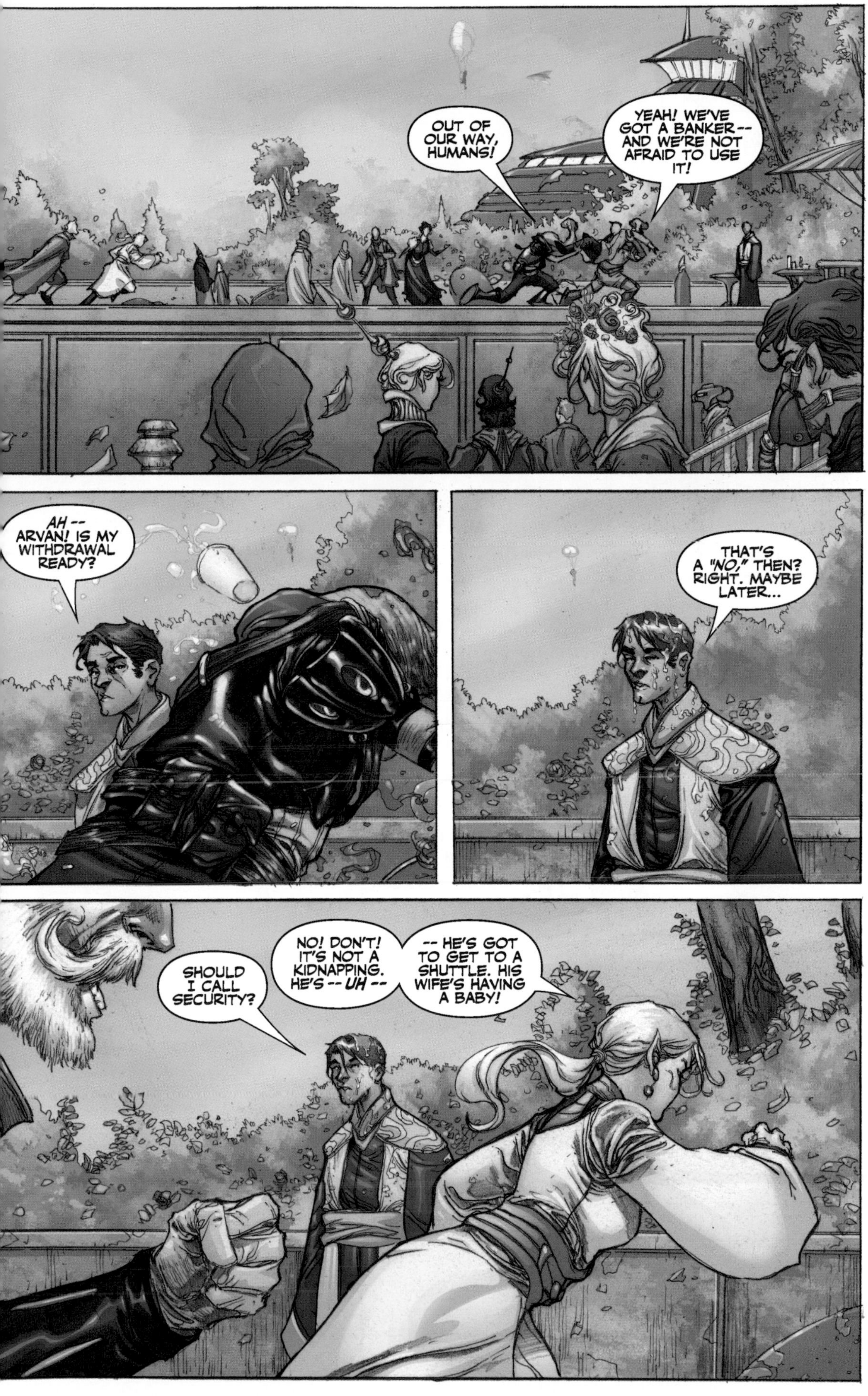
OUT OF OUR WAY, HUMANS!
YEAH! WE'VE GOT A BANKER-- AND WE'RE NOT AFRAID TO USE IT!
AH -- ARVAN! IS MY WITHDRAWAL READY?
THAT'S A "NO," THEN? RIGHT. MAYBE LATER...
SHOULD I CALL SECURITY?
NO! DON'T! IT'S NOT A KIDNAPPING. HE'S -- UH --
-- HE'S GOT TO GET TO A SHUTTLE. HIS WIFE'S HAVING A BABY!

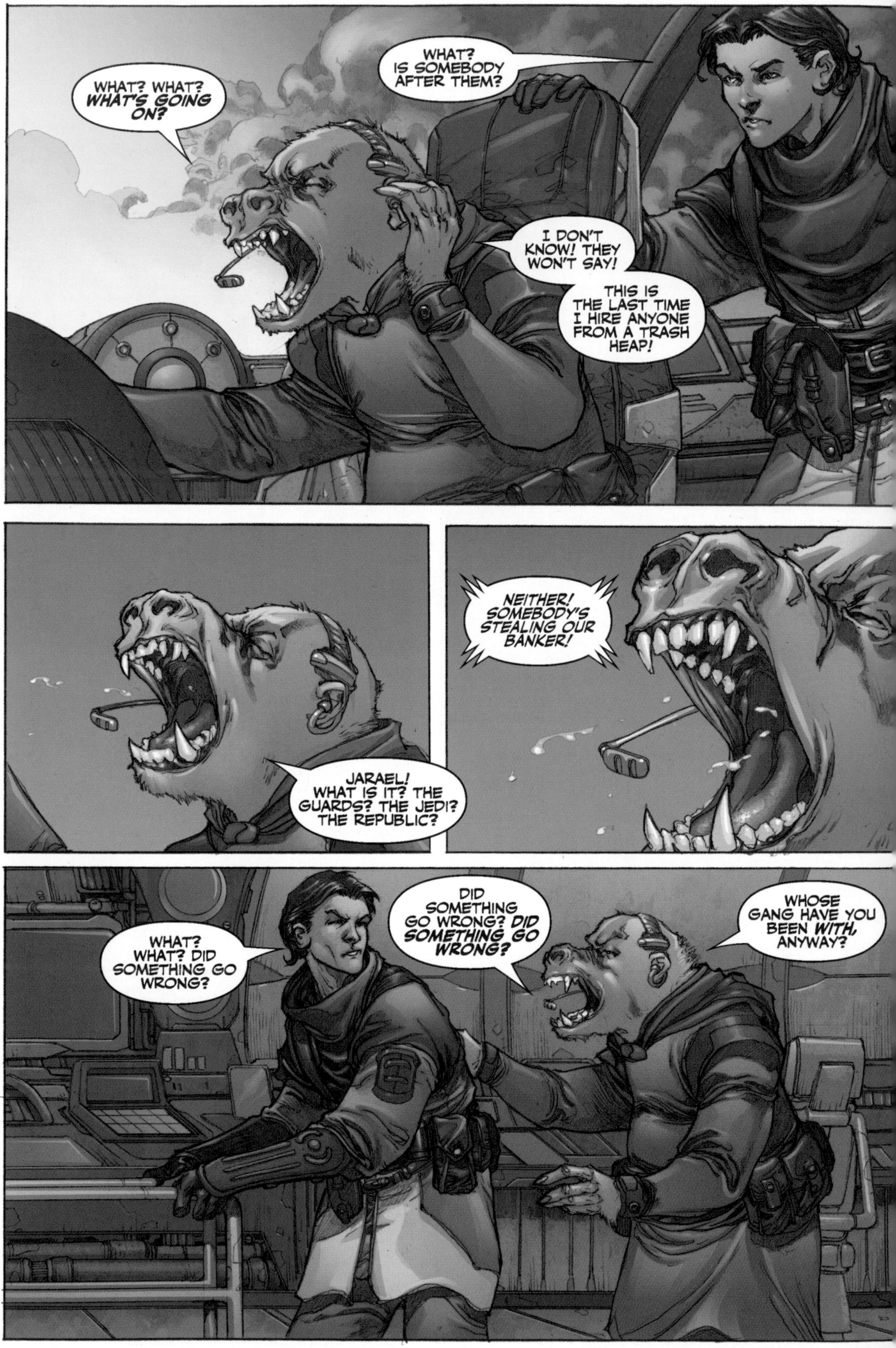
WHAT? WHAT? *WHAT'S GOING ON?*
WHAT? IS SOMEBODY AFTER THEM?
I DON'T KNOW! THEY WON'T SAY!
THIS IS THE LAST TIME I HIRE ANYONE FROM A TRASH HEAP!
JARAEL! WHAT IS IT? THE GUARDS? THE JEDI? THE REPUBLIC?
NEITHER! SOMEBODY'S STEALING OUR BANKER!
WHAT? WHAT? DID SOMETHING GO WRONG?
DID SOMETHING GO WRONG? *DID SOMETHING GO WRONG?*
WHOSE GANG HAVE YOU BEEN *WITH,* ANYWAY?

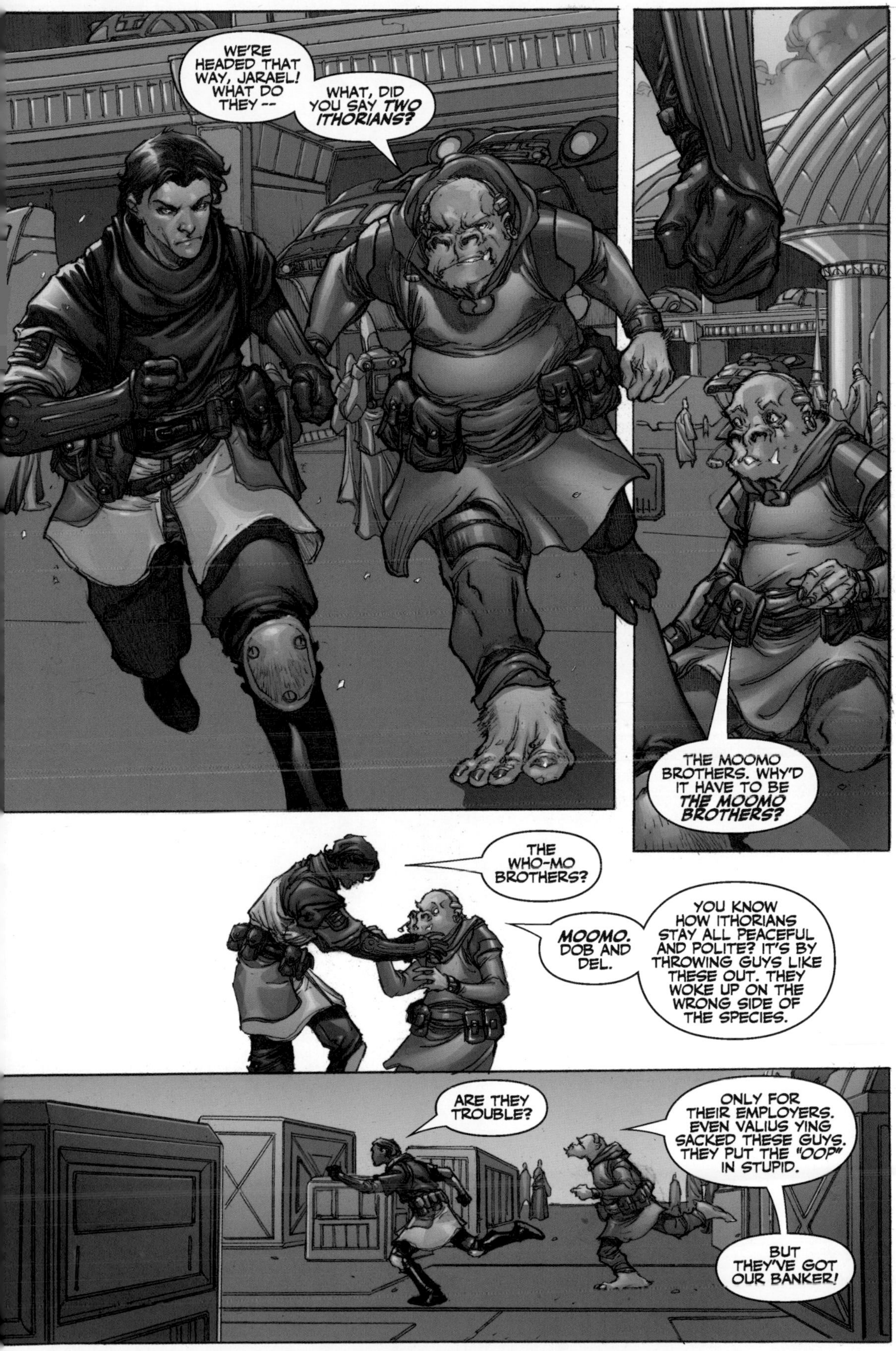
WE'RE HEADED THAT WAY, JARAEL! WHAT DO THEY --
WHAT, DID YOU SAY TWO ITHORIANS?
THE MOOMO BROTHERS. WHY'D IT HAVE TO BE THE MOOMO BROTHERS?
THE WHO-MO BROTHERS?
MOOMO. DOB AND DEL.
YOU KNOW HOW ITHORIANS STAY ALL PEACEFUL AND POLITE? IT'S BY THROWING GUYS LIKE THESE OUT. THEY WOKE UP ON THE WRONG SIDE OF THE SPECIES.
ARE THEY TROUBLE?
ONLY FOR THEIR EMPLOYERS. EVEN VALIUS YING SACKED THESE GUYS. THEY PUT THE "OOP" IN STUPID.
BUT THEY'VE GOT OUR BANKER!

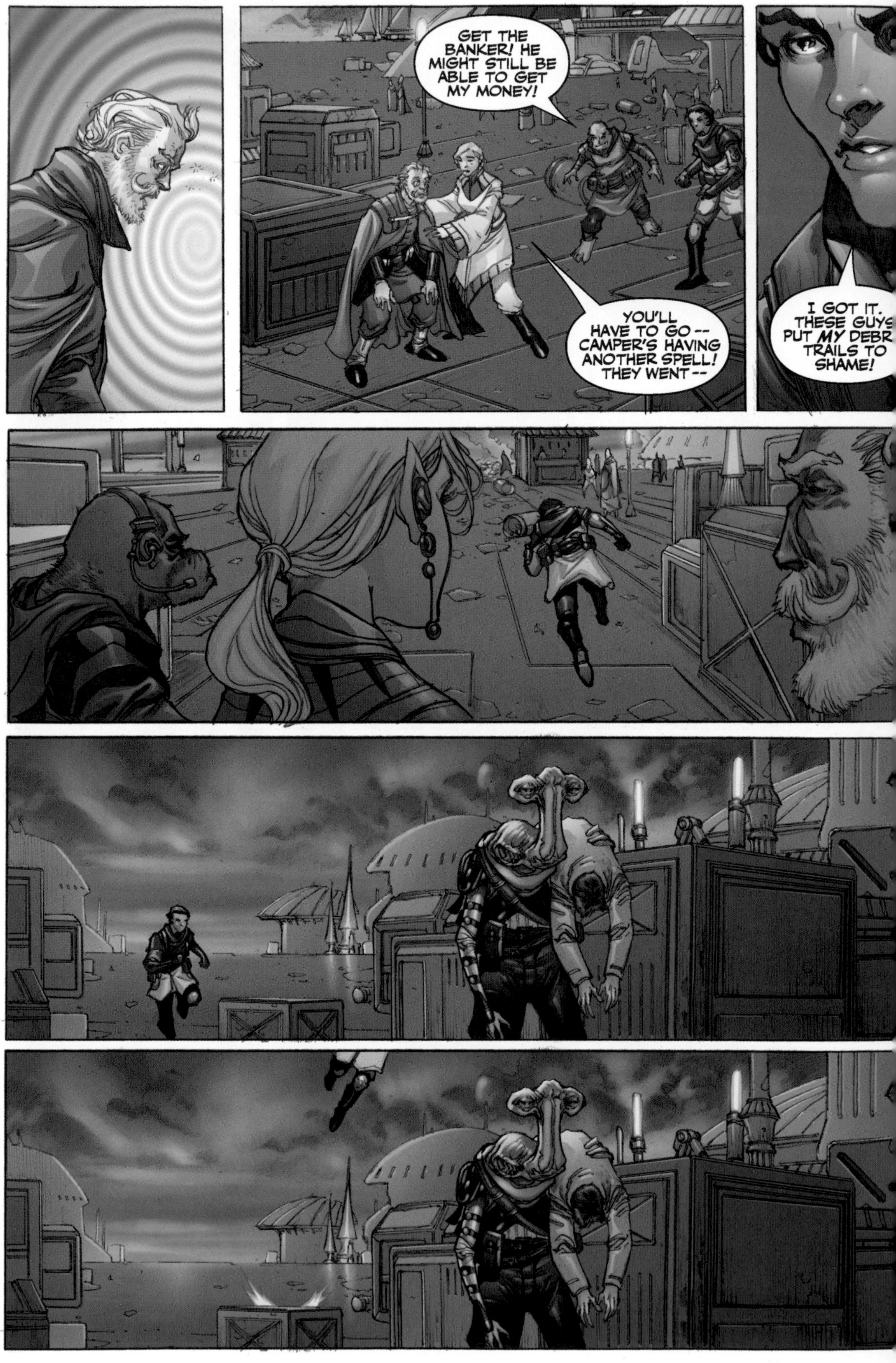
GET THE BANKER! HE MIGHT STILL BE ABLE TO GET MY MONEY!
YOU'LL HAVE TO GO -- CAMPER'S HAVING ANOTHER SPELL! THEY WENT --
I GOT IT. THESE GUYS PUT MY DEBR TRAILS TO SHAME!

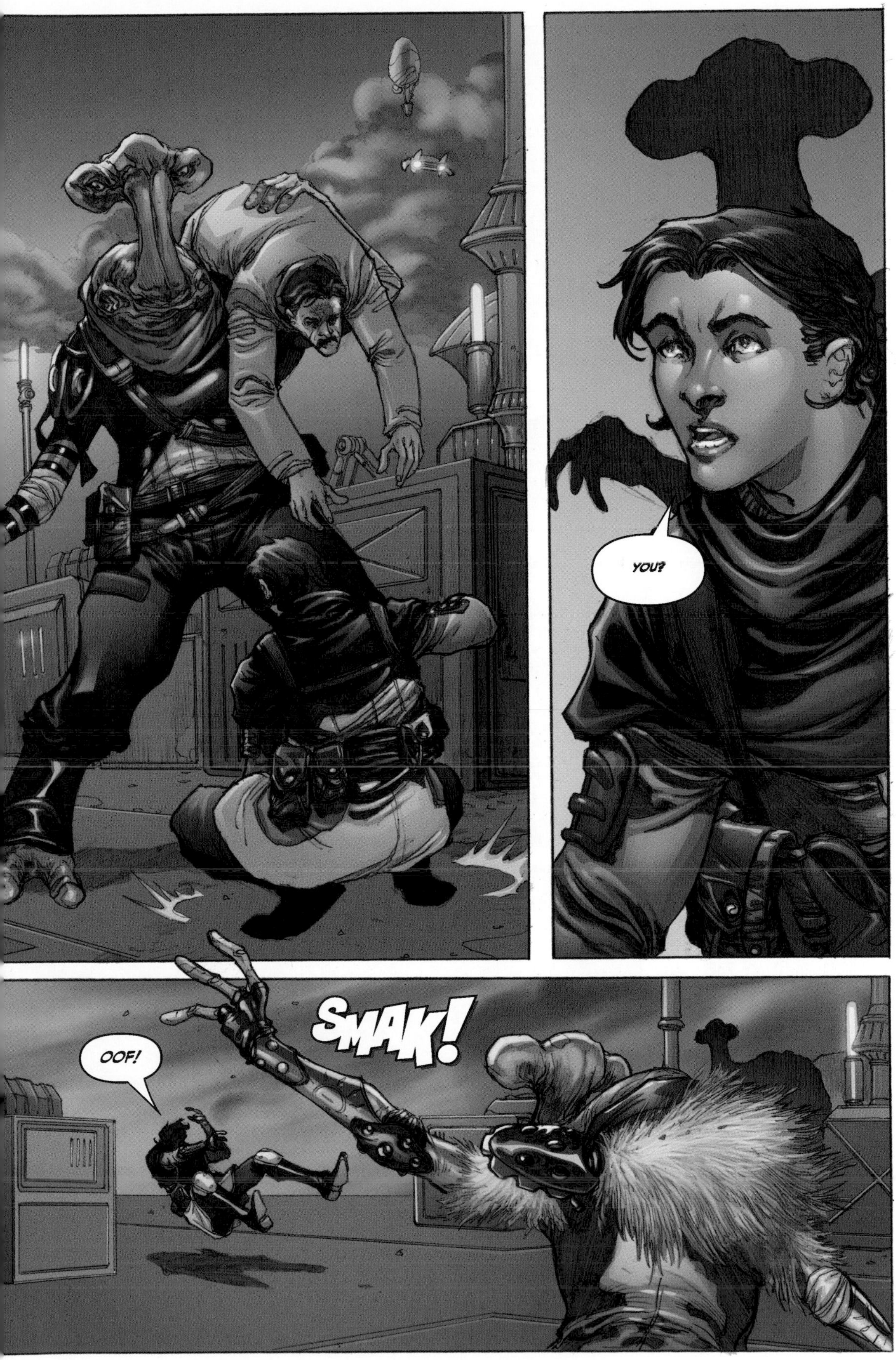
YOU?
SMAK!
OOF!

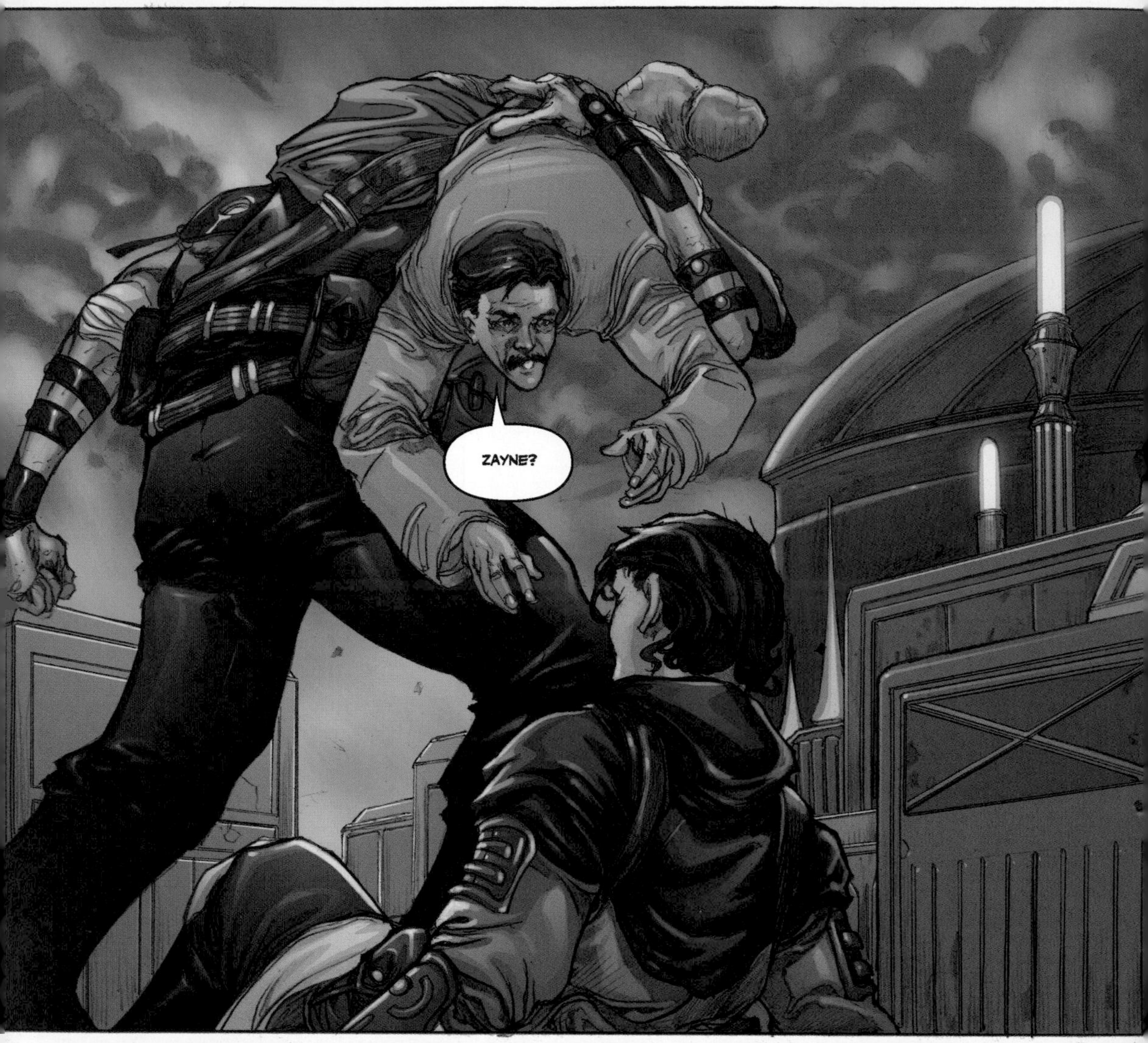
ZAYNE?

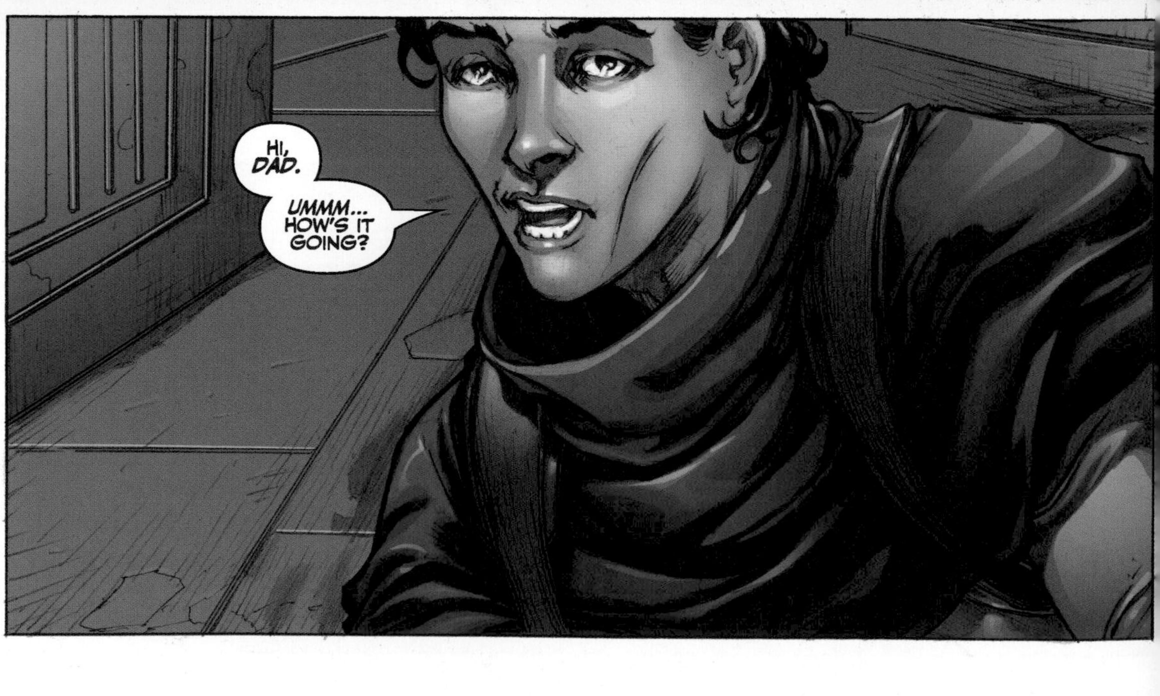
HI, DAD.
UMMM... HOW'S IT GOING?

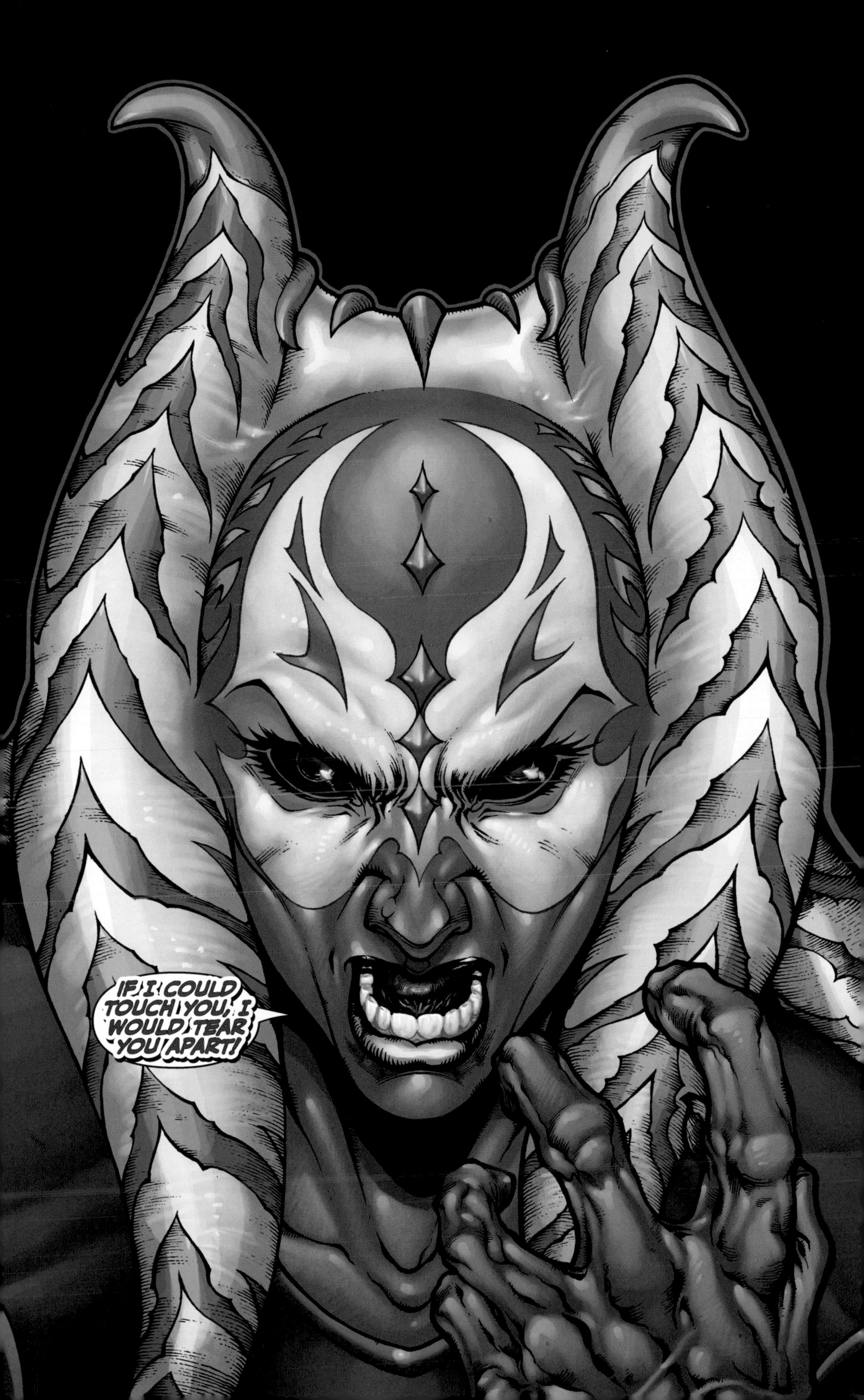
IF I COULD TOUCH YOU, I WOULD TEAR YOU APART!

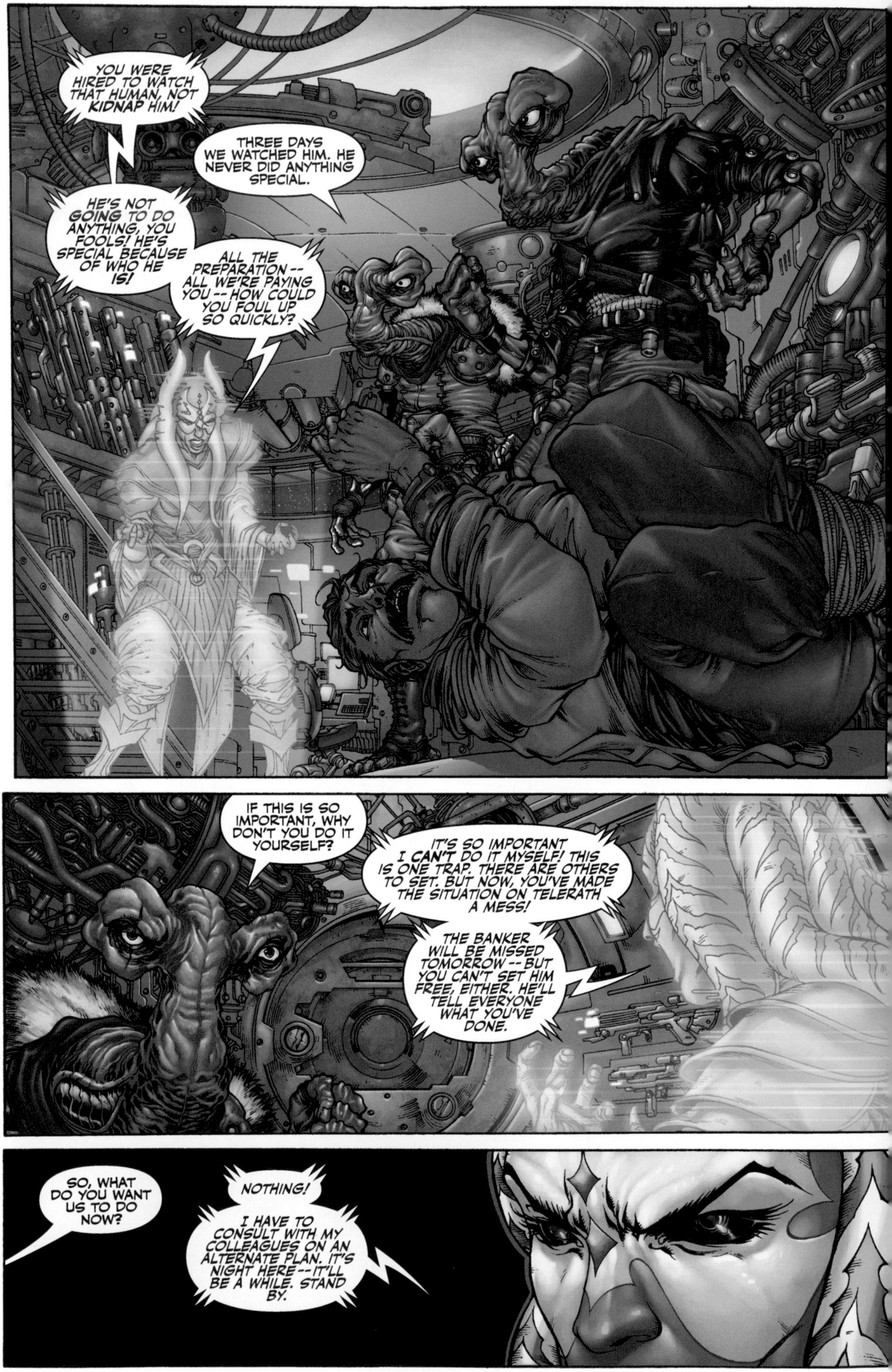
YOU WERE HIRED TO WATCH THAT HUMAN, NOT KIDNAP HIM!
THREE DAYS WE WATCHED HIM. HE NEVER DID ANYTHING SPECIAL.
HE'S NOT GOING TO DO ANYTHING, YOU FOOLS! HE'S SPECIAL BECAUSE OF WHO HE IS!
ALL THE PREPARATION -- ALL WE'RE PAYING YOU -- HOW COULD YOU FOUL UP SO QUICKLY?
IF THIS IS SO IMPORTANT, WHY DON'T YOU DO IT YOURSELF?
IT'S SO IMPORTANT I CAN'T DO IT MYSELF! THIS IS ONE TRAP. THERE ARE OTHERS TO SET. BUT NOW, YOU'VE MADE THE SITUATION ON TELERATH A MESS!
THE BANKER WILL BE MISSED TOMORROW -- BUT YOU CAN'T SET HIM FREE, EITHER. HE'LL TELL EVERYONE WHAT YOU'VE DONE.
SO, WHAT DO YOU WANT US TO DO NOW?
NOTHING!
I HAVE TO CONSULT WITH MY COLLEAGUES ON AN ALTERNATE PLAN. IT'S NIGHT HERE--IT'LL BE A WHILE. STAND BY.

IT'S NIGHT HERE, TOO. WE'LL SLEEP ON IT.

NO, YOU WON'T! I DON'T SLEEP, SO NOBODY SLEEPS! STAY WHERE YOU ARE --

-- AND DON'T DO ANYTHING!

SHE'D BE A HAPPIER PERSON IF SHE GOT MORE SLEEP.

I'D BE HAPPIER IF YOU SHUT YOUR MAW.

WHAT'RE YOU TALKING ABOUT MA FOR? IF SHE WAS HERE SHE'D SWAT YOU IN THE HEAD!

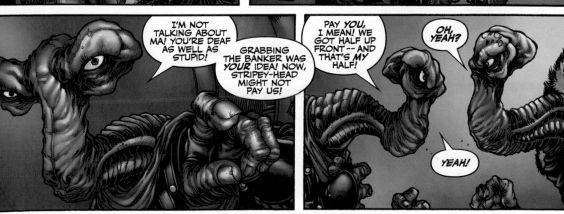

I'M NOT TALKING ABOUT MA! YOU'RE DEAF AS WELL AS STUPID!

GRABBING THE BANKER WAS YOUR IDEA! NOW, STRIPEY-HEAD MIGHT NOT PAY US!

PAY YOU, I MEAN! WE GOT HALF UP FRONT -- AND THAT'S MY HALF!

OH, YEAH?

YEAH!

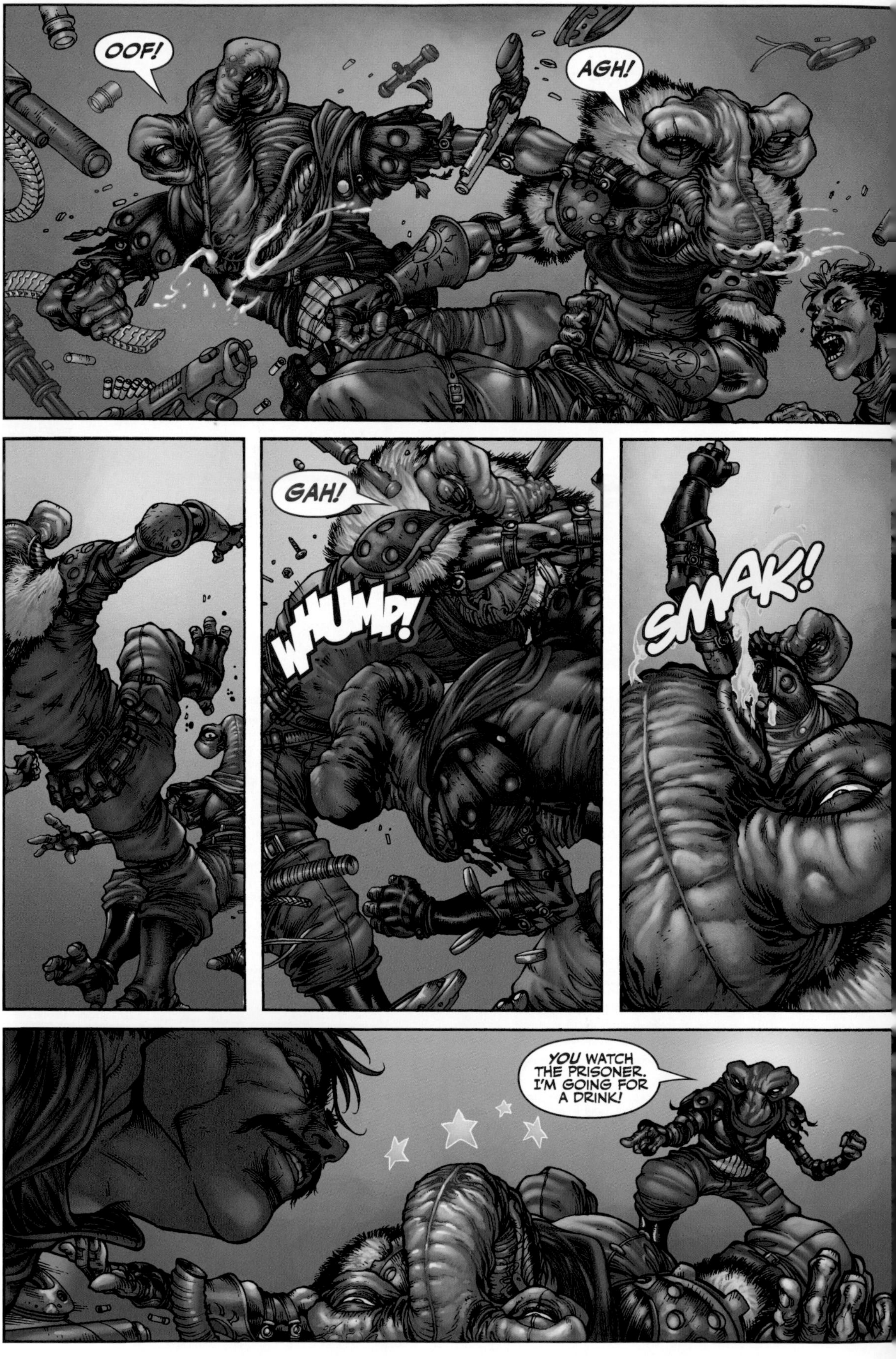
OOF!
AGH!
GAH!
WHUMP!
SMAK!
YOU WATCH THE PRISONER. I'M GOING FOR A DRINK!

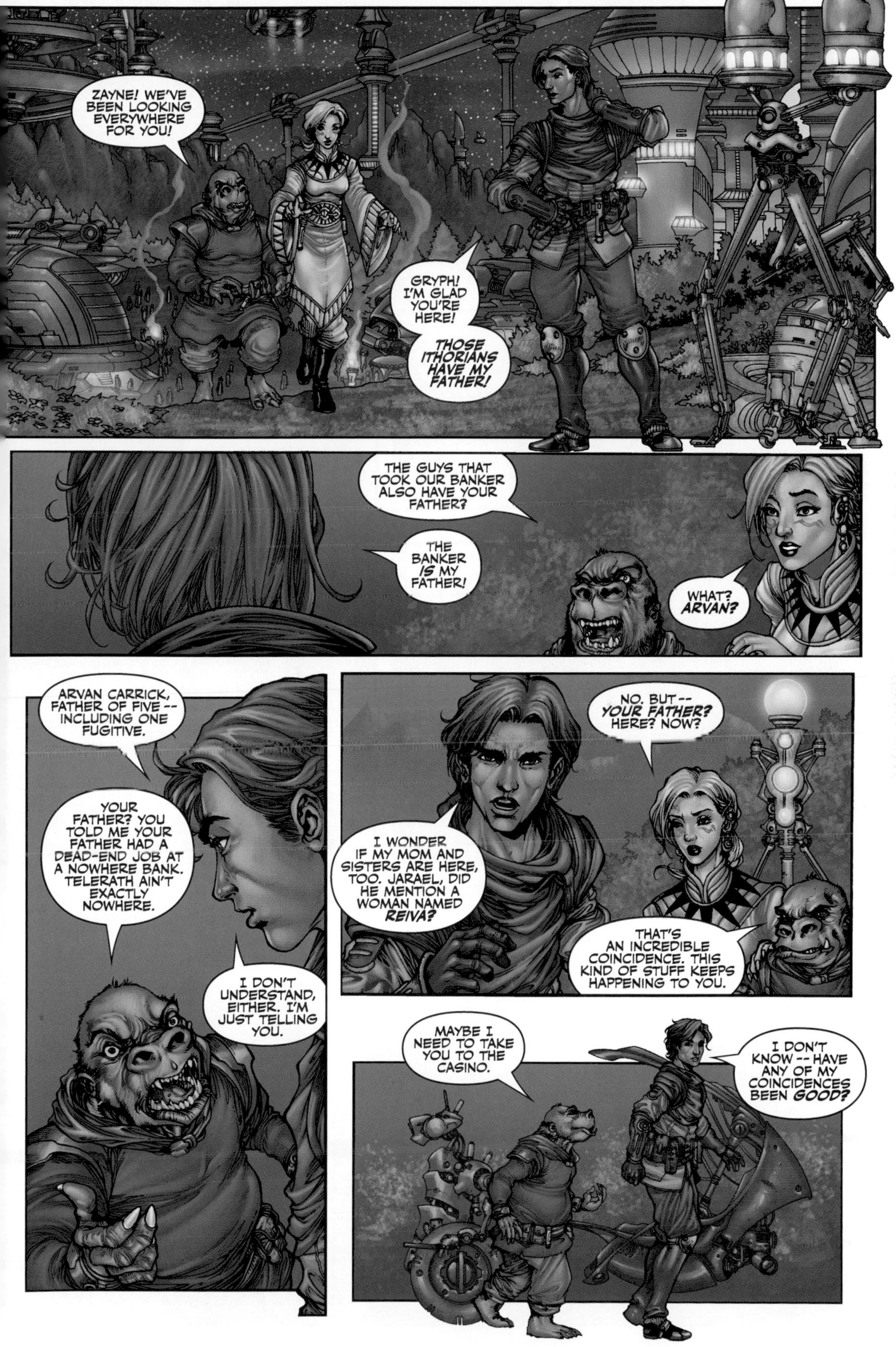
ZAYNE! WE'VE BEEN LOOKING EVERYWHERE FOR YOU!
GRYPH! I'M GLAD YOU'RE HERE!
THOSE ITHORIANS HAVE MY FATHER!
THE GUYS THAT TOOK OUR BANKER ALSO HAVE YOUR FATHER?
THE BANKER IS MY FATHER!
WHAT? ARVAN?
ARVAN CARRICK, FATHER OF FIVE -- INCLUDING ONE FUGITIVE.
YOUR FATHER? YOU TOLD ME YOUR FATHER HAD A DEAD-END JOB AT A NOWHERE BANK. TELERATH AIN'T EXACTLY NOWHERE.
I DON'T UNDERSTAND, EITHER. I'M JUST TELLING YOU.
NO. BUT -- YOUR FATHER? HERE? NOW?
I WONDER IF MY MOM AND SISTERS ARE HERE, TOO. JARAEL, DID HE MENTION A WOMAN NAMED REIVA?
THAT'S AN INCREDIBLE COINCIDENCE. THIS KIND OF STUFF KEEPS HAPPENING TO YOU.
MAYBE I NEED TO TAKE YOU TO THE CASINO.
I DON'T KNOW -- HAVE ANY OF MY COINCIDENCES BEEN GOOD?

BUT IT DOESN'T MAKE SENSE!

I MEAN, WHY WOULD ANYONE WANT TO KIDNAP MY FATHER, OF ALL PEOPLE?

TO GET TO *YOU.*

NO. *NO!* I CAN'T BELIEVE THAT--NO MATTER HOW BADLY MY MASTERS WANT TO CATCH ME. JEDI, HIRING BOUNTY HUNTERS? I CAN'T IMAGINE ANY RESORTING TO THAT.

AND TARGETING FAMILIES IS JUST BEYOND THE PALE.

OH, AND KILLING PADAWANS IS RIGHT THERE ON THE GOOD JEDI *"TO-DO LIST"!*

MAYBE THEY THOUGHT THIS WOULD FLUSH YOU OUT. IT'S AMAZING THAT WE LUCKED INTO YOUR DAD OURSELVES BEFORE THE TRAP WAS SET.

I GUESS THE FORCE IS WITH ME.

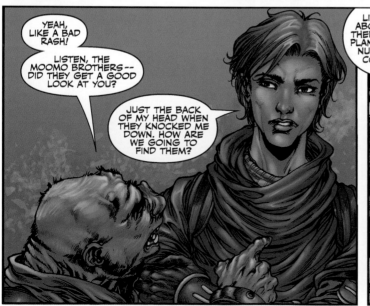

YEAH, LIKE A BAD RASH!

LISTEN, THE MOOMO BROTHERS-- DID THEY GET A GOOD LOOK AT YOU?

JUST THE BACK OF MY HEAD WHEN THEY KNOCKED ME DOWN. HOW ARE WE GOING TO FIND THEM?

LIKE I SAID, I KNOW ABOUT THESE GUYS. IF THERE'S A TENT ON THIS PLANET SELLING A MIND-NUMBING SUBSTANCE, COUNT ON THEM TO SMELL IT.

LET'S HIT THE *LAST RESORT.* THERE MIGHT BE A WAY TO SALVAGE THIS JOB, AFTER ALL...

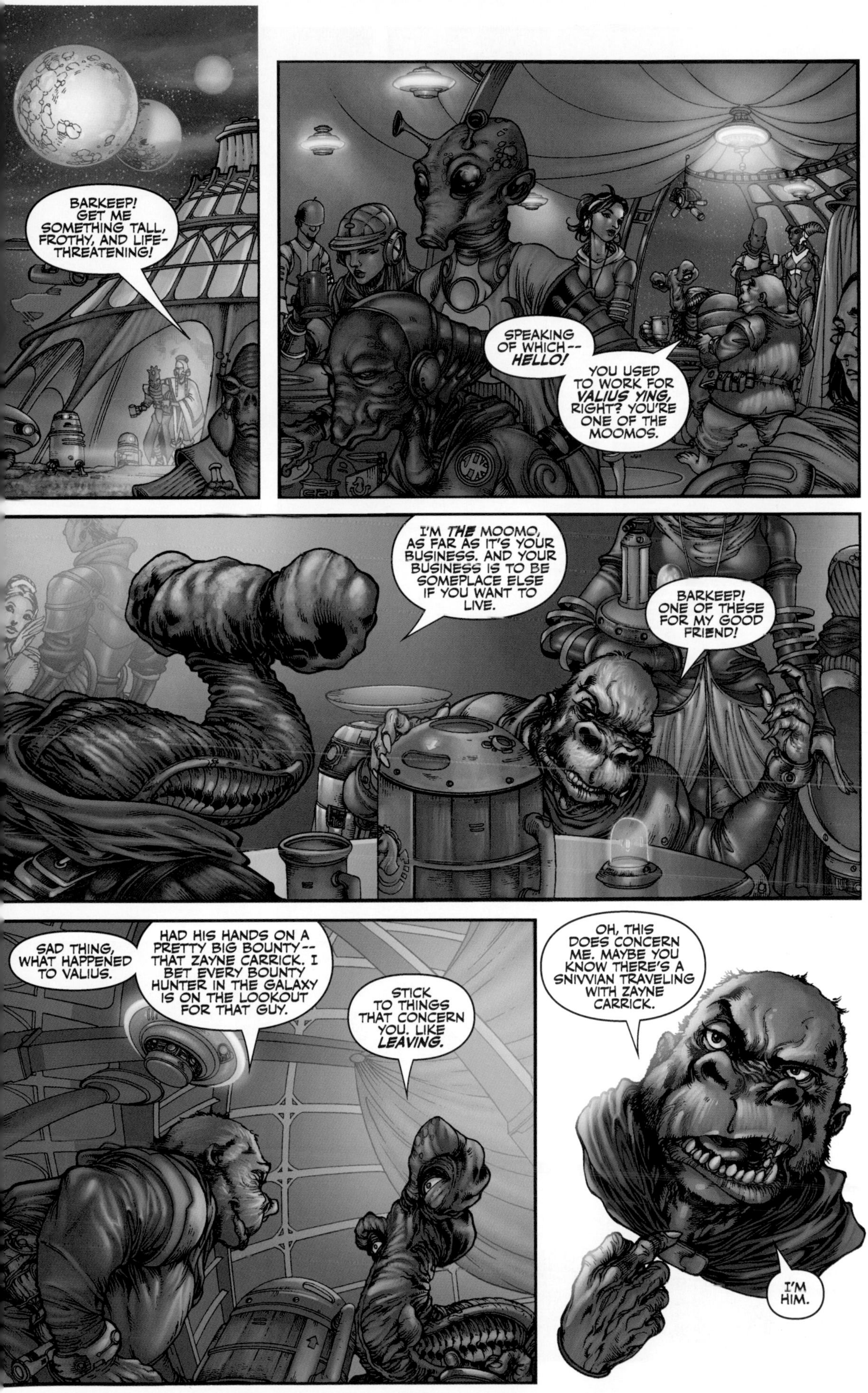
BARKEEP! GET ME SOMETHING TALL, FROTHY, AND LIFE-THREATENING!
SPEAKING OF WHICH-- HELLO!
YOU USED TO WORK FOR VALIUS YING, RIGHT? YOU'RE ONE OF THE MOOMOS.
I'M THE MOOMO, AS FAR AS IT'S YOUR BUSINESS. AND YOUR BUSINESS IS TO BE SOMEPLACE ELSE IF YOU WANT TO LIVE.
BARKEEP! ONE OF THESE FOR MY GOOD FRIEND!
SAD THING, WHAT HAPPENED TO VALIUS.
HAD HIS HANDS ON A PRETTY BIG BOUNTY-- THAT ZAYNE CARRICK. I BET EVERY BOUNTY HUNTER IN THE GALAXY IS ON THE LOOKOUT FOR THAT GUY.
STICK TO THINGS THAT CONCERN YOU. LIKE LEAVING.
OH, THIS DOES CONCERN ME. MAYBE YOU KNOW THERE'S A SNIVVIAN TRAVELING WITH ZAYNE CARRICK.
I'M HIM.

YOU DON'T SAY.

YEP, TELERATH'S JUST FILTHY WITH CARRICKS TODAY. THERE'S THE ONE I'VE GOT -- AND THE ONE *YOU'VE* GOT.

WHAT DO YOU KNOW ABOUT --

MY CARRICK'S WORTH A LOT MORE, I'LL BET.

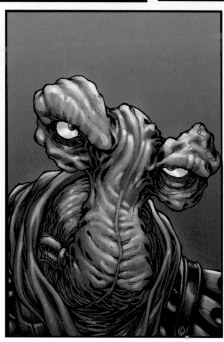

NO.

NO, NO. WE'RE ONLY BEING PAID FOR THE BANKER.

YEAH, BUT YOU DON'T WANT THE BANKER TO BANK. YOU WANT THE BANKER FOR BAIT.

WELL, IT WORKED. *ZAYNE CARRICK* IS *HERE.* HE'S IN MY SHIP RIGHT NOW.

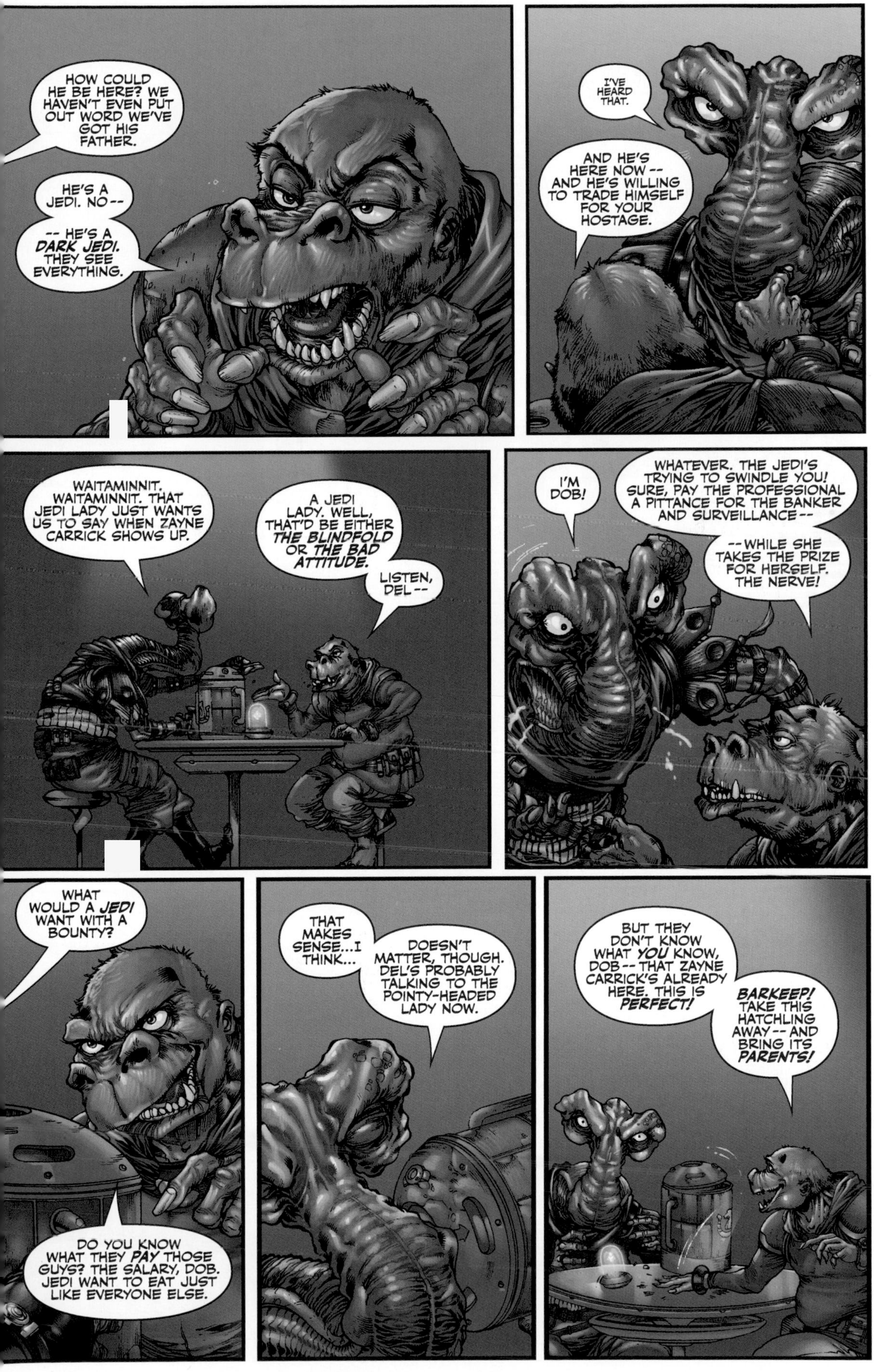
HOW COULD HE BE HERE? WE HAVEN'T EVEN PUT OUT WORD WE'VE GOT HIS FATHER.
HE'S A JEDI. NO--
-- HE'S A *DARK JEDI.* THEY SEE EVERYTHING.
I'VE HEARD THAT.
AND HE'S HERE NOW -- AND HE'S WILLING TO TRADE HIMSELF FOR YOUR HOSTAGE.
WAITAMINNIT. WAITAMINNIT. THAT JEDI LADY JUST WANTS US TO SAY WHEN ZAYNE CARRICK SHOWS UP.
A JEDI LADY. WELL, THAT'D BE EITHER *THE BLINDFOLD* OR *THE BAD ATTITUDE.*
LISTEN, DEL --
I'M DOB!
WHATEVER. THE JEDI'S TRYING TO SWINDLE YOU! SURE, PAY THE PROFESSIONAL A PITTANCE FOR THE BANKER AND SURVEILLANCE--
--WHILE SHE TAKES THE PRIZE FOR HERSELF. THE NERVE!
WHAT WOULD A *JEDI* WANT WITH A BOUNTY?
DO YOU KNOW WHAT THEY *PAY* THOSE GUYS? THE SALARY, DOB. JEDI WANT TO EAT JUST LIKE EVERYONE ELSE.
THAT MAKES SENSE...I THINK...
DOESN'T MATTER, THOUGH. DEL'S PROBABLY TALKING TO THE POINTY-HEADED LADY NOW.
BUT THEY DON'T KNOW WHAT *YOU* KNOW, DOB -- THAT ZAYNE CARRICK'S ALREADY HERE. THIS IS *PERFECT!*
BARKEEP! TAKE THIS HATCHLING AWAY -- AND BRING ITS *PARENTS!*

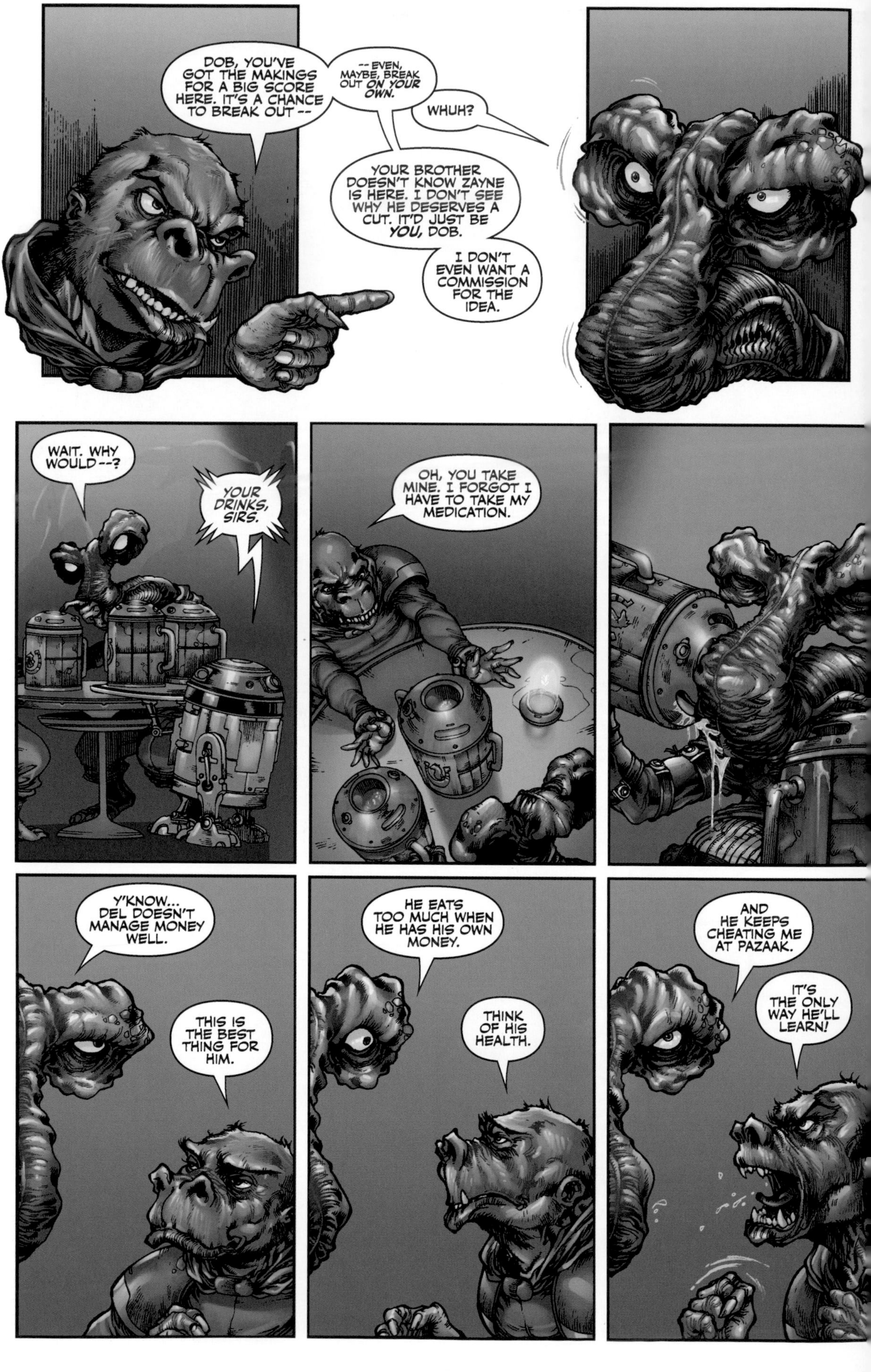
DOB, YOU'VE GOT THE MAKINGS FOR A BIG SCORE HERE. IT'S A CHANCE TO BREAK OUT --
-- EVEN, MAYBE, BREAK OUT *ON YOUR OWN.*
WHUH?
YOUR BROTHER DOESN'T KNOW ZAYNE IS HERE. I DON'T SEE WHY HE DESERVES A CUT. IT'D JUST BE *YOU,* DOB.
I DON'T EVEN WANT A COMMISSION FOR THE IDEA.
WAIT. WHY WOULD--?
YOUR DRINKS, SIRS.
OH, YOU TAKE MINE. I FORGOT I HAVE TO TAKE MY MEDICATION.
Y'KNOW... DEL DOESN'T MANAGE MONEY WELL.
THIS IS THE BEST THING FOR HIM.
HE EATS TOO MUCH WHEN HE HAS HIS OWN MONEY.
THINK OF HIS HEALTH.
AND HE KEEPS CHEATING ME AT PAZAAK.
IT'S THE ONLY WAY HE'LL LEARN!

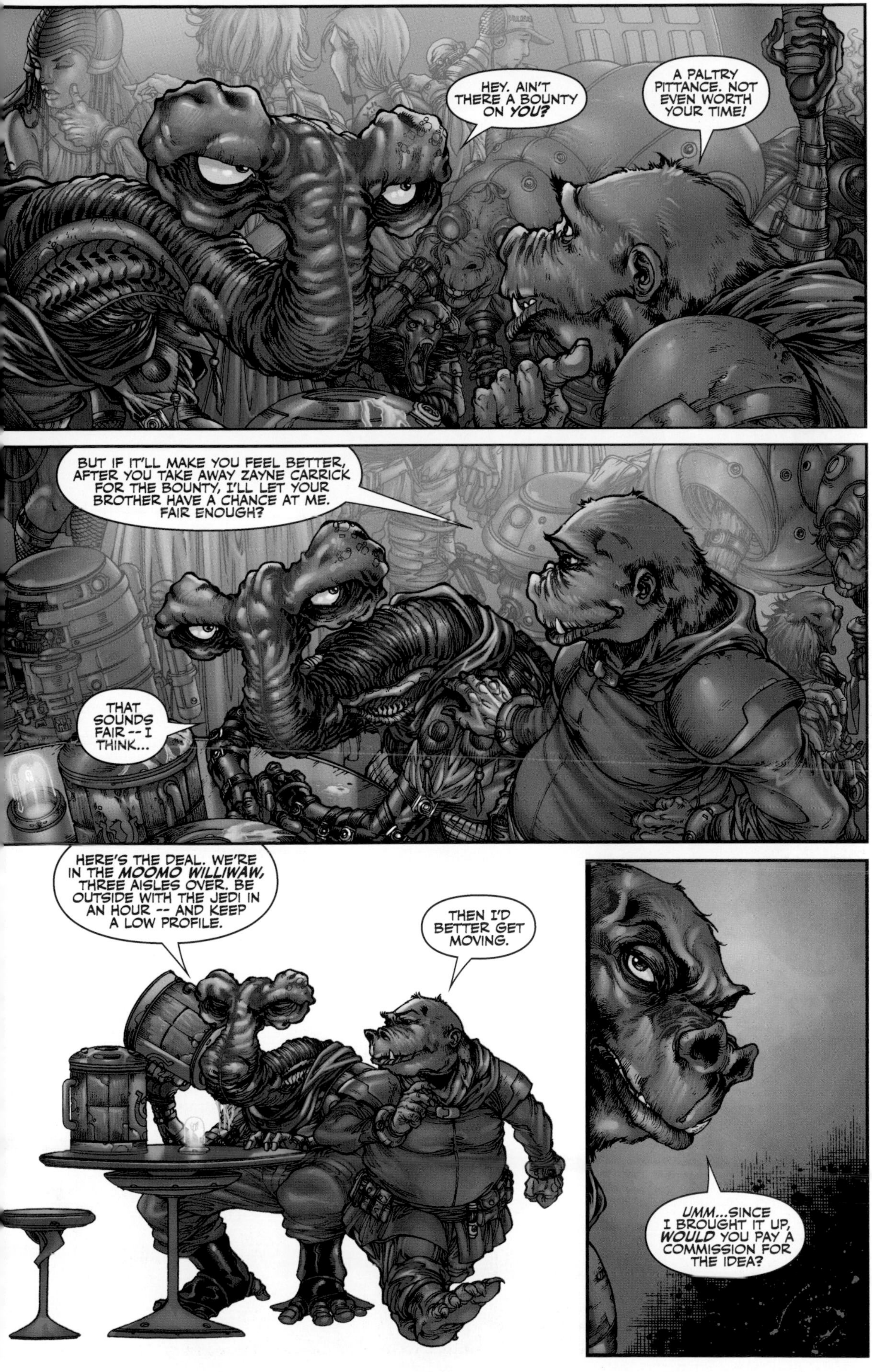
HEY. AIN'T THERE A BOUNTY ON *YOU?*
A PALTRY PITTANCE. NOT EVEN WORTH YOUR TIME!
BUT IF IT'LL MAKE YOU FEEL BETTER, AFTER YOU TAKE AWAY ZAYNE CARRICK FOR THE BOUNTY, I'LL LET YOUR BROTHER HAVE A CHANCE AT ME. FAIR ENOUGH?
THAT SOUNDS FAIR -- I THINK...
HERE'S THE DEAL. WE'RE IN THE *MOOMO WILLIWAW,* THREE AISLES OVER. BE OUTSIDE WITH THE JEDI IN AN HOUR -- AND KEEP A LOW PROFILE.
THEN I'D BETTER GET MOVING.
UMM...SINCE I BROUGHT IT UP, *WOULD* YOU PAY A COMMISSION FOR THE IDEA?

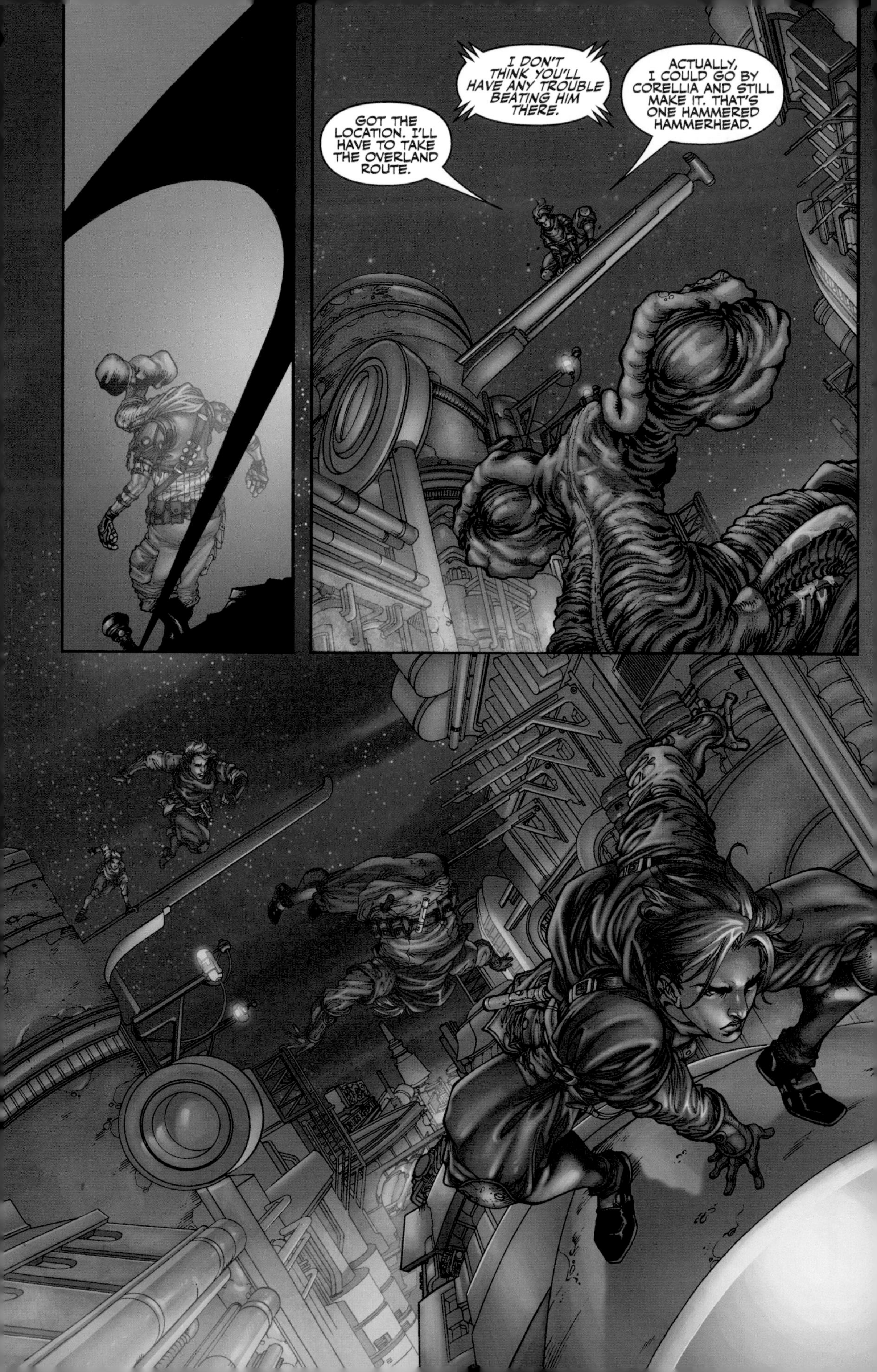
GOT THE LOCATION. I'LL HAVE TO TAKE THE OVERLAND ROUTE.
I DON'T THINK YOU'LL HAVE ANY TROUBLE BEATING HIM THERE.
ACTUALLY, I COULD GO BY CORELLIA AND STILL MAKE IT. THAT'S ONE HAMMERED HAMMERHEAD.

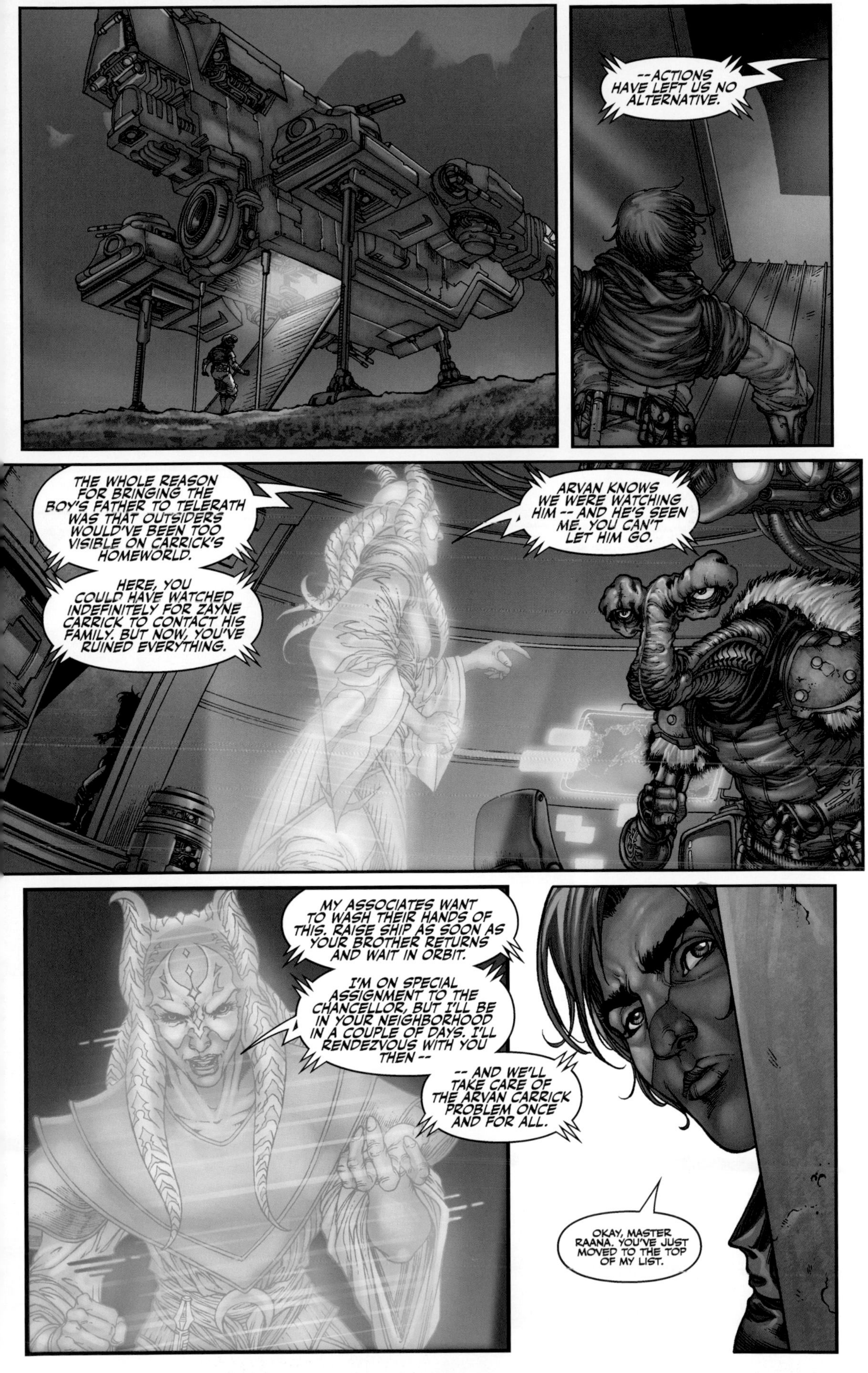
--ACTIONS HAVE LEFT US NO ALTERNATIVE.
THE WHOLE REASON FOR BRINGING THE BOY'S FATHER TO TELERATH WAS THAT OUTSIDERS WOULD'VE BEEN TOO VISIBLE ON CARRICK'S HOMEWORLD.
HERE, YOU COULD HAVE WATCHED INDEFINITELY FOR ZAYNE CARRICK TO CONTACT HIS FAMILY. BUT NOW, YOU'VE RUINED EVERYTHING.
ARVAN KNOWS WE WERE WATCHING HIM -- AND HE'S SEEN ME. YOU CAN'T LET HIM GO.
MY ASSOCIATES WANT TO WASH THEIR HANDS OF THIS. RAISE SHIP AS SOON AS YOUR BROTHER RETURNS AND WAIT IN ORBIT.
I'M ON SPECIAL ASSIGNMENT TO THE CHANCELLOR, BUT I'LL BE IN YOUR NEIGHBORHOOD IN A COUPLE OF DAYS. I'LL RENDEZVOUS WITH YOU THEN --
-- AND WE'LL TAKE CARE OF THE ARVAN CARRICK PROBLEM ONCE AND FOR ALL.
OKAY, MASTER RAANA. YOU'VE JUST MOVED TO THE TOP OF MY LIST.

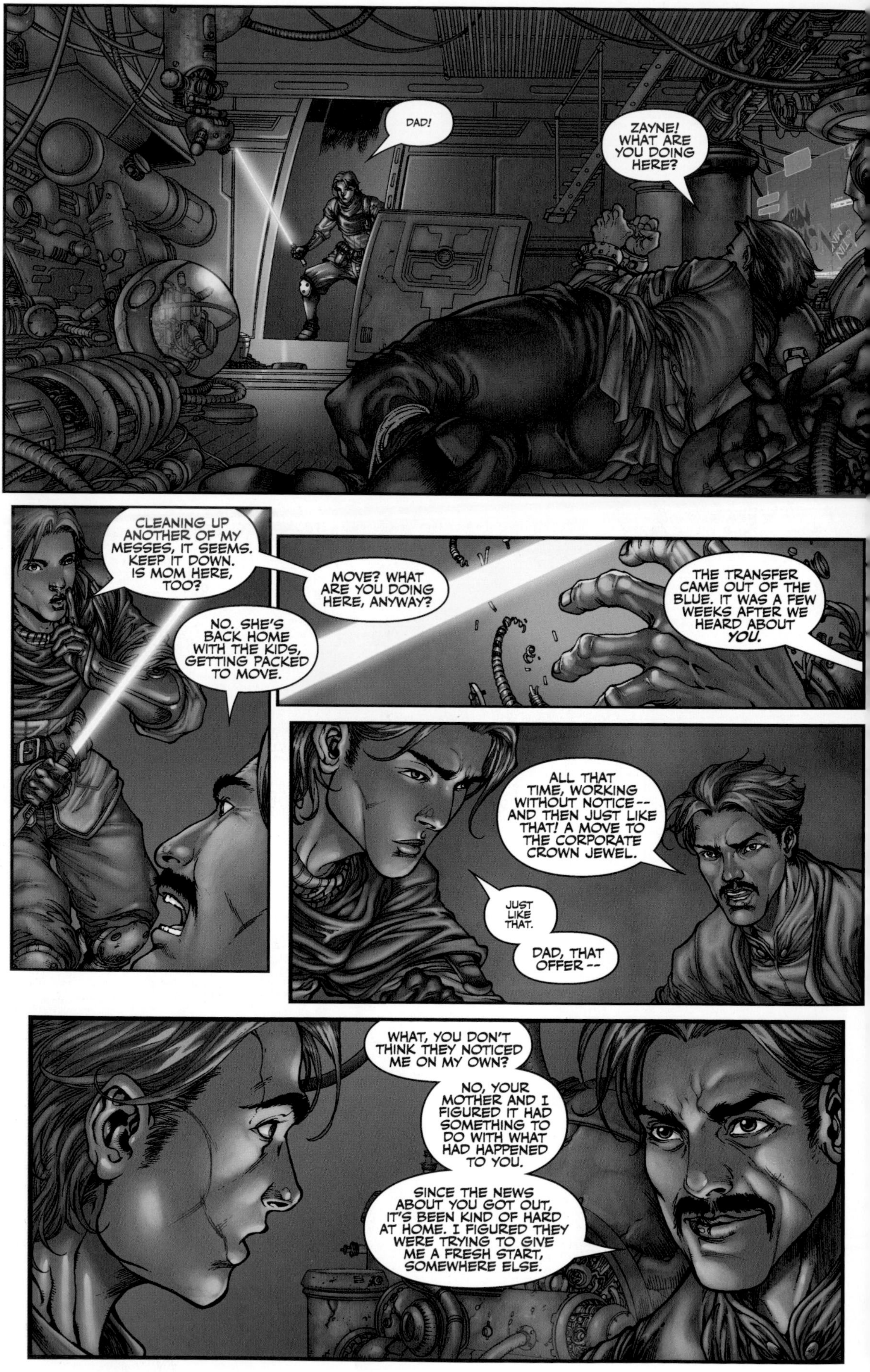
DAD!
ZAYNE! WHAT ARE YOU DOING HERE?
CLEANING UP ANOTHER OF MY MESSES, IT SEEMS. KEEP IT DOWN. IS MOM HERE, TOO?
NO. SHE'S BACK HOME WITH THE KIDS, GETTING PACKED TO MOVE.
MOVE? WHAT ARE YOU DOING HERE, ANYWAY?
THE TRANSFER CAME OUT OF THE BLUE. IT WAS A FEW WEEKS AFTER WE HEARD ABOUT *YOU.*
ALL THAT TIME, WORKING WITHOUT NOTICE-- AND THEN JUST LIKE THAT! A MOVE TO THE CORPORATE CROWN JEWEL.
JUST LIKE THAT.
DAD, THAT OFFER --
WHAT, YOU DON'T THINK THEY NOTICED ME ON MY OWN?
NO, YOUR MOTHER AND I FIGURED IT HAD SOMETHING TO DO WITH WHAT HAD HAPPENED TO YOU.
SINCE THE NEWS ABOUT YOU GOT OUT, IT'S BEEN KIND OF HARD AT HOME. I FIGURED THEY WERE TRYING TO GIVE ME A FRESH START, SOMEWHERE ELSE.

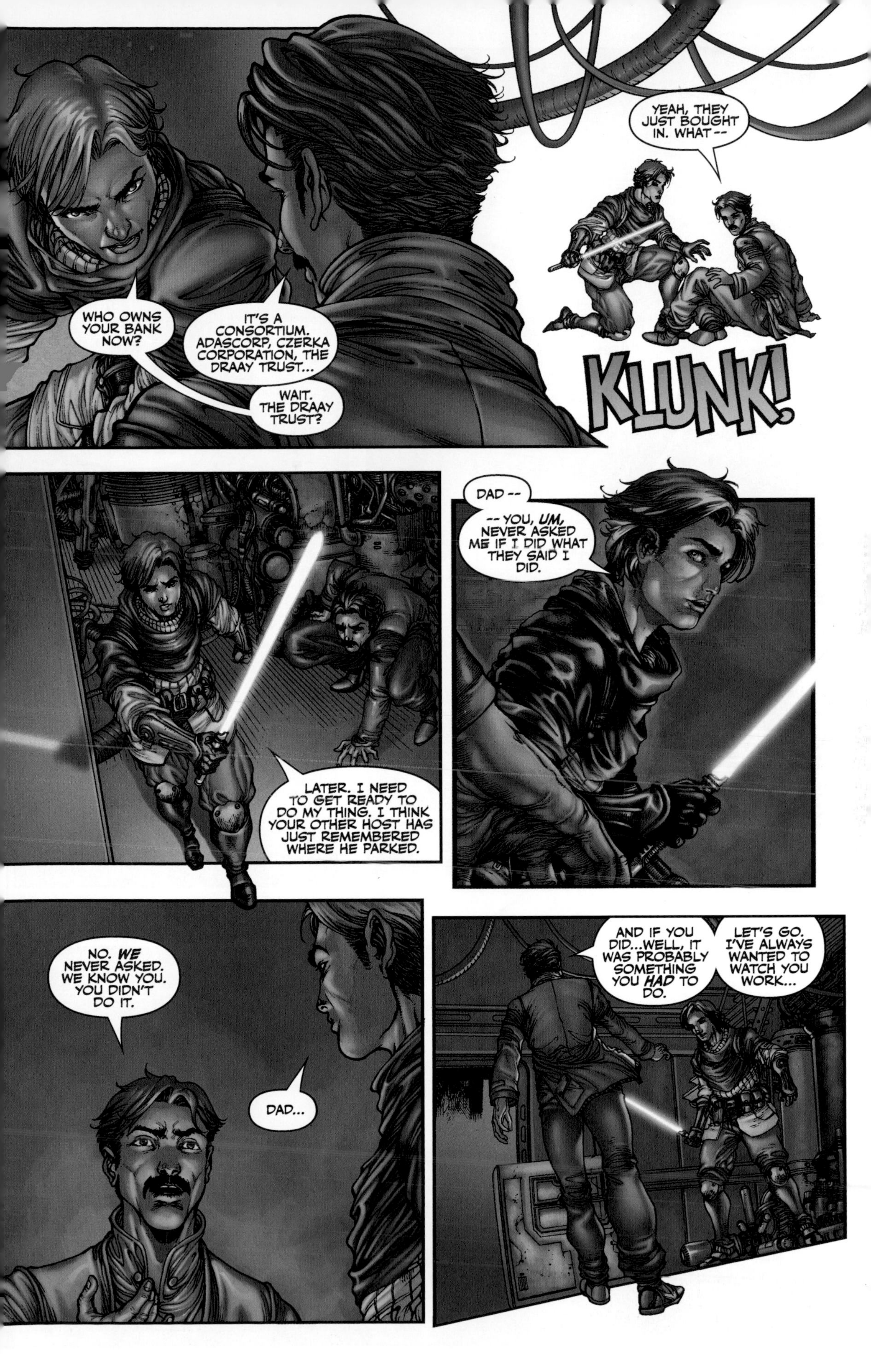
WHO OWNS YOUR BANK NOW?
IT'S A CONSORTIUM. ADASCORP, CZERKA CORPORATION, THE DRAAY TRUST...
WAIT. THE DRAAY TRUST?
YEAH, THEY JUST BOUGHT IN. WHAT --
KLUNK!
LATER. I NEED TO GET READY TO DO MY THING. I THINK YOUR OTHER HOST HAS JUST REMEMBERED WHERE HE PARKED.
DAD --
-- YOU, UM, NEVER ASKED ME IF I DID WHAT THEY SAID I DID.
NO. WE NEVER ASKED. WE KNOW YOU. YOU DIDN'T DO IT.
DAD...
AND IF YOU DID...WELL, IT WAS PROBABLY SOMETHING YOU HAD TO DO.
LET'S GO. I'VE ALWAYS WANTED TO WATCH YOU WORK...

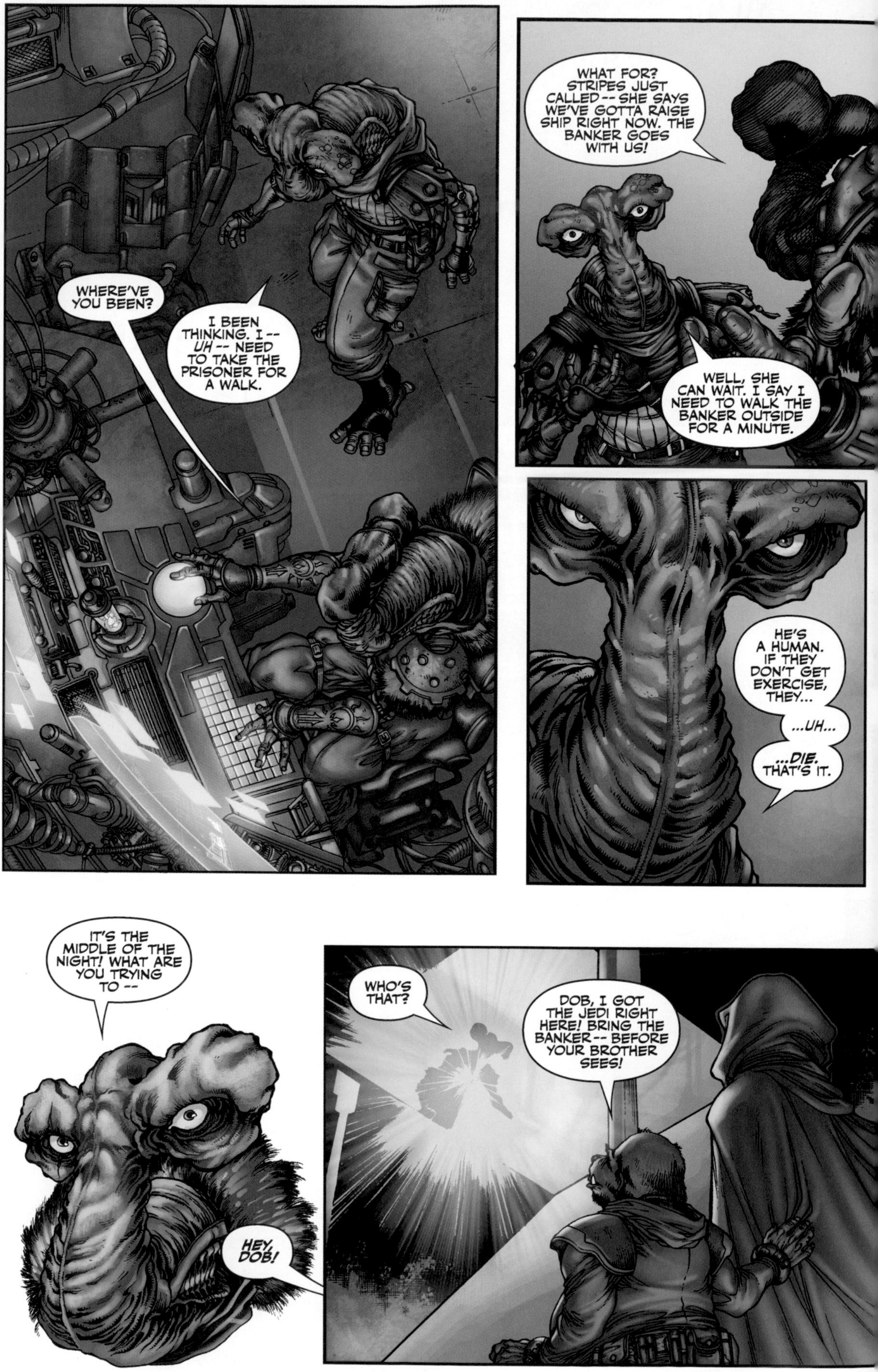
WHERE'VE YOU BEEN?
I BEEN THINKING. I -- *UH* -- NEED TO TAKE THE PRISONER FOR A WALK.
WHAT FOR? STRIPES JUST CALLED -- SHE SAYS WE'VE GOTTA RAISE SHIP RIGHT NOW. THE BANKER GOES WITH US!
WELL, SHE CAN WAIT. I SAY I NEED TO WALK THE BANKER OUTSIDE FOR A MINUTE.
HE'S A HUMAN. IF THEY DON'T GET EXERCISE, THEY...
...UH...
...*DIE*. THAT'S IT.
IT'S THE MIDDLE OF THE NIGHT! WHAT ARE YOU TRYING TO --
HEY, DOB!
WHO'S THAT?
DOB, I GOT THE JEDI RIGHT HERE! BRING THE BANKER -- BEFORE YOUR BROTHER SEES!

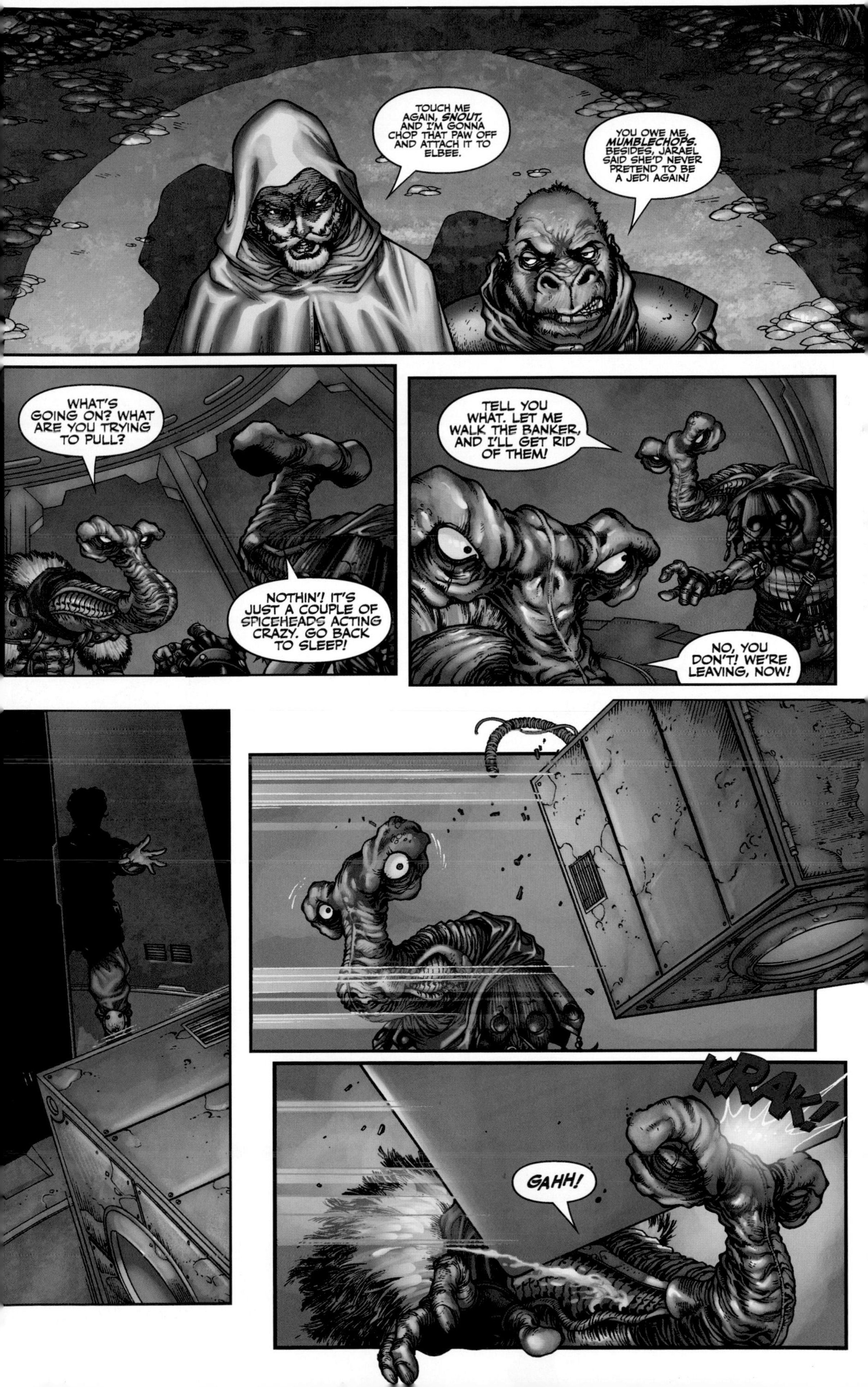
TOUCH ME AGAIN, SNOUT, AND I'M GONNA CHOP THAT PAW OFF AND ATTACH IT TO ELBEE.
YOU OWE ME, MUMBLECHOPS. BESIDES, JARAEL SAID SHE'D NEVER PRETEND TO BE A JEDI AGAIN!
WHAT'S GOING ON? WHAT ARE YOU TRYING TO PULL?
NOTHIN'! IT'S JUST A COUPLE OF SPICEHEADS ACTING CRAZY. GO BACK TO SLEEP!
TELL YOU WHAT. LET ME WALK THE BANKER, AND I'LL GET RID OF THEM!
NO, YOU DON'T! WE'RE LEAVING, NOW!
KRAK!
GAHH!

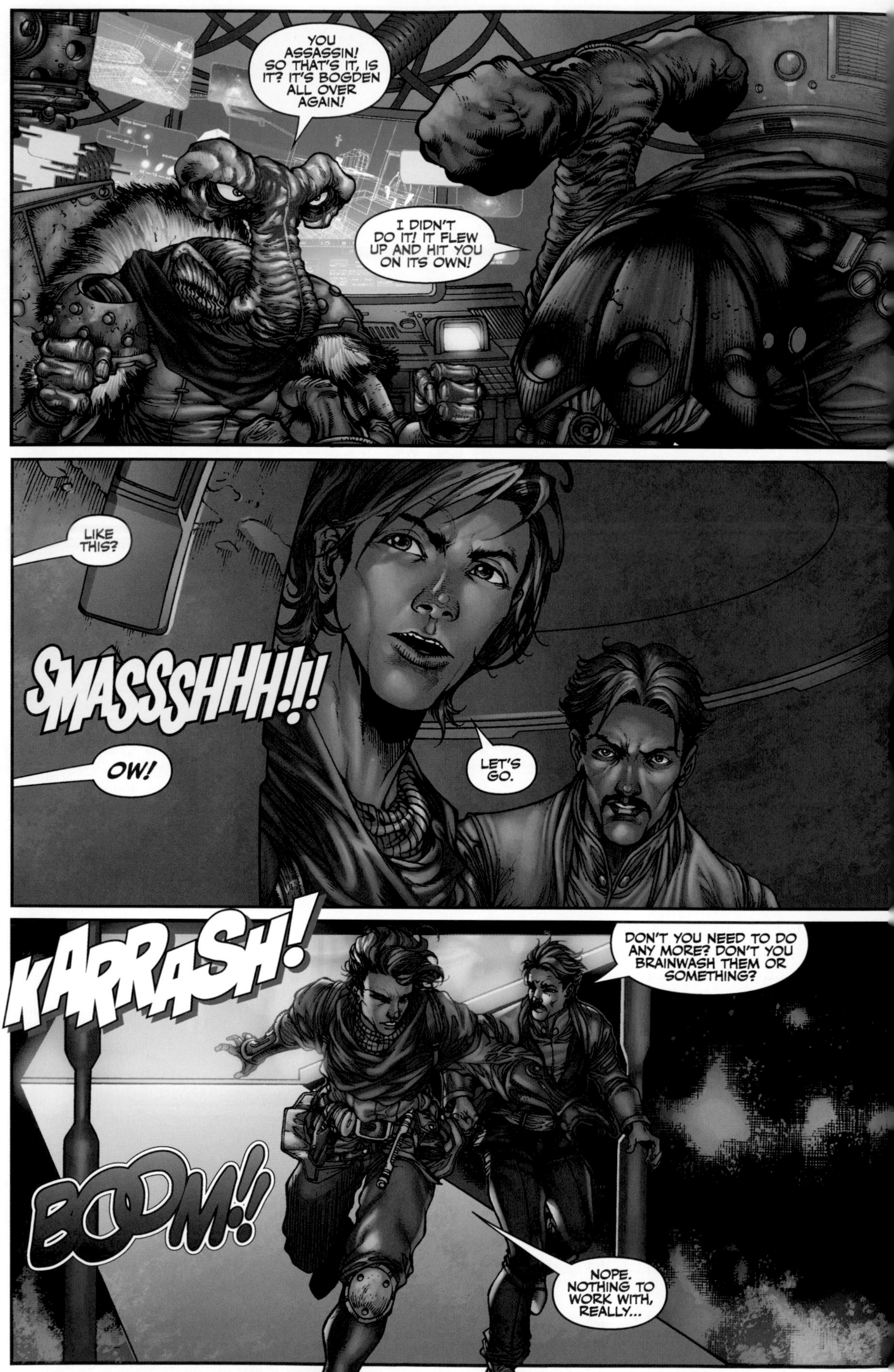
YOU ASSASSIN! SO THAT'S IT, IS IT? IT'S BOGDEN ALL OVER AGAIN!
I DIDN'T DO IT! IT FLEW UP AND HIT YOU ON ITS OWN!
LIKE THIS?
SMASSSHHH!!!
OW!
LET'S GO.
KARRASH!
DON'T YOU NEED TO DO ANY MORE? DON'T YOU BRAINWASH THEM OR SOMETHING?
BOOM!!
NOPE. NOTHING TO WORK WITH, REALLY...

LATER...

-- IT'S GOOD TO MEET YOU, MARN. AND YOUR DROID, THERE?

ELBEE. DON'T MAKE HIM GET UP--

-- HE'S ONE OF THE NEW KIND OF DROIDS THAT DOESN'T LIKE TO MOVE.

WELL, THE GOOD NEWS FROM THE OFFICE IS I HAVEN'T BEEN MISSED YET. I SHOULDN'T HAVE ANY PROBLEM GOING TO WORK AND PROCESSING THE BARON'S --

-- ER, CAMPER'S REQUEST. THAT'LL UNLOCK HIS ACCOUNT --

MY ACCOUNT!

-- YOUR ACCOUNT, THEN. I'LL CASH YOU OUT AND HAVE A SECURITY DROID DELIVER IT ALL HERE IN HARD CURRENCY.

YOU KNOW, KID, I THINK I HIRED THE WRONG CARRICK. I NEVER HAD AN INSIDE MAN AT A BANK BEFORE.

AND YOU DON'T, NOW. HE'S GIVING US WHAT WE CAME HERE FOR AND THAT'S ALL.

AND I'M NOT SURE HOW LONG DAD SHOULD STAY HERE ANYWAY. IF THE BANK REALLY SENT HIM HERE TO BE BAIT FOR ME --

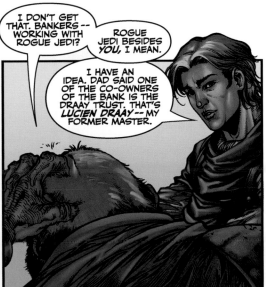

I DON'T GET THAT. BANKERS -- WORKING WITH ROGUE JEDI?

ROGUE JEDI BESIDES YOU, I MEAN.

I HAVE AN IDEA. DAD SAID ONE OF THE CO-OWNERS OF THE BANK IS THE DRAAY TRUST. THAT'S LUCIEN DRAAY -- MY FORMER MASTER.

WAIT. LUCIEN'S ONE OF *THOSE* DRAAY'S? HE'S GOT MONEY?

YES AND NO. THE DRAAYS WERE TURNING OUT PROFITS LONG BEFORE THEY STARTED TURNING OUT JEDI.

EVERY TIME A DRAAY WAS KNIGHTED, THE MARKETS SHOOK.

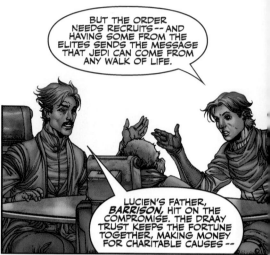

BUT THE ORDER NEEDS RECRUITS -- AND HAVING SOME FROM THE ELITES SENDS THE MESSAGE THAT JEDI CAN COME FROM ANY WALK OF LIFE.

LUCIEN'S FATHER, *BARRISON*, HIT ON THE COMPROMISE. THE DRAAY TRUST KEEPS THE FORTUNE TOGETHER, MAKING MONEY FOR CHARITABLE CAUSES --

-- WHILE KEEPING IT SAFE SHOULD ANY NON-JEDI HEIRS COME ALONG. BUT LUCIEN SHOULDN'T HAVE ANY INTEREST OVER HOW THE TRUST IS RUN, RIGHT?

NO, HE SHOULDN'T. BUT IT WOULD EXPLAIN A LOT, DON'T YOU THINK?

I THINK I SHOULD HAVE RUN OFF WITH *LUCIEN* INSTEAD OF YOU. YOU'RE BROKE!

THAT REMINDS ME. NOW THAT YOU'RE GETTING ALL THIS MONEY, GRYPH --

-- PAY ME.

AHEM. YOU JUST SAID THE JEDI WEREN'T INTO THE WHOLE MATERIAL THING.

I'M A HENCHMAN, NOT A JEDI. I HENCH, YOU PAY. NOW PAY ME.

THERE'S NOTHING LEFT TO BELIEVE IN ANYMORE.

HERE, THIS AMOUNT SEEMS FAIR.

MY HAND SLIPPED! MY HAND SLIPPED!

THIS HAS ALL BEEN VERY HARD ON MY NERVES...

GRYPH!

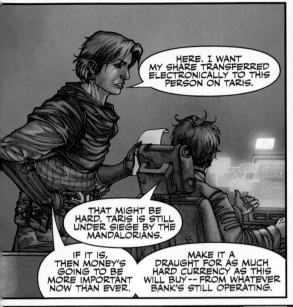

HERE. I WANT MY SHARE TRANSFERRED ELECTRONICALLY TO THIS PERSON ON TARIS.

THAT MIGHT BE HARD. TARIS IS STILL UNDER SIEGE BY THE MANDALORIANS.

IF IT IS, THEN MONEY'S GOING TO BE MORE IMPORTANT NOW THAN EVER.

MAKE IT A DRAUGHT FOR AS MUCH HARD CURRENCY AS THIS WILL BUY -- FROM WHATEVER BANK'S STILL OPERATING.

I SHOULD BE ABLE TO DO THAT. WHAT THEN?

THEN YOU NEED TO CALL YOUR MANAGEMENT AND TELL THEM YOU'VE HAD A CHANGE OF HEART -- THAT YOU WANT TO GO SOMEWHERE ELSE.

TAKE A LOOK.

THERE?!

IT'S THE ONLY WAY. I'M NOT SURE HOW FAR THIS CONSPIRACY GOES -- BUT THIS IS NEAR SOMEONE I STILL THINK I CAN TRUST.

THEY'LL HAVE A HARDER TIME MOVING AGAINST YOU THERE.

I HAVE A LOT TO DO BEFORE THIS IS OVER -- AND I NEED TO KNOW YOU'RE ALL SAFE.

I'M SORRY THIS HAS AFFECTED YOU. I KNOW IT'S NOT WHAT YOU HAD IN MIND FOR YOURSELF.

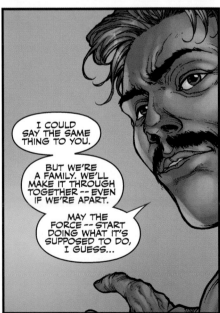

I COULD SAY THE SAME THING TO YOU.

BUT WE'RE A FAMILY. WE'LL MAKE IT THROUGH TOGETHER -- EVEN IF WE'RE APART.

MAY THE FORCE -- START DOING WHAT IT'S SUPPOSED TO DO, I GUESS...

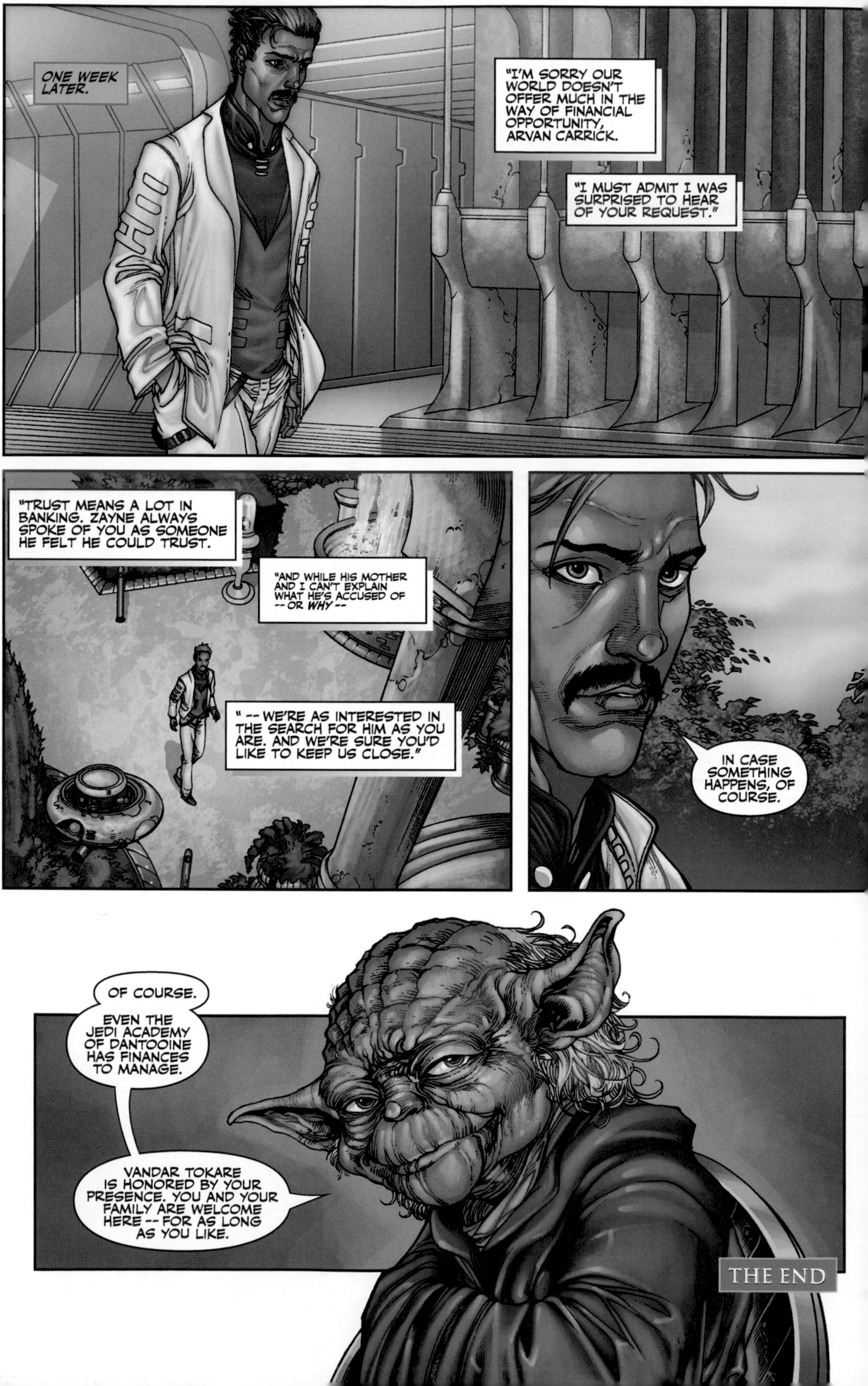
ONE WEEK LATER.
"I'M SORRY OUR WORLD DOESN'T OFFER MUCH IN THE WAY OF FINANCIAL OPPORTUNITY, ARVAN CARRICK.
"I MUST ADMIT I WAS SURPRISED TO HEAR OF YOUR REQUEST."
"TRUST MEANS A LOT IN BANKING. ZAYNE ALWAYS SPOKE OF YOU AS SOMEONE HE FELT HE COULD TRUST.
"AND WHILE HIS MOTHER AND I CAN'T EXPLAIN WHAT HE'S ACCUSED OF -- OR WHY --
" -- WE'RE AS INTERESTED IN THE SEARCH FOR HIM AS YOU ARE. AND WE'RE SURE YOU'D LIKE TO KEEP US CLOSE."
IN CASE SOMETHING HAPPENS, OF COURSE.
OF COURSE.
EVEN THE JEDI ACADEMY OF DANTOOINE HAS FINANCES TO MANAGE.
VANDAR TOKARE IS HONORED BY YOUR PRESENCE. YOU AND YOUR FAMILY ARE WELCOME HERE -- FOR AS LONG AS YOU LIKE.
THE END

STAR WARS®
CLONE WARS

Experience all the excitement and drama of the Clone Wars! Look for these trade paperbacks at a comics shop or bookstore near you!

VOLUME 1:
THE DEFENSE OF KAMINO
ISBN: 1-56971-962-4 / $14.95

VOLUME 2:
VICTORIES AND SACRIFICES
ISBN: 1-56971-969-1 / $14.95

VOLUME 3:
LAST STAND ON JABIIM
ISBN: 1-59307-006-3 / $14.95

VOLUME 4:
LIGHT AND DARK
ISBN: 1-59307-195-7 / $16.95

VOLUME 5:
THE BEST BLADES
ISBN: 1-59307-273-2 / $14.95

VOLUME 6:
ON THE FIELDS OF BATTLE
ISBN: 1-59307-352-6 / $17.95

VOLUME 7:
WHEN THEY WERE BROTHERS
ISBN: 1-59307-396-8 / $17.95

VOLUME 8:
THE LAST SIEGE, THE FINAL TRUTH
ISBN: 1-59307-482-4 / $17.95

VOLUME 9:
ENDGAME
ISBN: 1-59307-553-7 / $17.95

To find a comics shop in your area, call
1-888-266-4226

For more information or to order direct:
• On the web: darkhorse.com
• E-mail: mailorder@darkhorse.com
• Phone: 1-800-862-0052.
• Mon.-Fri. 9 A.M. to 5 P.M. Pacific Time

*Prices and availability subject to change without notice.

STAR WARS © 2006 Lucasfilm Ltd. & ™ (BL8004)

STAR WARS
CLONE WARS
ADVENTURES

Don't miss any of the action-packed adventures of your favorite STAR WARS®
characters, available at comics shops and bookstores in a galaxy near you!

 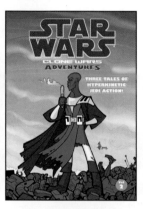  

Volume 1	Volume 2	Volume 3	Volume 4
ISBN-10: 1-59307-243-0	ISBN-10: 1-59307-271-6	ISBN-10: 1-59307-307-0	ISBN-10: 1-59307-402-6
ISBN-13: 978-1-59307-243-8	ISBN-13: 978-1-59307-271-1	ISBN-13: 978-1-59307-307-7	ISBN-13: 978-1-59307-402-9

Volume 5	Volume 6	Volume 7	Volume 8
ISBN-10: 1-59307-483-2	ISBN-10: 1-59307-567-7	ISBN-10: 1-59307-678-9	ISBN-10: 1-59307-680-0
ISBN-13: 978-1-59307-483-8	ISBN-13: 978-1-59307-567-5	ISBN-13: 978-1-59307-678-8	ISBN-13: 978-1-59307-680-1
			Coming in June!

$6.95 each!

To find a comics shop in your area, call 1-888-266-4226

For more information or to order direct: • On the web: darkhorse.com • Phone: 1-800-862-0052 Mon.-Fri. 9 A.M. to 5 P.M. Pacific Time.
• E-mail: mailorder@darkhorse.com *Prices and availability subject to change without notice.

STAR WARS © 2004—2007 Lucasfilm Ltd. & ™ (BL 8012)